'Contemporary': Architecture and Interiors of the 1950s

'contemporary'

architecture

and

interiors

of

the

1950s

Lesley Jackson

For Ian

Phaidon Press Limited
Regent's Wharf
All Saints Street
London N1 9PA

First published 1994
Reprinted 1995
Reprinted in paperback 1998,
1999, 2000

© 1994 Phaidon Press Limited

ISBN 0 7148 3757 1

A CIP catalogue record for this book is available from the British Library

Printed in Hong Kong

Page 2 *View of living room in Case Study House number 21, Los Angeles, designed by Pierre Koenig in 1958. This house was radical in its use of steel I-beams for its structural framework and ribbed steel decking for its roof, features which were deliberately left exposed on the interior.*

Page 5 *View of the sundeck of the Rose Seidler house, Turramurra, NSW, Australia designed by architect Harry Seidler in 1950. Born in Austria, Seidler trained under Walter Gropius at Harvard and worked with Marcel Breuer in New York before emigrating to Australia in 1948, bringing with him the latest ideas from the Modern Movement.*

contents

Charles and Ray Eames sitting in the double-height open-plan living room of Case Study House number 8 which they designed for themselves ☞ at Pacific Palisades, Los Angeles, between 1945 and 1949. The interior includes furniture by Charles Eames, paintings by Ray Eames, and a rich, colourful collection of rugs and artefacts.

View of the open plan living room ☞ of Case Study House number 9 designed by Charles Eames and Eero Saarinen for John Entenza, the editor of Arts and Architecture *magazine, between 1945 and 1949. Slight changes in level indicate subdivisions within the room.*

During the 1950s the term 'Contemporary' was widely used in Great Britain and the USA to describe the new fashion for modern design. The choice of the word 'Contemporary' to characterize buildings and domestic products that were consciously forward-looking rather than traditional, reflected a desire on the part of society to avoid dwelling on the past, and to re-affirm instead its faith in the future. Buildings and products designed in the 'Contemporary' style were thus confident, life-affirming and optimistic. This was a remarkable period for young architects and designers to be embarking upon their careers: the opportunities for original creative expression were unparalleled, and the attitude of the public towards modern design was more positive and receptive than at any time since the Art Nouveau movement at the turn of the century.

The 'Contemporary' style did not just materialize out of thin air at the end of World War II, however; it evolved in a direct line of descent from the Modern Movement of the 1920s and 1930s. During this period, Modernist architects had striven to create a 'style without a style' by casting off the oppressive influence of historical revivalism, or eclecticism as it was known in the USA, and although the somewhat austere, pared-down aesthetic of Modern Movement architecture did not prove popular with the general public during the early years, the advent of Modernism did at least draw public attention to the worst excesses of nineteenth century design. It certainly helped pave the way for the acceptance of the new 'Contemporary' approach to architecture and design which would capture the public imagination after the war. The 'Contemporary' style was a modified version of Modernism, which recognized that it had a clear and distinctive visual identity and never strove to present itself as a 'style without a style'. To refer to 'Contemporary' design as a style, therefore, is not to belittle its achievements in relation to the high-minded ideals of Modernism, nor to imply that its creators were solely interested in aesthetics, but to recognize its strong visual impact.

The achievements of the 1950s in the field of architecture and design are long overdue for recognition and reappraisal and, by treating the period seriously, highlighting its dynamism and creativity, and illustrating the main breakthroughs in architecture and interior design, that is what this book sets out to do. In the field of domestic architecture, the book concentrates largely on the first decade after the war because it was during this period that the main trends were established which would dominate design during the late 1950s and early 1960s. The cut-off point for the book is 1962, because I feel that this date marked a turning point in the direction of modern design, after which the spirit of youthful innocence and exuberance which had characterized the early post-war period was, to a certain extent, lost. Popular culture, consumerism and the teenage revolution of the late 1950s and early 1960s are subjects not included in this book, as these are well covered elsewhere and have, in any case, tended to receive attention at the expense of other equally important and interesting aspects of the period in recent years. Nor is this a book about nostalgia: that would be to diminish the outstanding architectural achievements of the period and to undermine the importance of 'Contemporary' design.

Although the main subject of the book is the design and decoration of individual houses, the architecture of public buildings is discussed in the chapter called 'Society Goes Contemporary'. This is not just the story of the achievements of the big-name architects of the period, however; the book introduces many less well-known figures and aims to illustrate the general application of the 'Contemporary' style within society as a whole. The USA, which was at the forefront of developments in domestic design during the 1950s, is given deserved prominence, but the contributions of British and mainland European architects and designers are also recognized, especially those of the Scandinavians who played such an important role at this time. To the architects, designers and manufacturers of today, the achievements of the 1950s could act as an example and an inspiration. For those readers who are new to the subject, this book will act as a stimulus for further investigation.

Lesley Jackson, May 1994

Villa Savoye, Poissy, France, ⟨⟩ designed by Le Corbusier and Pierre Jeanneret in 1930, is a definitive example of Modern Movement architecture. In the Modernist house, design was pared down to the essentials.

1. the birth of the 'contemporary' style

'It is significant that the modern aesthetic of architecture is born elsewhere than in the ateliers of architects. It is born in factories and laboratories, in places where new things for daily use, without precedents, are created; where tradition has no influence, and there is no aesthetic prejudice.'

FRS Yorke, The Modern House (sixth edition), 1948

During the first half of the twentieth century, art and architecture were gradually transformed by the influence of the Modern Movement. Although Modernist ideas were slow to catch on initially, by the early post-war period, Modernist thinking had revolutionized the approach to the design of both the domestic dwelling and the workplace. Unlike its predecessors, Modernism was not intended to be yet another style in an ever-changing historical sequence; it was a rejection of the very concept of change and style. The Swiss architectural historian, Sigfried Giedion, advised against using the word 'style' altogether when describing modern architecture because of the formalistic notions that this word

THE MODERN
HOUSE

SIXTH EDITION, REVISED   F. R. S. YORKE

Above *Cover of the book*
The Modern House
*by F R S Yorke, first
published in 1934, which
documented the rise of the
Modern Movement in
Europe. The sketch on the
front jacket of the revised
edition of 1948 shows
a couple relaxing on the
flat roof of their house.*

Opposite *Three views
of Le Corbusier and Pierre
Jeanneret's beautifully
proportioned Villa Savoye
at Poissy in France, built
in 1930. Important
Modernist features include
the narrow reinforced
concrete pillars or* pilotis
*which support the
cantilevered first floor; the
simple, unadorned box-like
form of the building; the
extensive use of windows;
the flat roof, and first-floor
terrace garden.*

implied. What Modernism was trying to promote, he wrote in *Space, Time and Architecture* (1963 edition), was 'an approach to the life that slumbers unconsciously within all of us', meaning that it entailed fundamental rather than superficial change. Allegiance to the Modern Movement involved the complete rejection of historicist ornament and aesthetics. In their place, progressive architects and designers, such as the pioneering teachers at the Bauhaus in Germany during the 1920s, called upon their students and colleagues to adopt a more detached, clinical and scientific approach to the creation of buildings and objects. Henceforth, they said, objectivity and functionalism were to be the order of the day, and 'factories and laboratories' were to provide the new models for the office and the home. In the much quoted words of Le Corbusier, one of the leading protagonists of the Modern Movement, the modern house was to be a *'machine à habiter'*, (a machine for living in), and the workings of that machine were to be carefully formulated to meet the requirements of real human activities in a changed and changing world.

The design of the modern house first began to take shape in Europe and America during the first thirty years of the twentieth century, led by pioneers such as Walter Gropius, Marcel Breuer, Ludwig Mies van der Rohe and Frank Lloyd Wright. Its emergence was well documented in the illuminating and perceptive survey first published in 1934 by the British architect, FRS Yorke, called *The Modern House*, which was revised and reprinted six times over the next fourteen years. The first revised post-war edition recorded the construction of fifty architect-designed private houses built between 1926 and 1948 in the USA and Europe. In his introduction to the book, Yorke argued passionately for the functional basis of the modern house:

We can no longer afford to build the house that makes bad use of space, or to employ ornamental devices to counteract weaknesses in basic design. Anything that is for use must be, above all else, efficient, and the design of the modern house is based on the principle of utility – it is fundamentally a thing for use.

As the cumbersome lifestyle and the anachronistic values of the Victorian and Edwardian eras collapsed in the wake of World War I, there was an increasingly vigorous assault on the accepted visual norms of architecture by the pioneers of the Modern Movement. What was revolutionary about the thinking of progressive architects between the wars was to conceive of the house from the inside out, to suggest that its exterior shape should be determined by its interior structure. Yorke described this approach as:

...a plan that is consistent with the new outlook on life, the new mode of living... The architect, working from the plan, outwards to the exterior, finds there is a new external expression, that there can be no compromise between the plan that is made for service and the symmetrical or picturesque façade.

Underlying this idea was an acceptance of the need to base the choice of rooms and their layout on the actual requirements of the users; in

other words, for the activities of the inhabitants to determine the structure of the house, rather than for the physical limitations of the house to set arbitrary limitations on its subsequent use. Consequently, in order to understand the modern house – and this applies equally to buildings of the 1940s and 1950s as to those of the 1920s and 1930s – it is often necessary to begin from the inside out, by analyzing the nature of the interior. From the outside, even the most successful modern house might appear incomprehensible; but from the inside it should always seem supremely logical. Yorke declared:

> The modern architect does not force upon the house a symmetry or a geometric scheme if neither symmetry nor geometry is necessary to the purpose of his project. He does not cover it with decorations borrowed from the 'styles' or with modernistic ornaments invented by catchpenny commercial fashion makers.

Thus, according to Yorke, the inhabitants of a truly modern house should be able to enjoy the comfort, not of sham ornament and false decoration, but of function perfectly matched to need.

As a result of changes to the interior structure and layout of the modern house, the appearance of the exterior changed dramatically. It lost its pitched roof and became rectilinear in form, based on a play of planes and recesses in an abstract, sometimes Cubist, formation. In some cases, the design aesthetics of the modern house could be directly linked to developments in contemporary art, as in the Schroeder House in Utrecht, built by Gerrit Rietveld in 1924, which reflected the ideas of painter Piet Mondrian and the Dutch De Stijl group. In the words of the architect, quoted in *Modern Houses of the World* by Sherban Cantacuzino, his aim was to use 'elementary forms, simple spaces and primary colours exclusively, because they are so fundamental and because they are free of associations.' It is interesting to note that Rietveld's justification for the choice of primary colours for the decorative scheme, because they were 'free of associations', was identical to the reasoning of other European Modernist architects that there should be no decoration at all.

Clearly, there were widely differing views on this point, even at this early stage, as witnessed by the functional yet overtly decorative approach to architecture and interior design adopted by Frank Lloyd Wright in the USA. What united the two camps, however, was their shared recognition of the need for coherence within the design of a building, whether this included decorative elements or not. This was in stark contrast to the stylistic eclecticism of Victorian architects. It was the quality of coherence within his own work that Wright was to refer to in Cantacuzino's book as 'organic', by which he meant the creation of a single unified and fully integrated aesthetic; or, as he put it, 'Always *of* the thing, never *on* it.'

During the more relaxed years after World War II, when the Modernist ideas were being disseminated in a more pragmatic way with less purist zeal, Wright's theories about organic architecture were to seem increasingly relevant, with the result that the adoption of a more Wrightian approach by many American architects underpins the wider public acceptance of the Modern Movement at this time.

Above and Opposite *Three views of the Schroeder House in Utrecht designed by Gerrit Rietveld in 1924. Although the exterior is mainly white, some of the primary colours used to* *decorate the interior have been carried through to highlight details of the exterior structure. During the 1950s, colour would again play a vital role in architecture.*

Above and Opposite *The Ennis House, designed by Frank Lloyd Wright, was one of a series of houses built by Wright in Los Angeles during the early 1920s using decorative relief-moulded pre-fabricated concrete blocks. Wright's use of pattern and texture in architecture would find renewed favour during the 1950s.*

Right *The Storer House, another of Frank Lloyd Wright's so-called 'textile block' houses in Los Angeles, was constructed from patterned concrete blocks held together by steel rods. The blocks, left exposed on the interior, became a dominant component of the decorative scheme. In this way Wright achieved an 'organic' unity between the interior and the exterior of his buildings.*

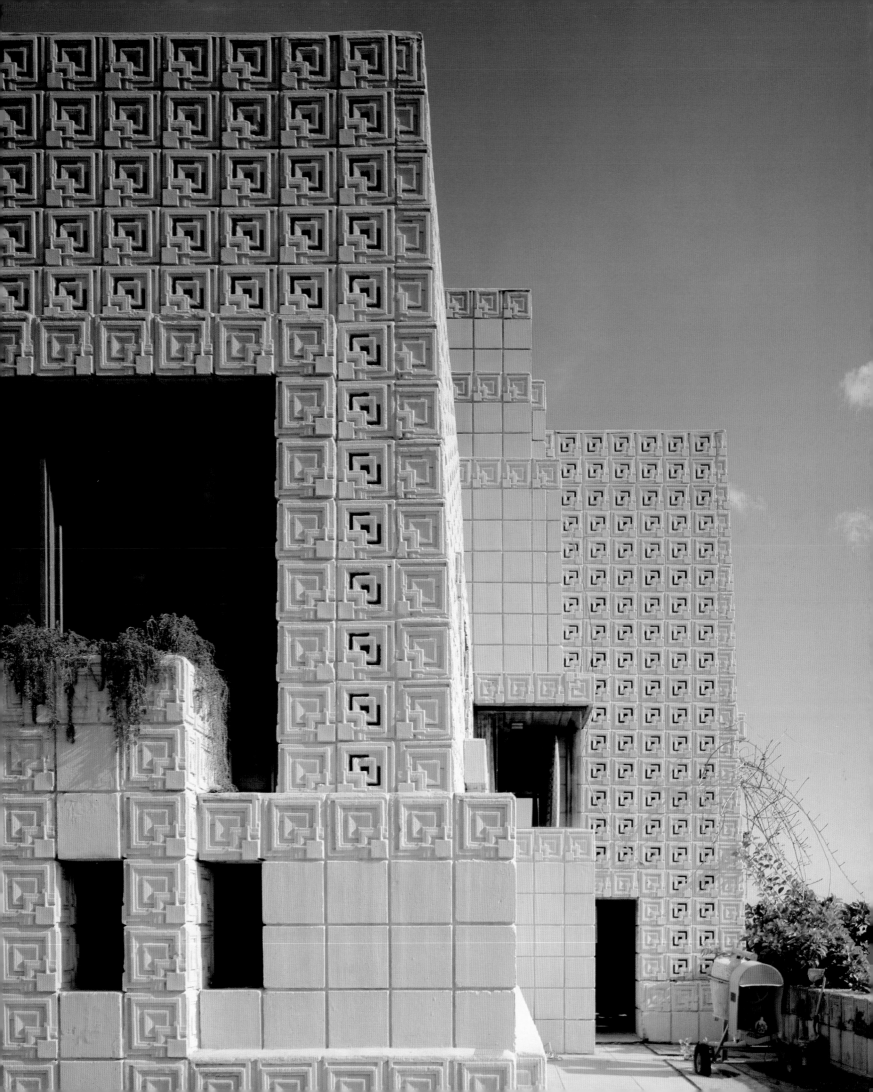

The Tomkins House in Long Island, designed by Marcel Breuer in 1945, shows how Breuer's work mellowed after he emigrated to the USA. By the mid-1940s his aesthetic vocabulary had broadened to incorporate stylistic features such as decorative brickwork and coloured paintwork, both of which would have been regarded as anathema during the early years of the Modern Movement in Europe – the era of the clinical white box.

The attempt by pioneer European Modernist architects to create a 'style without a style' had ultimately proved rather elusive, as new buildings of the 1920s and 1930s soon developed shared physical characteristics with a clear formalistic identity. This arose partly because of similarities in the choice of building materials and partly as the inevitable outcome of the aesthetic vision shared by the creators of these new buildings. As soon as visual ideas start to be repeated, they inevitably emerge as a recognizable style linked to a particular period in time. Even when the architect has consciously sought to eliminate decorative elements from his work, the public will focus on those physical characteristics and immediately identify them as a style.

It is also inevitable that distinctive new design styles will soon be imitated, and in this respect the buildings of the Modern Movement were no exception. In fact, because the Modernist house of the 1930s looked so obviously different from the traditional dwelling, it was particularly easy for the less scrupulous architect or speculative builder to create a 'moderne' house which superficially resembled it. The term 'moderne' describes the superficial pastiche of Modernism by commercial builders and manufacturers. It was just one of several fashionable styles of the 1930s, and is also sometimes now referred to as 'Art Deco', although the term 'moderne' was used at the time, whereas 'Art Deco' was coined retrospectively. The staunch Modernist, FRS Yorke, dismissed these 'speculatively built "Moderne Houses"' as part of the fashion for 'moderne' Art Deco design, characterized in Britain by 'jazz wallpapers, cubist vases and angular glassware'.

The idea that aesthetics alone were sufficient to make a building truly modern was a fallacy also exposed by Howard Myers in his foreword to George Nelson and Henry Wright's influential book, *Tomorrow's House*, in 1945: 'The notion that the contemporary approach to design involves flat roofs and corner windows and the exclusion of rambler roses is one kind of nonsense this book aims to expose.'

Retrospectively, however, the argument about the distinction between modern and 'moderne' design during the 1930s was largely academic because, at the time, modern architecture of any sort was the exception rather than the rule. Widely influential as were the pioneering architects of the Modern Movement after World War II, before this period their ideas were absorbed only by an elite composed of their close colleagues and their wealthy clients. Ironically, it was the war itself that produced a climate more favourable to modern architecture during the late 1940s and early 1950s. It was the approach of war, too, which caused the displacement of several key individuals, such as Mies van der Rohe, Walter Gropius and Marcel Breuer, from Germany to the USA during the 1930s. Here, they were able to practise more freely than they had been able to in Europe, to see more building projects come to fruition and to disseminate their ideas through teaching the next generation of American architects. In this way, their influence was greatly extended and their ideas gained wider currency. Furthermore, although materials shortages were widespread in the USA, there was less disruption to the construction industry there than in Europe during the 1940s. In spite of problems, therefore, more progress was made towards the consolidation and development of Modernist ideas in America during this period than was possible in Europe. The common-sense approach to design and architecture proposed by Nelson and Wright in *Tomorrow's House* in 1945 soon became widely accepted in the USA because it was more readily appreciated there that 'a house, like any other product, is the result of design and production processes. Looked at in this way, home is no different from a pencil sharpener or a tractor. It shares with them the characteristic of being an item of consumer use.'

The most significant change to the layout of the modern interior was open planning; an idea pioneered by Le Corbusier that began to take hold during the 1930s and was to become standard practice during the 1950s and 1960s. According to Yorke: 'The convenience and simplicity, and incidentally much of the charm of the modern interior are due to open planning, and the consequent intercommunication between rooms in the living quarters.'

The basic principle of open planning was that it was no longer considered necessary to erect permanent physical barriers between every room. Some divisions could be removed entirely, others could be of a more impermanent nature, in the form of accordion screens, for example, or sliding glass doors. Some walls clearly remained desirable, such as those dividing living areas from sleeping areas and, of course, those isolating areas, such as bathrooms, where special privacy was required. Other walls were now non-essential, however, and had continued to be erected out of habit rather than necessity. Thus, in the modern house the dining room might merge with the living room, and the living room with the study, while staircases to the upper or lower floors might rise into or out of any of these quarters. The idea that rooms should be more broadly multi-purpose, available for use in one form or another twenty-four hours a day, and also that the definition of function needed to be even more flexible, were a reflection of the increasingly informal lifestyles and decreasingly elastic budgets of the 1950s.

Although most of those who commissioned architect-designed private houses during the 1930s were wealthy and could still afford to employ live-in servants at this date, the scale of the average middle-class household was, on the whole, greatly reduced after World War I, so that the general trend was towards the self-servicing house, which was easy to maintain and did not require significant outlay on domestic upkeep. This trend continued after World War II, when the female head of the household often took on the housework instead of employing a maid. Thus it became imperative for housework to be not only manageable but also minimal. 'We do not need large houses,' noted Yorke, 'for we have neither large families to fill them nor domestics to look after them... and because servants are scarce we rely upon mechanical devices and efficient organization to lighten work in the home.' Given that servants had become scarce even before World War II, it was a reflection of the unusual wealth and status of the average client of a Modernist house of the 1930s, that so many illustrated in *The Modern House* still retained living quarters for a servant of some description. By the 1950s, this was rapidly becoming an anachronism.

Another Victorian convention gradually eroded during the 1930s was the location of living rooms on the ground floor and bedrooms and bathroom on the first floor. Modern architects realized that the

Below *Diagram from Le Corbusier's* Précisions *illustrating the advantages in terms of space gain in flat-roofed houses that are built on raised pillars with open plan interiors, over pitched-roofed houses with partition-like interior dividing walls.*

Bottom *Detail of the interior of Le Corbusier's Villa Savoye at Poissy showing how the architect put into practice his theories about open planning. A fluid 'free plan' is created partly through the use of ramps between floors, and partly through the reduction in the number of interior walls and doors.*

Right *Here, in the Villa Savoye, the conventional house plan is reversed, with the main reception room being raised onto the first floor above the garage and service rooms. From the first floor living room, which is 45 ft/13.7m long, there is direct access from one side onto a paved roof terrace. This is shielded and made more private by the continuation of the exterior wall. There is also another roof garden at the top of the house over the first floor rooms. In designing these facilities, a greater fluidity of movement was envisaged between acitivities taking place indoors and outdoors.*

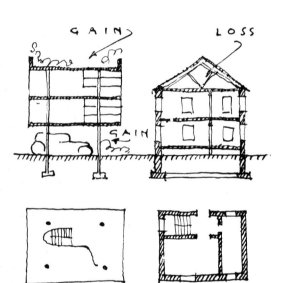

Above *The attractive paved terrace garden on the first floor of the Villa Savoye. The terrace takes up approximately one third of the available space at this level, which is an indication of the importance which the architect* *attached to it, and the significant role that he envisaged it would play in the lives of the people occupying the house. Access to the terrace is via one of the large sliding windows in the living room.*

first floor, being lighter and airier, was often the prime site within the house, and that it made sense to locate the primary living area there, rather than the secondary sleeping quarters. Le Corbusier had recommended that houses should be raised on pillars or *'pilotis'*, so that the ground floor rose to first-floor level and the service quarters, previously located in the cellar, were also brought above ground.

Although such arrangements were by no means the rule, it did become much more common to find the conventional internal layout altered in the modern house of the 1930s, with some or all of the bedrooms located on the same floor as the main living room. This challenging of tradition was also extended to the position of the garden, which was sometimes to be found, not at the foot of the house, but on the balcony or the roof instead. This feature was a favoured ploy of Le Corbusier in several of the houses built in France during his partnership with his cousin Pierre Jeanneret during the 1930s. In fact, Le Corbusier described the inversion of the traditional house plan in terms of his idealized vision of a floating city:

> The plan of the modern house can be reversed. The reception-rooms will be at the top, in direct communication with the roof garden, in the fresh air, away from the street with its dust and noise, in full sunshine. The roof becomes a solarium, and the demands of modern hygiene are satisfied. Generalization: the whole ground surface of the town is free, available for walking on. The ground is in a sense doubled; transported aloft, right in the sun.

Flat roofs first came into vogue between the two World Wars. According to Cranston Jones, writing in *Architecture Today and Tomorrow* (1961), the reason for this was that 'the image of flat-topped cubes on stilts... captured the public imagination.' The practical reason for flat roofs, however, was that the attic or loft area under the pitched roof was now considered to be a waste of space, and the roof itself, if level, could serve as an additional outdoor room for summer use. Le Corbusier described the flat-roofed house as having a 'free' plan and the pitch-roofed house as having a 'paralysed' plan, because the former gained so much space at ground level and at roof level. During the 1930s, in central Europe in particular, there was an obsession with healthy living and the need to spend time outdoors exercising or sunbathing, an attitude manifest in the moral fervour of Le Corbusier's remarks about 'hygiene'. Consequently, many houses were built with roof terraces, or with extended balconies at first-floor level leading off from the main living room, for use as an outdoor gymnasium, or a sun lounge. The advantages of these were also extolled by Yorke:

> The demand for out-of-door sleeping and exercise space on porch or roof follows the realization of the value of light and air and the large window... People who have flat roofs, easily accessible, find it possible to enjoy the sunshine from March to October.

Often, in addition to internal staircases, floors were connected by exterior ramps or steps, thereby emphasizing the idea of the half indoor-half outdoor house.

Above *Modern Movement architects prided themselves on designing houses that were tailored to the needs of modern living. The Caneel House in Brussels, designed by L H De Koninck in 1931, had* two roof terraces, one of which was fitted out as an open-air gymnasium. This feature reflects the importance attached to sunbathing and outdoor exercise at this date.

One of the great achievements of Modern Movement architecture was to increase the amount of natural light in buildings. Above *The Seagram Building in New York, designed by Mies van der Rohe in 1958,* demonstrates the concept of curtain wall window systems as applied to a tall office block. Here, glass is used as the main cladding material in place of masonry.

Right *Le Corbusier's Villa Savoye of 1930 has both ribbon windows running in a band around the house at first-floor level and large curtain wall windows which open from the first-floor living room onto a roof terrace.*

Closely linked with the growing interest in sunbathing and physical exercise that developed during the 1930s, and ideas about how facilities for such activities could be incorporated within the modern house, was a new emphasis on making the interior lighter through the installation of larger windows. From the 1930s onwards windows were to become an increasingly dominant feature of both the interior and the exterior of modern buildings, growing not only in size but also in number. In fact, it could be said that the 1930s was the decade in which window-mania first took hold within the architectural fraternity – a love affair which has continued ever since, with mixed success.

With the development of 'ribbon' window systems in the 1930s – in which bands of small or medium-sized panes were set at the same level in strips or 'ribbons' around the building – there was a rapid increase in the overall ratio of window to wall. After the war this culminated in the ubiquitous 'curtain-wall' window cladding of office blocks, and the controversial glass-walled houses designed by Mies van der Rohe and Philip Johnson in the USA. The original intention had been simply to reduce the physical barriers between the indoors and the outdoors: to allow light in, while keeping the elements out. Increasing the amount of light inside the house was considered as essential to good health as was physical exercise out of doors. During the 1930s, as a symbolic rejection of the often dark and gloomy houses of the late nineteenth century, the opening-up of the modern interior to natural light took on quasi-moral overtones, hints of which are captured in the comments by Yorke:

> In earlier times sunlight was regarded as harmful rather than beneficial; it was considered a stimulant to the growth of bacteria and windows were made small deliberately and placed away from the sunny side... Through medical research we have learnt better, and today sunlight is accepted as healthy and desirable; we take sun-baths and even artificial sun-ray treatments, we like large windows, and sometimes fill them with special glass to admit the ultra-violet rays.

In the most deluxe and well-equipped modern houses of the 1930s elaborate mechanisms were devised so that even the barrier of the main living room window could, on occasion, be removed. At the press of a button, the window would glide down into a cavity below, operated by an electric pulley system. Smaller windows, now more often made with steel rather than wooden frames, were designed to be more flexible in their methods of opening: special hinges enabled them to be opened fully outwards, or runners allowed them to be slid along behind an adjacent fixed pane.

Another striking feature of the modern house was the carefully considered inter-relationship between the building and its surroundings. If the house was in an urban setting, the main living quarters were usually separated from the immediate neighbourhood through being raised up above street level. If it was in a rural environment, a deliberately dramatic site was sometimes chosen, so that the building could be integrated into the countryside. Similar trends were to continue in the 1950s in increasingly exaggerated forms, so that urban

Opposite, Above and Following Page
Following the lead of Mies van der Rohe with his controversial glass-walled Farnsworth House at Illinois (see page 60-61), designed in 1946 but not completed until 1950, Philip Johnson built his own Glass House at New Canaan, Connecticut, in 1949. This single storey steel-framed house has no exterior walls, just floor to ceiling windows, so there is no visual obstruction between the interior and the surrounding landscape. The Glass House attracted extensive media coverage at the time, and although few clients were as bold as Johnson in wishing to live in what could be described as a goldfish bowl, the initiative did encourage other architects to increase the number and scale of the windows in the buildings they designed.

buildings became taller and more detached from their surroundings, and rural buildings became increasingly daring in the attempted interaction between the man-made and the natural environment.

This was a characteristic which had been exploited by Frank Lloyd Wright and which was seen in its most extreme and 'organic' form in the Kaufmann House of 1936 built at Bear Run, Pennsylvania. The house was known as Fallingwater because it was literally built over a waterfall. In it, living rooms opened directly out onto terraces and the architect made extensive use of uninterrupted horizontal windows to emphasize the closeness of the indoors to the outdoors. It was at Fallingwater, too, that Wright began to experiment with cantilevered structures and to explore the structural potential of reinforced concrete as a building material. Fallingwater projects on several planes over the waterfall and the rocks below. During the 1930s, cantilevering was largely used, as here, as a demonstration of the technical prowess of modern architectural engineering. During the 1950s, architects began to use it less heroically, as a means to an end, rather than as an end in itself.

When the main living room was at ground level or opened onto a terrace, large floor to ceiling picture windows were often installed to bring the drama of the landscape right into the living room. An outstanding example of this was the Tugendhat Haus of 1930 at Brno in the Czech Republic designed by Mies van der Rohe which had a 'Fenesta' steel-framed picture window, electrically operated so that it could be made to disappear entirely below floor level at the push of a button. A sign of increasing maturity after the war, however, was the integration of the non-dramatic landscape into the house, which made the most of even the modest suburban garden, for example.

Architects practising in North America, being physically distanced from the war, were able to continue to develop the concept of the modern house largely uninterrupted during the 1940s. This included both native and emigré architects, between whose work a fusion now began to take place. During the course of this decade, inauspicious as it was for architects and designers working in Europe, a new confidence emerged in the USA. As a result, by the 1950s, North America had clearly taken the lead in the development of modern architecture: the European-born Modern Movement had been overtaken by American 'Contemporary' architecture. In 1945, as soon as the hostilities were over, the architect George Nelson and Henry Wright, the editor of *Architectural Forum*, published *Tomorrow's House – A Complete Guide for the Home Builder*, an extremely influential book which instructed the reader in planning a new home, remodelling an old house and making the best use of the latest materials, equipment and appliances. The main aim of the book, as clearly stated in the foreword by Howard Myers, was to suggest an alternative to the generally accepted notions of what a house could offer its inhabitants. In particular, the authors were keen to refute the idea that modern houses were somehow uncomfortable and that the only sort of new house that could possibly be comfortable was one based on a traditional model. Myers was also quick to point out the glaring inconsistency of modern taste:

This book challenges not most, but all of the sweet-scented nostalgia on the domestic scene. Despite its persuasive manner, it is going to

Opposite and Above *Fallingwater House, Bear Run, Pennsylvania, designed by Frank Lloyd Wright in 1936. This virtuoso house was noteworthy for the way in which the man-made structure was so masterfully integrated with the landscape, and for Wright's adventurous use of reinforced concrete for the cantilevered terraces. What finally emerged as the 'Contemporary' style in the USA after World War II was a combination of the technical bravado of Wright, and the finesse of architects from the European Modern Movement, such as Mies van der Rohe.*

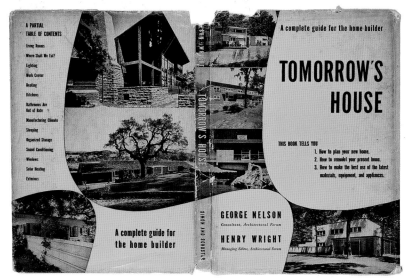

Top *Tugendhat House, Brno, Czech Republic, designed in 1930 by Mies van der Rohe. This house had large, electrically-operated 'Fenesta' steel windows in the living room which could be lowered into the ground at the press of a button.*

Above *The cover of Tomorrow's House – A Complete Guide for the Home Builder by George Nelson and Henry Wright. Published in 1945, this book heralded the arrival of 'Contemporary' architecture in the USA after the war.*

disturb many readers who keep their milk in the latest refrigerator, drive to business in the newest car, but persist in thinking that a Cape Cod cottage remains the snappiest idea in a home.

The great tradition in building, as Nelson and Wright pointed out in *Tomorrow's House*, was not to copy the styles of the past, but to work in a confidently modern idiom. In their view, architects only moved forward by developing forms expressive of their particular age, not by staying still or regressing. The authors conclude with a deliberately paradoxical statement: 'We are in favour of modern houses, not because they are modern, but because they are traditional.'

In both Europe and the USA, during the 1920s and early 1930s, one overt sign of allegiance to the Modern Movement was in the choice of building materials and, in particular, the preference for man-made materials, such as steel and concrete, over natural materials, such as stone and wood. Reinforced concrete, in which rods of steel were embedded in pillars or beams of concrete, provided a major technical breakthrough, opening up new structural possibilities because of its increased strength. As a result, from the 1930s onwards, the basic engineering of modern buildings could be radically reviewed. Architects of the day were so enthusiastic about these exciting new engineering opportunities that they literally waxed lyrical, not only on the technical merits of their materials, but on their aesthetic charms as well. Yorke enthused:

Steel and concrete have their own form and their own beauty. The new materials and the revolutionary systems of construction based upon their properties make it possible for us to plan our buildings according to our needs, with freedom and economy, with immense spans and slender supports, with cantilevered façades, so that the traditional sense of dimension, proportion and scale is destroyed, for not only is the internal organization affected, but the external form also. The form is the result of the plan, the construction, and the materials, not of a preconceived idea of what a building should look like, or an essay in a popular style.

Progressive architects, such as Le Corbusier, felt creatively inspired by their new materials, because it was these that gave them the freedom to plan their buildings in the logical and rational way in which they believed modern architecture should be designed.

From a technical point of view, the most important breakthough was that, whereas it was the load-bearing walls which had previously carried the weight of a building, now the narrow steel or reinforced concrete posts and beams took all the weight, so that what was inserted inbetween them could be simply infill. This infill did not need to be either strong or thick, its main purpose being for insulation. It was, in fact, more like a skin, while the steel and concrete framework formed the skeleton. It followed, therefore, that architects could decide to make this skin of entirely different materials from those that had previously been considered standard, and this, in turn, drastically altered the physical appearance of buildings. Once again, technical breakthroughs had resulted in a revised aesthetic code.

Modernist houses of the 1930s, however, undoubtedly had a more restricted visual vocabulary than 'Contemporary' houses of the 1950s. Many were somewhat clinical in appearance, being typically rendered in stucco painted white, and their clean, precise appearance meant that the 1930s Modernist house sometimes bore a closer resemblance to a health centre or a laboratory than to a conventional home. This clinical aesthetic was often carried through into the design of the interior too, which was also almost invariably painted white or cream throughout as well, and tended to be as free from decorative detailing and embellishments as the exterior. The over-riding impression of both the interior and exterior was of hygiene, precision, orderliness and control.

All this changed after the war when Modernist architecture became more expressive in colour, shape and mood. During the 1950s the 'rules' were relaxed as it came to be recognized that houses could be practical without being humourless, and as it began to be appreciated that the introduction of a variety of colours, textures and patterns in the form of exterior cladding and interior decoration added important elements of visual stimulation which could make a house or an apartment block much more pleasurable to live in. The introduction of such decorative features led to the emergence of the 'Contemporary' style of the 1950s which combined the fundamentals of Modernism with a more upbeat and dynamic exploration of the visual potential of applied art.

The main difference between architecture of the 1930s and the 1950s was that whereas before the war buildings incorporating decorative features had tended to be dismissed by serious architects as frivolous or 'moderne', after the war decorative art, as incorporated into the fabric of the building and as used in the adornment of its interior, was treated much more positively. Furthermore, the growing influence of contemporary art on design after World War II opened up new possibilities for greater visual expression in architecture. Although the majority of public and private buildings continued to be rectilinear in form, the previously rigorous and rather inflexible conventions of Modernism were, in some instances, softened by the influence of organic sculpture. Sometimes this could be seen directly in the adoption of overtly plastic or consciously expressive shapes within the form of buildings; at other times it was manifested indirectly through the integration of works of sculpture in public buildings.

Aesthetics were only one aspect of the much wider changes that were to take place in architecture and interior design after the war, however: it was not simply a question of changing taste and fashion but of fundamental shifts in attitude – social, political and psychological. The most significant factor to bring about radical change was, of course, the war itself. The massive physical destruction inflicted on so many European cities meant that governments were faced with an acute housing shortage during the late 1940s. In addition, because of the displacement of large populations, the shortage was on an unprecedented scale. Modern architecture, with its concern for functionalism and for economical use of space, with its scientific approach to human and technological engineering and with its common-sense, rational exploitation of new building materials, was now suddenly viewed as an essential ally in tackling this momentous problem. Suddenly, the theory

Above *House on the Danube in Hungary designed by Ludwig Kozma in 1935. Not only was the structural framework of this house constructed using reinforced concrete, but the floors and the roof were as well. In places, the concrete was left exposed, revealing the impress of the shutters used to contain it while it was being poured.*

Following Page *The Buck House designed by Rudoph Schindler in 1934. Schindler, like Richard Neutra, was of Austrian origin. After emigrating from Europe they both settled on the West Coast of the USA where they played a significant role in the development of modern architecture in that area. During the early 1930s both men were clearly working in what was known as the 'International Style'.*

and the practice of Modernism began to make sense so that when, for example, the first new high-rise blocks of flats were erected in London after the war on estates such as Roehampton, they were warmly welcomed both by the authorities who had funded them and by the people for whom they provided a much-needed home.

Much of the public hostility to modern architecture that had inhibited progress in Europe before the war now evaporated in the face of overwhelming social need. Furthermore, although the planning of individual houses still offered architects greater creative scope, many began to feel that it was also their duty to address the problem of low-cost housing and to endeavour to tackle this problem creatively as well. This accounts for the outstanding quality of some of the architects working for or with local authorities during the 1950s, including talented individuals such as Sven Markelius in Sweden and Le Corbusier in France. At this time, a common sense of purpose motivated the architects of public housing schemes in some socialist countries, such as Sweden and Britain, and their lead in this field was much admired elsewhere. In spite of the enormous pressure on governments at this time to house people as quickly as possible, most local authority-employed architects working in Britain in the early 1950s found that it was possible to achieve their goal in a positive and creative way, without abandoning the newly established functional basis of their creed.

As well as providing the impetus for huge social change, the war also gave a new purpose and direction to pioneer European Modernist architects and designers of the 1930s such as Breuer, Gropius and Mies van der Rohe, who had hitherto been struggling for recognition. After the war, although mostly no longer working in their native countries, these individuals now received public and professional recognition which, through the commissions they were awarded, and the influence they exerted in their new teaching posts, enabled their message to reach a much wider audience. Henceforward, Modernism was treated with much greater respect.

What made the post-war 'Contemporary' style different from the pre-war Modern style was that the war had changed social needs and attitudes and this was reflected by the shift in design priorities during the late 1940s. Functionalism was still of primary importance, but there was a less hard-edged clinical analysis of what was deemed functional, and a wider range of options for how a functional house could be created. After World War II national characteristics also came more visibly to the fore in terms of the choice of building materials, so that whereas during the 1930s the International Modern style was fairly uniform – an all-white exterior being virtually de rigueur; after the war, although basic structures and frameworks might be similar – the choice of exterior finish often varied enormously. The British, for example, were attached to brick and stone; the Americans and the Scandinavians preferred timber; the Italians had a special liking for tiled exteriors; and the South Americans responded positively to the challenge of raw concrete. While the basic structure of 'Contemporary' houses in different parts of the world had many common elements, regional variations in cladding, for example, meant that houses now retained their own distinct identities.

The interior of the 'Contemporary' house differed from its Modernist predecessor in its increased attention to decorative detail, both in the fabric of the building, where the architect took the leading role, and in the choice of furniture and furnishings, where the decisions of the house-owner came to the fore. This shift was noted by the architectural writer Wolf von Eckardt in 1961 when he noted in *Mid-Century Architecture in America*: 'At first it seemed as though the only alternative to masquerading buildings in historic costumes was to present them in a state of pristine nudity. But that was by no means all there was to it.' The pre-war Modern house had had an aura of exclusivity because it was often architect-designed both inside and out and particular attention was paid to achieving consistency and homogeneity between the interior and the exterior. The more active role played by the owner of the 'Contemporary' house made it crucially different in mood and character, as well as an expression of greater democracy. Also, there was a subtle shift of emphasis away from the Modernist idea of the house as a machine – a concept which many people found too impersonal and even vaguely disturbing – to a more people-centred approach. According to Nelson and Wright, people 'began to forget about the "machine" as an end in itself and to think more about what it could do for better living.'

One explanation given at the time for the widespread public hostility towards modern architecture during the 1920s and 1930s was that it reflected a resistance on the part of society to change. This was especially pertinent as the likelihood of a second World War became more of a possibility. Nelson and Wright reflected on this in *Tomorrow's House*: 'We can see... why modern houses were greeted at the outset with such violent outbursts of disapproval. "Modern" was more than a way of designing houses – it was one more symbol of incomprehensible change. And every change these days seems to be a threat to personal and social stability.' By the 1950s, however, because of the revolution in social attitudes effected by the war and as a result of being deprived of choice for so long during and immediately after the hostilities, people relished the thought of change and welcomed the luxury of being offered greater choice. The public were consequently much more receptive to the wider and more adventurous range of 'Contemporary' architecture and design on offer during the 1950s.

After World War II there was a fundamental shift in the philosophy behind the creation of the 'Contemporary' house. Whereas during the 1930s architects had aspired to objectivity and distance in their approach to design – they liked to think of themselves as scientists engaged in some form of social experiment – the experience of the war brought with it the realization that people needed to be treated as human beings, and thus a more humane and expressive approach to architecture and design developed. Nelson and Wright were the first to express these changed perceptions when they wrote in 1945: 'Individuality is possible only in a modern house because no other approach to building expresses life as it is today. And without expression there is no individuality.'

Above *Interior of the Jones House in Los Angeles, designed by Quincy Jones and Frederick Emmons in 1955. With its pleasant interior courtyard garden and its varied wood, steel and concrete surfaces, this house typifies the more relaxed, expressive and individualistic qualities of 'Contemporary' architecture of the 1950s, which ensured that there was even greater spatial fluidity between the indoors and outdoors.*

Night-time view of Case Study House number 22 by Pierre Koenig, built in the dramatic setting of the Hollywood Hills in 1959–60. The glass-walled living room of this classic house ☞ cantilevers out over the hillside, so that the occupants of the room appear from the outside to be hovering over the city.

2. the house

'Where contemporary architecture has been allowed to provide a new setting for contemporary life, this new setting has acted in its turn upon the life from which it springs. The new atmosphere has led to change and development in the conceptions of the people who live in it.' **Sigfried Giedion, Space, Time and Architecture, 1963**

Although the 'Contemporary' style followed directly on from the Modern Movement, it was imbued with a different spirit. The war years marked a decisive break. Afterwards, Modernist architects and designers felt less embattled; the atmosphere in the design world was less uptight; and modern architecture was increasingly accepted by and integrated with society. One of the reasons for this was that post-war design was more people-centred, and 'Contemporary' architects were more generous in their assessment of the public's wider needs. They recognized, for example, that such needs extended beyond the provision of the basic functional necessities to encompass other equally important, but less rationally justifiable requirements, such as the demand for visual stimulation and

physical comfort — what Philip Will characterized in *Mid-Century Architecture in America* as 'warmth, texture and decoration'.

Although no less rigorous in their approach and no less determined in their ambitions than before the war, the majority of 'Contemporary' architects were more democratic in the audience they set out to reach, and more pragmatic in the standards to which they aspired on behalf of their clients. Many pursued an active interest in low-cost housing, for example, either on behalf of local authorities, or in partnership with commercial developers, and the profession as a whole deliberately sought to avoid being perceived as elitist and exclusive. A desire to encourage a greater three-way dialogue between architects, clients and users of modern buildings was reflected in comments made by Pier Luigi Nervi at the time:

> Everyone contributes to architecture: the client, with the exact definition of his requirements and the choice of designer; the architect in the function of interpreter or rather catalyst, of the deep and sometimes unconscious feelings of the society in which he lives; the general public, which judges a work of architecture with the immediacy which comes from the very fact of living in it or beside it and, by its verdict, influences succeeding developments in building.

Amongst the design fraternity, too, there was a strong desire to reach a wider audience, not just in terms of size but in social make-up as well. This they hoped to achieve by encouraging manufacturers to put good quality 'Contemporary' design into mass-production, thereby reducing the price to the consumer. These ideas had their origins in European initiatives of the 1910s to the 1930s – in the philosophy of the Deutscher Werkbund and the Bauhaus in Germany, for example, and in the promotion of Industrial Art in Britain and Sweden during the inter-war period – but it was during the 1950s that they came to fruition in real terms.

It was in the USA in the 1950s that many of the most significant early post-war developments took place, both in architecture in general, and in domestic architecture in particular. This was in part due to the arrival earlier in the century of several emergent figures from the European Modern Movement who had set up practices and began to teach. In the 1920s Eero Saarinen arrived from Finland along with Richard Neutra and Rudolph Schindler from Austria. In the 1930s they were followed by the famous trio from the Bauhaus, in Germany; Walter Gropius, Marcel Breuer and Ludwig Mies van der Rohe. Equally, however, it was due to the consolidation and expansion of an increasingly healthy native tradition, stimulated and presided over by the towering elder statesman of the American design world, Frank Lloyd Wright.

This dynamic cocktail of influences, triggered by the prospect of economic renewal following World War II, led to a flowering of native talent in the field of architecture and design in the USA during the late 1940s. Added to which, as the American public became more receptive to 'Contemporary' design during the 1950s, thereby stimulating the market, the USA emerged as one of the new design superpowers of the post-war era, along with Finland, Denmark,

Above *An early photograph of the Mutual Housing Association community development scheme at Brentwood, Los Angeles, built between 1946 and 1950, seen here before the site had been fully developed. This was a co-operative venture involving several hundred* *families who purchased an area of land in the Crestwood Hills, and then employed the architects Whitney Smith and Quincy Jones, and the engineer Edgardo Contini, to create a range of standardized house designs suitable for various sites.* Opposite *Because these houses were constructed of basic prefabricated components such as steel 'I' bars and concrete blocks, they were relatively low-cost. Exposed concrete blocks are clearly visible in this view of an interior.*

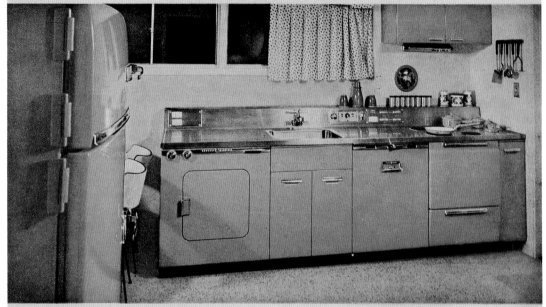

Top *Still from the film* Mr Blandings Builds His Dreamhouse *made in 1948, showing a modern house designed in the traditional Cape Cod style with a pitched roof and wooden shutters.* Above *Cover of the 1944 American publication,* Small Homes Guide, *aimed at veterans returning from the war. Because of the housing shortage at the end of World War II, there* was considerable public interest in architecture. Above Right *An advertisement for a range of American 'dream kitchen' appliances marketed by General Electric during the 1950s. 'Built-in custom kitchen-laundry centers' came as part of the standard fittings in the Country Clubber houses built by the developer, William Levitt (seen middle top), during the 1950s.*

Sweden and Italy. In the field of 'Contemporary' architecture, the USA was, for a time, the undisputed world leader.

Instrumental in creating a climate for change and encouraging a shift in public opinion were the editors of several leading architectural magazines, notably Henry Wright of *Architectural Forum*, Emerson Gable of *Architectural Record*, and John Entenza of *Arts & Architecture*. Although they were only able to reach a limited public through these magazines, they also engaged in a wider range of activities including publishing books on the subject of house design – both 'how-to' books and surveys of contemporary practice – which reached a much wider audience and helped to raise public awareness of the issues under discussion by specialists in the field. In so doing, however, they were not uncritical of their audience, as they felt that it was the American weakness of complacency that was inhibiting the wider acceptance of modern architecture and interiors. It was only by deliberately puncturing these complacent attitudes that they felt they could make a breakthrough. It is clear from the tone of Nelson and Wright in *Tomorrow's House* that the cowardly and often reactionary nature of the majority of potential American house-builders and homeowners before the war was considered the major hurdle to be overcome in converting the public to modern architecture. The perceived need for stimulation and guidance in this area was what prompted the somewhat didactic tone of Howard Myers in his foreword:

> Every mortgage banker should read it to make certain the houses he finances will retain high resale value ten, fifteen, twenty years from now. Every house builder should read it if he aspires to greater success than his smug competitor. Every real estate man should read it because it can add a new note of conviction to his plea for home ownership – of the right house. And every architect should read it if only to stiffen his backbone when he tells the client 'You cannot walk backwards into the future!'

The tactic employed by the authors themselves, however, was not to barrage their readers with talk of Modernism and the avant-garde, but to attempt to persuade them that what was being proposed was simply a matter of common sense. Interestingly, what distinguished this book from those that had preceded it and what made it uniquely American, was that functionalism was no longer presented as a pseudo-science but as a commercial imperative. This pragmatic approach was very different to the high-minded intellectual tone of the European Modernists during the earlier part of the century; it was clearly designed to appeal, in particular, to a more hard-nosed, business-minded American audience. It was directly to this audience that the authors now spoke, not, as in the case of Yorke and his contemporaries, simply to fellow architects. They had no desire to preach to the converted. Furthermore, Nelson and Wright perceived that during the first half of the 1940s a subtle change had been taking place in public attitudes in the USA as a result of the impact of the war. Since people were now more responsive to common sense and there was no longer any need to preach, a little light-hearted persuasion was all that was required in order to bring people round. Gradually, too, the somewhat off-putting adjective

'Modern', as supplied to the new style of architecture and design during the 1930s, with its connotations of elitism and exclusivity, was being dropped in favour of the more accessible 'Contemporary'. Whereas 'Modern' implied something rather remote and futuristic, 'Contemporary' suggested something directly relevant to today. The 'Contemporary' house, as it was becoming known during the early 1940s, therefore, was no longer being presented in an intimidating way, as an offshoot of modern art, but in a form that was more palatable. While the authors clearly hoped that their book would be 'provocative' – in other words, make people uncomfortable enough to question the received ideas that were commonplace before the war – it was also intended to be 'useful and convincing'. 'Contemporary' architecture, Nelson and Wright assured the public, was nothing to be alarmed about; 'the swing towards the modern' was the most sensible course for society as a whole to follow.

Equating the American public with a patient suffering from a psychosomatic illness, what Nelson and Wright prescribed initially was the verbal equivalent of a good dose of salts. This they administered in the form of an amusing exposé of the aesthetic foibles and prejudices of the middle classes, drawing attention in particular to the inconsistency of the public's response to modern design, which they found acceptable in the form of a mechanical gadget such as a fridge or a car, but unacceptable when applied to a house. Houses were judged by inherited or received notions about aesthetics and social conventions, rather than by their suitability for the task in hand. Focusing their attack on the cherished American ideal of the Cape Cod style house, the authors first painted an idyllic picture of 'a quaint little white cottage, shyly nestling in a grove of old elms or maples, bathed in the perfume of lilacs...', only to demolish this as 'a dream'. They then pointed out rather bluntly that, 'When people attempt to realize it today, what they actually get is either a cheap imitation or an outrageously expensive fake. And in the end the whole thing is given away by the late model Buick at the front door... or by the kitchen ventilating fan, or a television aerial, not to mention the tiled bath and the streamlined kitchen.' The reference to the streamlined kitchen is significant, because it was through the increasingly irresistible appeal of improved facilities such as these that a proportion of the American public was eventually won over to the idea of the all-round streamlined fully 'Contemporary' house. It was, in fact, the desirability of the 'Contemporary' kitchen that partly accounted for the growing popularity in the 1950s of the 'Contemporary' house, both in the USA and elsewhere. Furthermore, it was undoubtedly the attraction of the American dream kitchen, with its Formica-topped built-in fitted units, its generously proportioned fridge, and its wealth of labour-saving electrical gadgets, that made many Europeans so keen to emulate the American lifestyle.

In spite of their somewhat facetious attitude towards their readers, in promoting 'tomorrow's house' during the mid-1940s, Nelson and Wright saw themselves as catalysts, rather than initiators, of change. Their power, they felt, was in their ability to influence the speed at which change took place, rather than to determine its actual direction, and they were confident in predicting that, once the war was over, major changes would rapidly take place. This was a conclusion they reached from studying the media which, even by the mid-1940s, already projected an increasing number of images of modernity in relation to the home:

> We have been watching the advertisements, the movies, and the magazines, and the swing to the modern has definitely begun. All our tremendous apparatus for influencing public opinion is tuning up for a new propaganda barrage in favour of these new houses. A new fashion in homes will be created, and the public will follow.

By the early years of the 1950s the predicted trend had been confirmed. When the editors of *Architectural Record* published a survey entitled *A Treasury of Contemporary Houses* in 1954, the concept of the 'Contemporary' house had obviously been widely accepted. In the introduction to this book by Emerson Gable, his comments on the stylistic changes that had been taking place in American domestic architecture since the war capture something of the excitement and exuberance of the period:

> House design today is in a state of delightful confusion. Confusion because ideas seem to change so rapidly, or maybe because there are so many ideas, so many new things to work with. Delightful because we want our houses to be delightful. You might even say that delight is the current fashion.

Young American architects took their work extremely seriously, clearly revelling in the creative opportunities which had suddenly opened up for them after the war, and responding in an overtly enthusiastic way. Many had felt frustrated that their careers had been held back by the war, and the pleasure of being able to practise their art without restraint at last was a new and thrilling experience: it was as though architecture itself was deregulated. By this date, too, there were many new materials coming on to the market – some developed for military purposes during the war – acting as a spur for technical experimentation. For some, this was a major incentive in its own right; others were content simply to be able to pursue their work creatively using traditional materials. It was this varied mixture of responses and solutions to the challenge of modern architecture that produced what Emerson Gable characterized as the situation of 'delightful confusion' which prevailed at this time.

That 'Contemporary' houses were being extensively built in the USA during the early 1950s is indicated by the amount of material accumulated in *A Treasury of Contemporary Houses*: over fifty examples were from recent issues of the *Architectural Record*. Further evidence is provided by Gable's introduction in his reference to modern architecture, not as a recent development, but as something well-established that had taken hold 'many years ago... sweeping out the sentimental litter of by-gone styles'. According to Gable, modern architecture had emerged in response to the fact that the American public had become more discerning intellectually, rejecting the phoney in favour of the honest:

So architects set about developing an architecture that would satisfy our sharpened intellects. They began developing new forms, new materials and techniques, new aesthetics, new combinations of space, new ways to design houses for their purposes.

What was different from the 1930s, Gable pointed out, however, was the degree of emotional commitment. 'Variety' and 'delight' were identified as the two key characteristics of domestic architecture in the USA by the mid-1950s. Academic rules and rigid formulae were out of fashion: instead, architects were to be given a freer rein in order to enable them to create buildings that would give genuine pleasure and satisfaction to their owners. Gable claimed confidently that 'nowadays there is no dogma, intellectual or otherwise, against using whatever ideas may appeal to you'.

This was a prosperous time commercially in the USA, and as the consumer boom grew apace, the building trade and architectural profession prospered with it. According to Philip Will, president of the American Institute of Architects, writing in *Mid-Century Architecture in America* in 1961:

> We face the biggest building boom in any nation's history. The forces behind it – the rapid expansion of our population and the growing obsolescence of our cities – are irresistible. The question is not whether we will build on an unprecedented scale but how well we will do it.

As in Europe, intense pressure to house the fast-growing population resulted in an explosion of building activity during the late 1940s and the 1950s, typified in the USA by massive standardized suburban developments such as the Levittowns in New Jersey and Pennsylvania built by the entrepreneur William J Levitt. At times the scale of building activity and the momentum it generated threatened to result in a free-for-all, especially when unscrupulous developers became involved. However, such momentum could be constructive if channelled in the right direction, such as via publicly or commercially funded low-cost housing schemes. This was the motivation behind the many prototype architect-designed 'Contemporary' houses developed during the period, which were intended for mass production. In spite of the growing popularity of the 'Contemporary' style, however, very few developers would invest in housing schemes that were too overtly modern, so the majority of houses, although they contained many modern features within the interior, often had a conventional pseudo-Cape Cod cottage on the exterior.

It was during the Depression years of the 1930s, when the building trade was in recession, that many architects had begun to investigate seriously the idea of low-cost housing schemes. Ideally, the aim was to achieve the standardization of both components and designs. As the American architectural historian Esther McCoy explained retrospectively in *Blueprints for Modern Living*, 'when practice wanes, theory flourishes... Architects who matured in the 1930s were dedicated to the ideal of architecture as a social art... by the 1940s the true path was through standardization.' Out of these experiments grew the remarkable

Top and Far Right
Lake Success, Levittown, Long Island, NY, 1949. The entreprenurial developer, William Levitt, scored a huge public success during the early post-war period with his massive suburban estates, known as Levittowns. Built on huge tracts of land in New York, Pennsylvania and New Jersey, each estate housed tens of thousands of people. Levitt's low-cost houses were built extremely quickly using standardized components and factory-type production methods. Hoards of visitors were attracted to view each new range of model houses.

Levitt catered to all tastes: some dwellings had flat roofs in the 'Contemporary' style but many were built with pitched roofs in more traditional styles.
Above *In 1949 King Vidor made a film called* The Fountainhead, *about the vacillating*

fortunes of a Modernist architect. The architect, played by Gary Cooper, was loosely based on Frank Lloyd Wright, as this still from the film, showing a Modernist house in the style of Wright, clearly shows.

case study house 5

Whitney R. Smith, A. I. A., Architect

THIS IS THE FIFTH OF A CONTINUING SERIES OF STUDIES BY NINE NATIONALLY-KNOWN ARCHITECTS FOR ARTS & ARCHITECTURE'S CASE STUDY HOUSE PROGRAM. THESE HOUSES WILL BE BUILT THROUGH THE MAGAZINE AS CLIENT AS SOON AS IS PRACTICABLE AFTER THE LIFTING OF WARTIME RESTRICTIONS.

initiative of the Case Study House programme in Los Angeles. The brainchild of John Entenza, the editor of the enlightened West Coast magazine *Arts and Architecture*, these houses were commissioned over a twenty-year period from the mid-1940s to the mid-1960s, and were conceived originally as prototypes for low-cost housing using standardized mass-produced components. Although with the return to commercial prosperity and full employment during the 1950s the programme ultimately changed direction and began to cater for the needs of a more affluent society, the early houses bear witness to a high degree of bold experimentation of a non-commercial kind.

Entenza had bought *Arts and Architecture* in 1938, taking over as editor two years later. Under his guidance a hitherto idiosyncratic regional magazine was transformed into a mouthpiece for the Modern Movement in America, with an international profile. It also took on a stylish new graphic identity created by Herbert Matter and Alvin Lustig. Aesthetics also played an important role in the Case Study Houses: the scheme was not just about functionalism and 'fitness for purpose', but about the creation of what Entenza referred to as a 'good environment'. This encompassed both the interior and exterior appearance of the house, as well as its workability from the inhabitants' point of view. However, in some ways the aims of the scheme were rather vague and open-ended, which was why, even at the outset, the various architects involved adopted such different approaches, and why, after some time had elapsed, it began to depart from its original premise – the creation of low-cost housing in a 'Contemporary' idiom.

As with so many initiatives of the early post-war period, there was something of a missionary fervour about the Case Study House programme when it first started. Initially this led to some misunderstanding about the motives behind the programme: some suggested that it was just a propaganda exercise while others dismissed it as an advertising ploy on behalf of the building trade designed to boost its business. What seems to have actually motivated Entenza to undertake such a difficult, expensive and demanding project, however, was the desire to consolidate the progress he had already made through *Arts and Architecture* magazine in raising public awareness about the issues involved in modern architecture. He was particularly concerned to inhibit back-sliding on the part of the public to their former position of complacency. In the words of Esther McCoy, 'The Case Study House programme was based on the assumption – the fear – that architecture at the end of the war would fall back into its eclectic rut.'

What Entenza was trying to prevent was a return to the false ideal of the Cape Cod dream cottage and other forms of historical revivalism, or eclecticism as it was described at the time, so prevalent during the 1930s. Through building the Case Study Houses, Entenza was hoping to demystify and popularize the aims of the Modern Movement, to open up its products to public view and its aims to public scrutiny. His aspirations were one step on from those of Nelson and Wright: instead of simply writing about the idea of 'Tomorrow's House', he decided to press ahead and build it instead. In this way he hoped to bring the message home to people that, if they were going to build a dream house, it should be in a 'Contemporary' rather than a traditional style. By putting actual examples of 'Contemporary' houses on

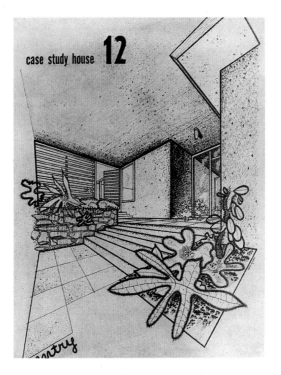

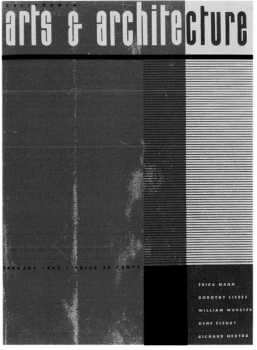

Opposite and Top Left *Two pages from* Arts and Architecture *magazine featuring the designs for Case Study Houses number 5 and number 12, commissioned from Whitney Smith in 1945 and 1946 respectively. Although neither of these houses was ever actually built, many others were, and the programme as a whole helped to raise public awareness of 'Contemporary' architecture in the USA during the early post-war period.* Bottom Left *Cover of* Arts and Architecture *magazine, February 1942, designed by Alvin Lustig. A stylish new graphic identity was created for the magazine by Alvin Lustig and Herbert Matter after John Entenza assumed the editorship in 1940. Five years later he embarked on the ambitious Case Study House programme.*

view, complete with complementary furniture and furnishings, he was demonstrating in real terms that 'Tomorrow's House' was available today. This prospect was clearly an attractive one, because when the first six houses were opened to the public in 1946-7, they attracted 368,554 visitors. In the end, although only two-thirds of the Case Study Houses were actually built, all the designs were published.

Several of the architects involved in the programme, such as Richard Neutra and William Wurster, were already well established by the 1940s but the majority were relatively young and unknown. Charles Eames, who built a house for himself with his wife Ray at Pacific Palisades, and Eero Saarinen, with whom he collaborated on a house for John Entenza on an adjacent site (Case Study Houses numbers 8 and 9 respectively, built between the years 1945 and 1949), were still at the early stages of their careers. These two architects had achieved earlier success by jointly winning the Organic Furniture Competition held by the Museum of Modern Art in New York in 1940. Younger still were Craig Ellwood and Pierre Koenig, whose proto-high-tech Case Study Houses of the mid- to late 1950s set new standards of sophistication and modernity for the decade.

Whereas in some cases the actual clients and their precise circumstances were known in advance of the design being commissioned, other houses were originally designed for imaginary clients. Richard Neutra, in Case Study Houses numbers 6 and 13, called his imaginary clients the Omegas and the Alphas. Each family had their own fictitious client profile, detailing the number of people, their relationships, their finances and their habits. Before the houses could be built, however, they had to be matched to an actual rather than an imaginary client, at which point the plans were often modified.

One characteristic which all the houses shared was technological experimentation. Sometimes this was embodied in the actual structure of the building itself, as in the steel-framed houses of Craig Ellwood, and sometimes in the choice of building materials, as in Pierre Koenig's use of steel decking. The desire to experiment was also reflected in the incorporation of new, often synthetic, materials into the interior, such as Formica on work surfaces and Naugahyde upholstery on furniture. Likewise, the prevailing interest in technology resulted in the installation of electric gadgets into many of the Case Study Houses, such as automated garage doors, hi-fi and television equipment, and multi-purpose kitchen appliances, such as the combined sink-cooker in Case Study House number 21. Sometimes technical innovation was pre-determined by the sponsorship of particular manufacturers, who provided free materials in the hope of benefiting from the resulting publicity, the Pioneer-Flintkote roof used on Case Study House number 7 by Thornton Abell being such an example.

Ideas about physical layout were also common to many houses in the scheme. These included open planning which was a Modernist feature and 'zoning' – the grouping together of related activities into areas of the house which were in close proximity (such as the kitchen and the workshop) and conversely, the strategic physical separation of areas of the house devoted to conflicting activities, such as music-making and sleeping. As very few of the thirty-six houses were originally designed with more than one storey, zoning took place

Top and Opposite *The Bailey House (Case Study House number 20), originally designed by Richard Neutra in 1947–8, with later additions in 1951 and 1958, also by Neutra. As a result of these modifications, the* house was extended from a rectangular block to an L-shaped structure, with the bedrooms isolated in a separate wing away from the main daytime living area – a good example of 'zoning'.

Above *The open plan living/dining room of Case Study House number 10 designed by Kemper Nomland and Kemper Nomland Jr in 1945–7, with its free-standing fireplace subtly demarking a division between the two different areas of the room.*

mostly by locating conflicting activities in different wings of either a cross-shaped or an L-shaped plan, or on opposite sides of an interior courtyard. It was because of new psychological ideas about social behaviour, therefore – and in particular the need to balance the pressure for sociability against the need for personal privacy – that new approaches to interior planning were adopted.

Perhaps the best known and most influential of the early Case Study Houses was number 8, designed by Charles and Ray Eames. One of the reasons why the house was so successful was possibly because it was peopled by the 'ideal' clients – the architects themselves. This meant that fewer compromises were necessary and also that freedom of expression and experimentation were recognized as being fundamental to the project. The house was built of pre-fabricated industrial steel framing with diagonal cross-bracing. Strongly rectilinear in form, the square panels with which it was clad were composed of a mixture of transparent and translucent glass and lightweight opaque materials, such as Cemesto board, asbestos and wood, painted in black, white or primary colours. Charles Eames apparently found it creatively stimulating to work within such fixed constraints, writing in *Arts and Architecture* in 1949: 'it is interesting to consider how the rigidity of the system was responsible for the free use of space and to see how the most matter-of-fact structure resulted in pattern and texture.'

Inside the house, many of the building materials were left exposed, such as the steel I-beams and the ribbed Ferroboard ceiling. The inside surfaces of the opaque, exterior cladding panels were covered with stiffened natural canvas, while one of the interior walls of the dramatic double-height living room and several other interior walls were finished with wooden panelling. The house was furnished throughout with furniture designed by Charles Eames, with paintings by Ray Eames and other Modernist artists, and with a rich array of colourful folk art, textiles and sculpture collected by the couple.

It is interesting to compare the Eames house with its partner, the Entenza house (Case Study House number 9), which although constructed using similar basic materials, followed a different pattern in terms of its aesthetic treatment. According to the *Architectural Forum*, the two houses were 'technological twins but architectural opposites'. In the Eames house the exposed structural framework was a primary feature of the overall design; in the Entenza house, the structure was played down on the exterior, while on the interior it was deliberately concealed under plaster and wooden panelling. There was also an antithesis between the two houses in terms of the spatial treatment of the main living room – so decisive in the creation of the overall atmosphere of a house. In the Eames house a sense of openness was created through the exaggerated height (17 ft/5.2 m) of the main living room, whereas in the Entenza house a sense of spaciousness was created through exaggerated length (36 ft/11 m). To avoid monotony, however, Eames and Saarinen exploited the ploy of creating variations in room level in different parts of the main living room; in the Entenza house this was achieved by introducing raised platform areas and built-in sunken seating units.

The decision as to whether to conceal the structure of the house or whether to leave it exposed was an issue which cropped up in other

Previous Page, Opposite and Above *The most famous of all the houses built as part of the Case Study House programme was number 8, designed by Charles and Ray Eames in 1945 and completed in 1949. Located in Pacific Palisades, an attractive suburb of Los Angeles, the house consists of two separate rectangular blocks, one for living, the other for working. Constructed entirely from prefabricated modular components as an exercise in mass-production techniques, the Eames House is the essence of simplicity. While its mainly white exterior recalls the pre-war Modern Movement, and there are echoes of Rietveld and Mondrian in the addition of primary colour highlights, in the lightness of its steel framework, its creative use of space and its relaxed mood, it is confidently post-war and 'Contemporary'.*

Above *The exaggerated length of this open-plan living room in Case Study House number 9 was designed by Charles Eames and Eero Saarinen for John Entenza, the editor of* Arts and Architecture *magazine, in 1945,* completed *in 1949. The layout of this room provides a complete contrast to the double-height living room of the Eames House* (opposite), *although both give an impression of luxurious spaciousness.*

Right *The geometric design and controlled use of colour on the exterior of the Eames House contrast with the luxuriance of the interior. A stunning array of rugs, plants, modern art and* objets trouvés *adorn the house, reflecting the wide-ranging interests of the owners. Among his many talents, Charles*

Eames *was also a documentary filmmaker, and one of his most successful short films was* 'House', *an intimate portrait of his house and its contents.*

Opposite *The dramatic double-height living room of the Eames House, with its floor to ceiling steel-framed windows.*

Opposite *The Entenza House is built on a lot adjacent to the Eames House at Pacific Palisades. This is a view from the terrace of the Entenza House looking through the trees towards the Eames House. Now, forty years on, the woodland is* considerably denser, so each house enjoys greater privacy. Also built on neighbouring lots were two other Case Study Houses: the Bailey House (number 20) by Richard Neutra, and Case Study House number 18 by Rodney Walker.

Above *The steel-framed entrance porch of the Entenza House, enlivened by decorative coloured panels around the doorway. The front of the house itself is faced with tongue-and-groove wooden cladding.*

Unnumbered Case Study House at Pacific Palisades, Los Angeles, designed in 1950 by Raphael Soriano, shown under construction and after completion. *Above The figure in the centre of the picture is Soriano himself. This photograph graphically illustrates the post and beam construction method* used in the building of the Case Study Houses, *whereby an open framework is erected which is then covered with layers of insulation and cladding.* Right *The sleek and sophisticated appearance of the completed interior belies the simplicity of the techniques and materials used.*

Opposite *Floor-to-ceiling windows create a sense of openness between the interior and exterior of the house. Although the surrounding site would have appeared rather bare initially, judicious planting would soon ensure that the house became more integrated with the natural environment.*

Case Study houses, as well as in the wider architectural debate taking place both in the USA and abroad. It was particularly pertinent to the work of another Case Study architect, Raphael Soriano, who, like Charles Eames, was committed to investigating the wider use of industrial materials in housing. In Soriano's Case Study House of 1950 (unnumbered) he used steel, glass and concrete for the structure, but deliberately disguised these raw materials on the interior with a variety of decorative finishes, including plaster, brickwork and wooden panelling on the walls and carpeting on the floor. From his earlier experience of the public's reactions during the 1930s, he had come to the conclusion that there would be less resistance to modern architecture if the architect paid more attention to the creation of warmer, softer surfaces on the interior. In some of his buildings, therefore, he chose to sweeten the pill.

Although impressed by the simple, steel-framed structures developed by Soriano, Craig Ellwood was less inclined to compromise when it came to the aesthetics of the interior, and sought to highlight rather than to hide the details of the structural steel framework. Ellwood, whose background was in engineering and who thus considered himself free of the conditioning to which other architects had been subjected during their training, believed that as a result, he was more inclined to experiment both technically and aesthetically. His Case Study Houses numbers 16, 17 and 18, built between 1952 and 1958, were all low-slung, flat-roofed, single-storey buildings, constructed largely from steel and glass, with the steel frames themselves left exposed throughout. The reason why Ellwood pursued this method of building was because, as he explained in the magazine *Progressive Architecture* in 1959, he believed that 'The increasing cost of labour and the growing lack of craftsmen – our expanding machine economy – will more and more force construction into the factory, where units will be manufactured for fast job assembly.' Although Ellwood's vision of factory-produced housing never really took off in the way he had imagined, at the time his response to this situation was to create minimalist designs based on simple, regular grid patterns. His open-plan interiors incorporated features such as movable wall-screens, the design of which were inspired by the purity and flexibility of traditional Japanese domestic architecture. Ellwood was also consciously working in the more recent tradition of the Modernist glass pavilion, which had been taken to an extreme in the design of the Farnsworth House in Illinois by Mies van der Rohe in 1946, a project which was completed and widely published in 1951, just prior to Ellwood's involvement in the Case Study programme. Ellwood's use of translucent glass panels to shield the terraces surrounding the building, and to screen the exposed core of the house, reflected a greater concern for the personal privacy of his clients, however, than was accorded by the uncompromising Mies van der Rohe. The houses built by Ellwood during the 1950s were highly sophisticated in their minimalism and it was this type of understated elegance that was to become the hallmark of the American 'Contemporary' Style.

Working on similar lines to Ellwood was Pierre Koenig, who designed two Case Study houses towards the end of the decade. Koenig was particularly committed to the use of steel as a building

Previous Page *Farnsworth House at Piano, Illinois, designed by Mies van der Rohe in 1946 but not completed until 1951. This house was clearly a source of inspiration for the Case Study architect, Craig Ellwood.*

Top and Above *Case Study House number 16 designed by Craig Ellwood, 1952–3. Philip Johnson and Mies van der Rohe were severely criticized for their glass-walled houses because their total lack of privacy made them impractical for*

sites in close proximity to neighbouring houses. Ellwood overcame this problem by erecting translucent glass screens around the courtyards surrounding his houses, which allowed the light in but prevented passers-by from seeing inside.

Left and Above *Craig Ellwood built three Case Study Houses, all variations on the theme of the Miesian glass pavilion: number16 in 1952–3 (left and opposite); number 17 in 1954–5 and number 18 in 1956–8 (above). Modular building* systems, *prefabricated components, translucent glass panels shielding the exterior, and the installation of Japanese-inspired screen-like partitions within the interior, were all hallmarks of Ellwood's style.*

Opposite *Case Study House number 21 designed by Pierre Koenig in 1958. Although constructed from materials that many would consider suitable only for industrial buildings, namely steel I-beams and ribbed steel decking, Koenig's two Case Study Houses project an appearance of high sophistication and refinement.*

Above *The early Case Study Houses built during the first decade after the war were fairly modest in size, intended for clients on moderate incomes. By the second half of the 1950s, however, living standards had risen considerably and consumer expectations were also higher. Here, Case Study House number 22, designed by Pierre Koenig in 1959–60, incorporates a swimming pool, for example. The setting, high up in the Hollywood Hills overlooking Los Angeles, is extremely dramatic.*

THE LOS ANGELES EXAMINER

pictorial **Living**

Section 4   Week of April 19, 1959

Special report on the house of steel Page 6

Louella Parsons tells why Bob Young stays at top Page 22

material, not only for the posts and beams of the structural framework, but also in the form of ribbed steel decking for the roof and walls. Not surprisingly, therefore, he too made the decision to leave the framework exposed on the interior as well as the exterior, the new technique of arc-welding being employed to ensure that the detailing of the joints was of an acceptably high standard.

Koenig's 1958 Case Study House (number 21), a small compact steel and glass box measuring only 1,320 sq ft/122.6 sq m, was described in *Arts & Architecture* as representing 'some of the cleanest and most immaculate thinking in the development of the the small contemporary house'. The architect is much better known for his Case Study House (number 22), designed the following year, however, which was dramatically photographed at the time by Julius Shulman, one of the leading architectural photographers of the day. This house took full advantage of a remarkable site on the promontory of a hill overlooking Los Angeles, with a clear 240 degree panoramic view over 100 square miles of the city and its environs. The sense of natural drama was further heightened by the cantilevering, not just of the roof overhang, but of the main living room itself, well beyond the edge of the hillside, so that it was suspended without visible means of support over the precipice below. According to the client, CH Stahl, quoted in *Blueprints for Modern Living*, 'The view dictated a contemporary style.' The spectacular success of the house both aesthetically and structurally was a tribute to Koenig's confidence in, and understanding of, his chosen material, steel. This house was one of the greatest triumphs of the Case Study programme and, because of the extensive publicity it received, through Julius Shulman's remarkable photographs, was highly influential in popularizing and raising the status of the 'Contemporary' style. It certainly gave a great boost to the building industry in the precipitous Hollywood Hills, showing how well-suited the building techniques of 'Contemporary' architecture were to this type of rough terrain. Furthermore, cantilevered 'Contemporary' houses of this type gave otherwise unusable land a higher commercial value, by harnessing a view that could otherwise not be easily exploited.

It is, therefore, somewhat surprising to learn that, successful as it had proved itself to be in the Case Study House programme, the technique of building steel-framed houses did not, in fact, become widespread in the USA during the 1950s. According to Esther McCoy, the main reason for this was the inflexible nature of the construction industry in North America at this date:

> The steel frame was too strict to lend itself to mass-production; the margin for error was too narrow and no scheduling procedure that mixed the wood carpenter and the steel carpenter was ever devised. For these reasons the steel house never became a common type.

These comments, and her summary of the impact of the Case Study programme as a whole from a contemporary standpoint in *Blueprints for Modern Living*, place this achievement within the social and political context of the time:

> The Case Study houses were an idealized mirror of an age in which

Above and Opposite Two similar views of Case Study House number 21, designed by Pierre Koenig in 1958, taken at different times of day from the porte-cochère which joins the house to the carport. The view towards the dining room and study from this angle highlights the aesthetic importance of the reflective pool, one of a series by which the house was surrounded as if by a moat. As with the houses of Craig Ellwood (see pages 62–3), a Japanese

influence is discernible in this example of Koenig's work, expressed here through the interplay of the variously paved terraces with the pool. In the picture opposite the window opening from the study onto the terrace has been slid back completely. The above picture was featured in an article on 'the house of steel' which appeared in the Pictorial Living section of The Los Angeles Examiner in April 1959, shortly after the house was completed.

Following Page Night view from the terrace of Case Study House number 22 by Pierre Koenig, 1959–60, with the spectacular panorama of Los Angeles laid out below. The Los Angeles Examiner commented in a feature on the house and its residents in 1960 that 'Los Angeles is their great, big front yard'.

Above, Right, Opposite and Following Page
Four different views of House B at La Jolla, California, which is one of a group of three dwellings forming Case Study number 23, known as the 'Triad', designed by Edward Killingsworth in 1959–60. This project was conceived as the trial run for a larger speculative housing development sponsored by the Amantea Company, and it was the first in the Case Study programme to address the issue of community planning. The houses were laid out in a triangular formation, the picture opposite being taken from House A. Unfortunately, the project was not well received in what was a notoriously conservative area, so the larger scheme never came to fruition along the lines originally intended.

an emerging pragmatism veiled Rooseveltian idealism. Conceived as low cost, the house prices soared as inflation grew. Standardized elements were generally used, often imaginatively, but they did not bring down costs; nevertheless there was an effort to arrive at the prototypical, if only in floor planning or detailing... The service the houses rendered went beyond any experimentation embodied in any of the first eight. It was rather a service to time and place.

Although the programme lasted through into the mid-1960s – the last Case Study houses to be built were a set of apartments by Alfred Beadle and Alan Dailey in 1963-4 – *Arts and Architecture's* commitment to the scheme was never quite as strong after the departure of John Entenza from the magazine in 1962. By this date, however, the magazine was largely preaching to the converted, as the principle of the 'Contemporary' style in domestic architecture had been widely accepted for a number of years.

When, in 1939, the American Institute of Architects had published a survey called *Residential Architecture in California*, houses in the modern style were hidden away at the back of the book, while the front was reserved for buildings in more traditional or 'eclectic' styles. By the early 1960s, however, when Von Eckardt compiled a new survey called *Mid-Century Architecture in America*, there no longer seemed any doubts or reservations about the American public's willingness to accept 'Contemporary' design: indeed, this book was an overt celebration of America's growing world supremacy in the field of architecture. By this date, the jibes of Nelson and Wright at the parochialism and conservatism of the American public would have seemed out of place. It was now assumed that most of the American middle classes were more discerning in their tastes. According to Henry Luce, whose address to the American Institute of Architects in 1957 is quoted in Von Eckardt's book: 'The twentieth-century revolution in architecture has been accomplished. And it has been accomplished mainly in America – no matter how great our debt to European genius.'

This new-found confidence and pride in the achievement of American architects, and in their hard-won independence from their European colleagues, shines through very clearly in *Mid-Century Architecture in America*. Not only is it apparent in the self-assured quality of its material, but in the triumphant tone of the commentary by its editor, Von Eckardt, who summarizes post-war developments thus:

No sooner has America embraced the new architecture than it has blossomed out into a richness and inventiveness that must, in retrospect, astound even its most daring prophets. Its stark, bare and square austerity, largely a gesture of protest against over-decorative eclecticism, has given way to a less self-conscious expression. Taking up the fundamental tenets of earlier 'modern', a new modified modern with three basic characteristics has developed. These characteristics are:

First, a totally new emphasis on the interior spaces of a building in terms of their usefulness, comfort, and beauty and their interrelationship. In the past, rooms within a building were rigid compartments. Interior spaces are more flexible and sometimes can be divided at will. They open and flow into one another in a dynamic rather than static relationship.

Second, there is a new indoor-outdoor relationship. The use (some complain of overuse) of glass has made it possible to bring nature's plants and greenery into the building, and extend the building out into nature. Planted plazas, interior courts, and terraces have brought nature into our urban working environment.

Third, our buildings appear lighter, often buoyant. Skyscrapers soar effortlessly into the air. Other buildings rest lightly on the ground as though to disturb it as little as possible. Even where they hug the earth and adapt to its contours, they avoid being massive and ponderous.

By the end of the 1950s, therefore, the climate of opinion in the USA described by Nelson and Wright in 1945 had altered so significantly that it was now the open-plan modern house rather than the traditional Cape Cod cottage that had caught the popular imagination. 'Tomorrow's House' of 1945 had become 'Today's House' of 1960. Ironically, by the end of the 1950s the 'Contemporary' house was so widely accepted in the USA that it had itself become a symbol of the establishment, projecting to the world the face of confident, post-war, expansionist America. In 1945 Nelson and Wright had written of the Cape Cod-style 'Dream House' that this phenomenon 'exists because to the person who has lost his capacity for independent thinking and feeling it represents authority, expert opinion, tradition and cultural solidarity with his fellows'. Within the space of a decade, the wheel had turned full circle and such comments had become equally applicable to the standard American 'Contemporary' house.

After the war it soon became apparent that the balance of international power had shifted – a shift which encompassed both military and economic activity. Furthermore, whereas before the war cultural ideas had generally travelled from Europe to America, after the war this situation was reversed and, for the first time, Europeans were forced to pay serious attention to what the Americans were doing.

In the massive programme of reconstruction that got underway in Europe after the war, Germany and Italy, the defeated countries, were major beneficiaries of American investment and, as in Japan, along with American money came a new American ideology about 'Contemporary' architecture, design and popular culture. Britain, however, although a victor in the war, was unable to benefit from such outside investment, and this, combined with the effect of continuing shortages of building materials and labour, severely inhibited progress in the field of domestic architecture up until the mid-1950s. It also put artificial constraints on the output of the manufacturing industry, much of which had to be channelled towards the export market during the early years after the war in order to revive the economy. During the second half of the 1950s, however, when consumer goods became more widely available and the British public had become prosperous enough to afford new houses, so they became more responsive to 'Contemporary' architecture and design. But here, as in the USA, the powerful force of tradition was still a major obstacle to be overcome before modern design could become more widely accepted.

Above *The Shulman House, Laurel Canyon, Los Angeles, designed by Raphael Soriano in 1950, seen here under construction. This house, built for the photographer Julius Shulman, is composed of two distinct blocks. On the left is the studio and on the right is the main house; the two are connected by a covered walkway. The modular steel-framed post-and-beam construction method is clearly visible here.*
Right *An advertisement for the Bethlehem Steel Company promoting steel-frame construction for 'Contemporary' houses.*

In *Tomorrow's House*, Nelson and Wright had drawn attention to the anachronistic situation that prevailed in the domestic building trade in North America before the war:

> The technical means for producing good houses have long been at hand. Today's house is the crudest kind of solution to the problem of gracious, civilized living; it is decades behind the industrial possibilities of our time. Tomorrow's house – the antithesis of everything we have said about today's – could be built right now by anyone who has the good sense and courage to tackle it.

Although technology in the form of new building materials and techniques had progressed significantly since the beginning of the century, aesthetic ideas had not kept pace and even appeared to be regressing. Because of this, few houses built between the wars made use of the advanced materials and techniques that were actually available; stylistically, the two were incompatible. However, with the acceptance of a new aesthetic after the war – the 'Contemporary' style – materials that had previously been considered unacceptably modern were now more widely adopted.

Whereas in the past most houses had been built with deep foundations in order to create the stability to build upwards, now relatively shallow concrete foundations could be laid, making domestic cellars a thing of the past, except in countries such as Sweden where they remained popular for other reasons. On top of these foundations, rather than building cavity walls around the perimeter, often just the basic skeleton of the house was erected at first in the form of a framework of posts and beams. Although steel-framed houses never became widespread, even in the USA, steel in reinforced concrete began to be widely employed in 'Contemporary' architecture, particularly in tall blocks of flats and offices, which required special strengthening. For individual houses, however, unless they were cantilevered or fully open-plan, a reinforced structure of this nature was not always necessary, and often the framework was built entirely of wood or a mixture of concrete or steel posts with wooden beams. However, even in the USA, where wood continued to be widely used throughout this period, the principle of first erecting a skeleton and then fleshing it out was generally accepted as the sensible way to build a 'Contemporary' house.

Only after the basic framework had been erected were the walls constructed, the substance of the in-fill being dependent on a number of factors, including local building traditions, the availability of materials and the nature of the climate. Traditional cavity walls remained popular in cold northern climates where insulation was important. In Britain, houses were often brick-faced on the exterior but lined on the interior with concrete 'Thermalite' insulation blocks, the cavity sometimes being filled with insulating foam. In Scandinavia and the USA, tongue-and-groove wooden panelling was extensively used, partly because of the easy availability of wood, and partly because it was considered so effective both in terms of insulation and for its aesthetic effect. In southern climates, in the absence of air-conditioning ventilation was required, along with materials that would reflect rather than absorb the heat, and for this reason concrete proved to be popular.

Above *A* brise soleil *system in use at the Kaufmann House built in 1946 in the Colorado Desert by Richard Neutra. In hot sunny climates it was essential to devise* *effective systems for reducing the amount of direct sunlight entering houses with curtain wall windows although, here, the* brise soleil *is used to provide shade on a terrace.*

Above *The Kunstadter House designed by George Fred Keck and William Keck at Highland Park, Illinois, in 1952 is a good example of a building planned on modular lines. This and the Pearson House* (right) *demonstrate that the adoption of a modular system of construction need not necessarily be restrictive or inhibit creativity, but can instead result in a balanced and disciplined design.*

Right *The Pearson House designed by Richard Gordon at Mamaroneck, New York, which was featured in* Architectural Record *in May 1954. An attractive screened terrace resembling a pergola runs the length of this L-shaped house, a feature which emphazises the modular structure of this elegantly proportioned building.*

In intensely hot climates, such buildings were often faced with *'brise soleils'*, or sun breakers, to reduce the amount of direct light penetrating the interior, and thereby avoid the build-up of heat, Le Corbusier's Unité d'Habitation in Marseilles being a good example. Wet climates required materials that would not rot or rust, therefore exposed untreated wood and metals that might corrode had to be avoided. This explains why wood was never widely adopted in Britain, because it needed to be regularly treated in order to prevent it from rapidly deteriorating. Dry climates, on the other hand, required materials that would not dry out and crack, making inorganic materials, such as stone, steel and glass, particularly appropriate. This accounts in part at least for the popularity of the steel-framed glass box model within the Case Study programme in Los Angeles. In spite of regional variations in cladding, however, 'Contemporary' houses throughout the world bore many similarities, because they so often shared the same structural basis.

What was refreshing about the 'Contemporary' approach to house design was its tendency towards simplicity. Many buildings, not just houses, but schools and office blocks too, began to be designed on a modular basis. Although on a large scale this might have led to monotony, on a domestic scale it often resulted in greater purity and clarity. Typical of this new approach was the single-storey L-shaped house built for Mrs Edward Pearson in Mamaroneck, New York, by Richard Gordon during the early 1950s. This house was originally featured in the magazine, *Architectural Record*, and subsequently appeared in *A Treasury of Contemporary Houses*. According to the commentary, 'the house is designed for especially simple construction. It is laid out on a 41/4 ft [1.3 m] module, with 6 x 12 in [15 x 30 cm] long leaf-yellow pine beams. The beams rest in steel straps welded to light structural steel T-columns imbedded in the poured concrete foundation. Beams are 81/2 ft [2.6 m] on centre, so that 4 x 8 ft [1.2 x 2.4 m] mahogany ceiling panels would go in place without cutting.' The large living room was in one arm of the L, the bedrooms were in another – a good example of 'zoning' – with the entrance and the kitchen at the junction of the two wings.

Although there were many shared characteristics to 'Contemporary' houses, there were no set rules, and the brief to create a 'Contemporary' house was interpreted in many different ways. The principle of modularity, for example, did not mean that all houses in which it was adopted looked the same; it simply provided a flexible grid framework, the actual layout of which could be infinitely varied. Proof of the fact that a modular structure need not be prominent, and could easily be disguised, is provided by another of the dwellings featured in *A Treasury of Contemporary Houses*: the house built for Sigmund Kunstadter at Highland Park, Illinois, by George Fred Keck and William Keck. This house, which won the 1953 Honor Award for the Best House Design (Chicago Chapter of the American Institute of Architects), was described in *A Treasury* in the following terms:

After stepping from his car under the *porte-cochère* which links house and garage, the guest enters a large, glass-enclosed central hall from which he may be received in the studio-library for quiet talk, in the living room area for a family or party visit, or may be shown directly to his guest room (normally the den) to freshen up before making an appearance. At first glance, the rooms appear to be rather freely disposed in plan, with interesting 'ins and outs' for the long façades, but closer analysis reveals a studied arrangement which places these elements within a rectangular structural cage consisting of eight uniform bays.

Whereas for the Modernist house of the 1930s a flat roof and white stucco walls were virtually *de rigueur*, there were no such restrictions on what the 'Contemporary' house should look like. Many did have flat roofs, but it was by no means prohibited to install a pitched roof, some of which were mono-pitched, others asymmetrical: it really did not matter, and it depended very much on the situation of the house. External finishes were similarly varied, and might be composed of brick, stone, wood panelling, or perhaps more likely a combination of two or three different materials. Monotony and clinical regularity were seen as passé; variety, creative irregularity and spontaneity were the new characteristics of post-war domestic architecture. According to Emerson Gable (in *A Treasury of Contemporary Houses*), because of the freedom and creative opportunities it offered young architects setting up their practices after the war, 'the house is today the best opportunity for individual expression, a fascinating problem of comprehensible size'.

3. the interior

'The virtues of the open plan have intrigued us all for quite a while, and stirred up a lot of arguments. By now, few can seriously question that it is a good method for gaining flexibility and a sense of space in today's smaller, more compact houses – and perhaps for lowering the cost.'

Emerson Gable, A Treasury of Contemporary Houses, 1954

The most distinctive and remarkable quality of 'Contemporary' architecture was its treatment of interior space. When walking into an architect-designed house of the 1950s today, it is the creative way in which the space has been handled that makes the deepest impression. The most striking feature of the 'Contemporary' interior was its sense of openness and airiness, even when the house itself was not very large, which was often the case, particularly in regulation-bound early post-war Britain. Clearly it was in this field that post-war architects made their most decisive contribution to the development of domestic architecture, a fact recognized by Sigfried Giedion in *Space, Time and Architecture:*

It is not the independent unrelated form that is the be-all of architecture today but the organization of forms in space: space conception. This has been true for all creative periods, including the present day. The present space-time conception – the way volumes are placed in space and relate to one another, the way interior space is separated from exterior space or is perforated by it to bring about an interpenetration – is a universal attribute which is at the basis of all contemporary architecture.

Nelson and Wright noted in *Tomorrow's House* that, 'Contemporary houses have been planned to provide an acceptable minimum of living facilities within an absolute minimum of space.' The successful 'Contemporary' architect, therefore, had to learn how to maximize the perception of size by removing some of those physical barriers, such as floors and walls, which had hitherto defined and delimited space. This was one of the features that distinguished the work of Peter Womersley, the most talented British domestic architect of the period. The architect wrote about his RIBA Bronze Medal winning house, Farnley Hey, in West Yorkshire (1953), in the *Ideal Home Yearbook* of 1957:

> The area of approximately 1,650 sq ft [153.3 sq m] contained within its walls appears to be much greater than it is in fact. The wide expanse of window, the outdoor terraces and porches that colonise space outside for the house, are partially responsible, but it is the planning and degrees of enclosure that account for the spaciousness of the building. Apart from a small landing between bedroom and bathroom, there is virtually no circulation space; the staircase is as much a piece of furniture as a link between the different levels of the house.

Even when the brief of the architect was more circumscribed, for example, when developing prototypes for low-cost mass-production housing in Britain towards the end of the war, the importance of the principle of open planning was clearly recognized. This is apparent in the commentary in the *Architectural Review* in 1945 on the experimental houses designed by British architect Frederick Gibberd the previous year for the British Iron and Steel Federation under the aegis of the Ministry of Works:

> They are frankly experimental in plan, structure, and material... Though in essence an adaptation of the yardstick plan, these houses have succeeded in introducing within their limited space of the required 850 sq ft [79 sq m] floor area, the sense of spatial freedom and flexibility which distinguishes contemporary work at its best. Every use has been made of the degree of plan emancipation provided by the system of frame construction. The ground floor has been planned as openly as possible. Each living unit can be combined with each of the others, giving a variety of choice for the owner... Another essentially contemporary feature about the house is the way in which the breakdown of the usual box-like rooms has been carried further and applied to the outside walls. The walled in effect of the normal fortress house has been overcome by joining

Top Living room of the Entenza House designed by Charles Eames and Eero Saarinen between 1945 and 1949. Floor-to-ceiling windows bring the maximum amount of light into the house. *Above* Outdoor dining terrace and adjoining carport of Case Study House number 21 in Los Angeles, designed by Pierre Koenig in 1958. The idea of creating a free flow of activity between the indoors and the outdoors was strongly encouraged by 'Contemporary' architects, particularly those working in warm climates such as the West Coast of the USA.

the interior with the garden through french windows leading on to a small paved terrace.

Although relatively insignificant in comparison with the initiatives taking place in the USA, where the domestic interior was being opened up more comprehensively, in post-war Britain these small steps towards open planning were highly significant.

This new physical openness had a liberating effect on the character of the house, as well as a considerable impact on the way it was used, encouraging a more relaxed and informal lifestyle. The decision to opt for the 'Contemporary' style revealed much, not just about the thinking of the architect, but also about the character of the commissioning clients. In *Tomorrow's House*, Nelson and Wright pointed out that badly designed houses were a poor reflection on the people who commissioned them: 'What is a house?... It is a perfect mirror of a society, most of whose members are desperately afraid of acting like independent individuals. Its weaknesses are social, not technical.' By the same token, when a house was deemed to have been designed successfully, it was because the owners had stated their real needs clearly to their architect, who had used these as a basis, rather than accepted or inherited design formulae. However, although the new open, airy interiors of the 1950s prompted their occupants to adopt a correspondingly unfettered lifestyle, this is not to imply that such an ambiance was easy to create. It certainly did not arise out of a casual, *laissez-faire* attitude on the part of the architect; indeed, the successful 'Contemporary' house was the product of an extremely exacting design process and a minute attention to detail, a fact belied by the naturalness and spontaneity of its final appearance.

In physical terms what created the sense of lightness and airiness was the introduction of open planning, a concept developed during the early part of the century by Frank Lloyd Wright in the USA and by Le Corbusier in France. In his foreword to *Tomorrow's House*, Howard Myers commented that, 'Perhaps the greatest virtue of tomorrow's house is that it frees the plan... from the arbitrary concepts which have gotten in the way of gracious living these many years.' By using the phrase 'gracious living' Myers appears, like Giedion, to be making a link back to the more creative use of space in earlier times, particularly the eighteenth century. Since, by the mid-twentieth century space had become something of a luxury as populations had swollen and as land had become more expensive, the creation of extra space – or at least of a sense of extra space – had become the first duty of the 'Contemporary' architect.

Open planning did not always mean removing all the interior walls, but often leaving only those that were structurally or socially necessary. The rationale of a room became expansion rather than containment, and the principle underlying the design of the interior as a whole was not to produce a cluster of separate boxes, but to create instead a series of interlinked and interrelated spaces, their size, shape, and position determined by their function.

Until the mid-twentieth century, it had been structurally imperative to install physical divisions between rooms in the form of interior load-bearing walls. As mentioned in the previous chapter, the technical

Top and Above *Two perspective drawings of Roundwood House, Middlesex, designed by Keith Roberts in 1956. In his proposals, the architect envisaged a lightness and physical openness extending right through from the entrance hall to the living/dining room, achieved by reducing the number of interior walls and installing plentiful windows. Throughout the ground floor it was suggested that there should be regular variations in surface patterns and textures for both floor-coverings and wall-coverings. In the drawing of the entrance hall, for example, the floor surface changes from stone flagging to wood, while of the two walls visible near the stairs, one is painted in blue, the other has a patterned yellow wallpaper.*

advances in structural engineering meant that this was no longer necessary, so that modern interiors could become more open in layout. Adapting both to the unfamiliar aesthetics of open planning, and also to changes in established patterns of behaviour took several decades, however. The technical means for building open-plan houses had been available well before its practical application was widely exploited, the main hindrance being the pressure of tradition and social conventions.

Even the most radical architects of the 1920s and 1930s – including those such as Mies van der Rohe who had pioneered the introduction of Modernism – still clung to some of the old conventions of house design. As discussed earlier, many felt obliged to install lightweight foldaway walls as temporary subdivisions within larger rooms, for example, not for justifiable practical reasons, but simply because of convention. Thus, an accordion-type wall might be pulled across the room during the meal time in order to separate the living area from the dining area. Furthermore, although the Modern house of the 1930s was likely to contain a combined open-plan living room/dining room area, there was still resistance to the idea of opening up the partition between the kitchen and the dining room. In middle-class households the kitchen was still perceived as a place for the servants and it was not considered socially desirable to connect the dining room with the kitchen.

Of the fifty house plans recorded in Yorke's international inter-war survey, *The Modern House*, almost all retained the kitchen as an entirely separate, enclosed room, always very much behind the scenes and often distanced from the dining room by a corridor. To emphasize this social division, many examples were illustrated in which the servants' living quarters were located directly adjoining the kitchen, in the same area as the pantry and the laundry, where most of the menial tasks would be carried out. The discovery of such socially retrogressive features in the 1930s avant-garde houses of architects such as Marcel Breuer, Le Corbusier, Walter Gropius and Mies van der Rohe comes as something of a surprise, but also shows what a transformation in thinking and lifestyle was brought about by World War II.

'Contemporary' architects of the 1950s, although not entirely dispensing with the formula of temporary screen-type subdivisions, embraced the concept of the open-plan idea more wholeheartedly and comprehensively. After the war, it became much more common in the USA, for example, to find the kitchen and dining room directly linked, and often with three rooms combined into one, in the form of a single living room/dining room/kitchen. Creating a sense of division without erecting physical barriers was one of the great challenges of 'Contemporary' interior design, various solutions to which were proposed by the younger generation of architects. One such solution was to subdivide these large multi-purpose rooms by means of the type of furniture or accessories that were installed, such as storage units or plant troughs, or by the way in which the furniture was positioned or grouped. Another means of suggesting natural subdivisions within a large room, which involved a visual rather than physical ploy, was to introduce changes in surface texture to characterize different areas. This might involve laying a variety of floor coverings, such as vinyl tiles for the kitchen, for example, and polished wood for the dining room and living room floor areas. Different wall coverings could also

Opposite *Richard Neutra succeeded in making his houses almost transparent in places by adopting from Frank Lloyd Wright the technique of creating frameless mitred window joints. Here, in the Moore House at Ojai, California, designed in 1952, this technique is used to great effect: there appears to be no physical division* between the house and the mountains.
Top and Above *Two views of the living/dining room of Case Study House number 20, the Bass House, in Altadena, Los Angeles, designed by Buff, Straub and Hensman in 1958. Various ploys are used in this open-plan room to denote the change in function between* different areas, without breaking up the freeflow of space. A finely woven translucent hanging is suspended between the dining table and the armchairs, for example, while the rug on the floor in front of the fireplace associates this area with comfort and relaxation.*

Above *Sunken built-in seating in the living room of Case Study House number 9, the Entenza House, designed by Charles Eames and Eero Saarinen between 1945 and 1949. The change in levels denotes a subdivision within the open-plan room.*

Right and Opposite *Interior courtyards of two 'Contemporary' houses in California. Opposite is Case Study House number 25 at Long Beach designed by Edward Killingsworth in 1962. Here, the double-height ceiling creates a sense of space and light, which is the ideal setting for a work of modern sculpture. The terrace courtyard of the Jones House on the right, designed by Quincy Jones and Frederick Emmons in 1955, contains some attractive planting which grows up through the opening in the roof.*

make a strong impression: there might perhaps be exposed stonework on the chimney breast, wooden panelling in the dining area, and a washable, patterned vinyl wallpaper in the kitchen. Slight changes of level between different areas of the room – even if only a matter of a single step upwards or downwards – could also suggest an alteration in mood, or imply a change of the room's function, without impeding the passage of its occupants or even interrupting the free flow of conversation. Such techniques served to break up and define distinct areas within what might otherwise have seemed a somewhat barn-like or monotonous open-plan room.

Open planning was by no means restricted to the kitchen/dining room/living room areas of the house: in most 'Contemporary' houses, the open-plan nature of the interior was apparent as soon as the visitor crossed the threshold. The entrance hall was also used as a vehicle for announcing that the visitor was entering a 'Contemporary' house. Instead of the usual narrow, constricted and often dark hall corridor, with stairs leading directly up from it to the first floor and with possibly an awkwardly-shaped broom cupboard tucked away under the stairs, the hall became an open and hospitable reception area, a foyer with vistas through into the main living room. Indeed, in the warmer climates of the USA, the hall sometimes opened on to an internal courtyard with plants; often it connected directly with the kitchen.

To liberate the hall and transform it into a lobby, the stairs were often re-positioned in the living room, thereby freeing space in the entrance for built-in cupboards of a regular shape. The idea of stairs rising directly from the living room might at first appear rather awkward, but the stairs themselves – almost invariably open-tread – formed an integral part of the open plan, and were often considered a design feature. This open-tread design made them look rather like the ladders between the decks of a ship – which further emphasized their new role as visual connectors between levels and played down their former role as a symbol of physical separation between floors. Also, because they were open rather than enclosed, the open-plan theme was extended to the first-floor level, with the landing, or the room with which they were connected upstairs, being visible from the ground floor.

Closely linked to the nature of the stairs and how they were integrated with the living room in order to extend the open plan, another feature of 'Contemporary' houses was to locate rooms at half-levels, rather than uniformly floor above floor. Sometimes this sort of arrangement arose out of physical necessity when, for example, the sloping nature of the site prompted the idea of a terraced interior. It was also often simply a way of adding visual interest, breaking up the potential monotony of an otherwise unrelieved open interior. In cross-section, such plans resulted in a staggered inter-leaved arrangement which had the effect of distancing certain rooms – even if only by a relatively short flight of steps – that would otherwise have been on the same floor and, conversely, of bringing some rooms closer that would otherwise have been on separate storeys.

Out of this multi-layered plan developed the concept of the mezzanine floor – a familiar feature today in public buildings, such as theatres, but now less common in the context of the home. In 'Contemporary' houses, mezzanine floors or balcony landings were

Three views of Farnley Hey, designed by Peter Womersley in 1953 as an experiment in Californian 'Contemporary' architecture in the setting of the Pennines in West Yorkshire. These photographs were taken recently and include several details modified from the original design, but in spirit Farnley Hey has changed little since the 1950s.

Opposite *Open-tread staircase connecting the living room with the mezzanine balcony. Staircases of this type were a standard feature of 'Contemporary' interiors in many different countries.* Top *Mezzanine balcony at first-floor level overlooking the double-height living room, originally intended as a 'minstrels' gallery' for*

music-making. The end wall, originally wood panelled, has been glazed by the present owners. Above *The dining room adjoining the kitchen with exposed rough stonework on one wall. The ceiling is lined with panelled wood and the floor is laid with polished stone flags.*

often installed in double-height living rooms, the juxtaposition creating one of the most dramatic interior design effects of the period. In the USA this effect was often added to enhance the excitement of an already spacious layout. In Scandinavia and Europe, where space was at a greater premium, the introduction of a double-height room within a house might appear to be an unnecessary luxury, but was in fact considered expedient in order to counteract the danger of the building as a whole seeming overly small and confined. Many architects clearly considered double-height rooms an attractive option because they were used by individuals as various in their expression as Le Corbusier in the apartments of his Unité d'Habitation block, Arne Jacobsen in low-cost housing schemes near Copenhagen, Charles and Ray Eames in their Case Study house in California and Peter Womersley in Farnley Hey, near Huddersfield. Womersley, in particular, consciously exploited the device to dramatic effect, as it not only created a large room with a double-height ceiling, but also a double-height picture window bringing even more of the Pennine landscape and sky, into the living room.

Apart from the potential reduction in building costs and an increase in living space, there were other practical and social reasons for the growing popularity of open planning during the 1950s. These were more apparent in the 'workstation' section of the house, namely the kitchen. Linking the kitchen to the dining room by means of a serving hatch, or designing these two rooms as one, facilitated the passage of food and the return of empty dishes from one area to another, thereby reducing time spent on the serving of food. It also meant that when cooking, the housewife was not isolated within a back room while her children and her husband enjoyed the freedom and the comfort of the lounge. Equally, when entertaining, the hostess was not cut off from her guests, but could continue to engage in conversation throughout the occasion. These benefits may appear of negligible and dubious importance today, but in the 1950s, when the role of the middle-class housewife was ambiguous, it meant that although women had taken on many of the household tasks formerly undertaken by domestic servants, they need not necessarily be hidden away and taken for granted in the way that the latter had been. The open-plan kitchen/dining room, therefore, could be seen as an acknowledgement of the more prominent and assertive role that women would seek to play in the future, both in the home and in the workplace.

Another feature of the open-plan house was the location of an open storage unit acting as a room divider between the kitchen and dining-room areas. Such a room divider might contain crockery, cutlery and glassware, and it would normally be designed so that the cupboards opened from both sides. In some instances, with high stools set up to the working surface, the room divider could also serve as a breakfast bar, a new concept that proved particularly popular in the USA, where it was soon to become a design feature in its own right. Room dividers could also be installed in living rooms to separate general relaxation areas from specialized study or music room areas. These usually took the form of storage units for books and magazines, display shelves for ornaments, or built-in casings for electrical equipment, such as radios, record players or televisions. Alternatively, they might take the form of a cocktail bar, another fashion which originated in the USA.

Two different examples of 'Contemporary' room dividers.
Top A low-level room divider installed between the living and dining room areas of the Pearson House designed by Richard Gordon at Mamaroneck, New York, during the early 1950s. The open shelves of this sideboard substitute are used for the display of ornaments.

Above A built-in cupboard unit separating the kitchen and dining room at Farnley Hey, West Yorkshire, designed by Peter Womersley in 1953. Opposite In the spacious interior of Case Study House number 22 in Los Angeles, designed by Pierre Koenig in 1959–60, open planning extends right through from the living room to the kitchen.

An island of kitchen units creates an informal divider between the kitchen and dining room areas and because the cupboards are as sophisticated in appearance as the furniture in the living room, there is no sense of incongruity in this arrangement.

Above and Right
Architects of the early post-war period went to some lengths to make the most of limited space. In the Engleberg House designed by Harry Harrison in 1949, an open-plan children's bedroom is fitted with foldaway partitions so that each child can sleep in the privacy of his/her own 'room' at night. The room is kitted out as both a playroom and a study, with as much furniture as possible being built-in.

For obvious reasons, it was neither sensible nor desirable for the whole house to be completely open plan. Bedrooms require peace and quiet and bathrooms demand privacy, for which reasons they were normally enclosed. Sometimes a child's bedroom might double up as play area, or there might be foldaway or sliding partitions between rooms to increase space during the day and provide secure enclosed areas at night.

Noise and lack of privacy were two of the more obvious drawbacks of open planning; problems which aroused widespread debate during the 1950s. In *The House and Garden Book of Small Houses*, of 1961, for example, the editor commented:

> After the war, open planning was eagerly seized upon as it seemed to provide the joy of long vistas and a really generous feeling of space, even in a small house. The problems of noise and distraction that are apt to arise when the various activities of parents and children are accommodated in one space can, however, be formidable. Architects have since had second thoughts about open planning and today's houses have learned something from the open plan and something from the self-contained formulas of our forebears.

One solution which offset some of the potential drawbacks, was to introduce into the design of the interior the American concept of zoning. As mentioned earlier, zoning involved the division of the house into functionally related areas, with 'like' activities located in close proximity, and 'conflicting' activities physically separated into distant parts of the house. As Nelson and Wright pointed out in *Tomorrow's House*, this was an idea that originally derived from town planning:

> Zoning has become a common word in our cities. To date, however, few people have tried to apply it to the house. In connection with the house, all it means is that certain major types of activities are grouped for maximum convenience and for privacy. A 'zoned' house will have one or two sleeping areas, isolated as much as possible from the noisier rooms. It will have a service group, including heater, laundry, and possibly a portion of the kitchen; and finally it will have the general living section, which may include outside as well as inside space.

As a direct result of the popularity of 'zoning', many American houses of the 1950s were conceived as single-storey dwellings, it being manifestly easier to separate different zones on one floor than on two. 'Zoning' also accounts for the common L-shaped and cross layouts of many American 'Contemporary' houses, as architects sought to locate the different zones in physically separate wings or branches of the house. Although, due to shortage of space, the adoption of 'zoning' did not become as widespread in Europe as it was in the USA during the 1950s, nevertheless, it did have an influence on the thinking of 'Contemporary' architects internationally.

As we have seen, therefore, the 'Contemporary' house was usually composed of a balanced combination of open and enclosed spaces, the nature and arrangement of which were determined by the functions of

Top and Above *Two views of the dramatically situated Farnley Hey in West Yorkshire designed by Peter Womersley in 1953. With its generous picture windows, its exciting, spacious double-height living room, its daring cantilevered mezzanine floor, and its 'zoned' bedroom and bathroom wing, Farnley Hey provides a classic example of 'Contemporary' architecture in Britain during the 1950s.*

Right *As a building material, glass has played an extremely important role in the development of modern architecture, particularly during the post-war period. Anonymous though such design elements might now appear, during the 1950s they made a significant contribution to the creation of the 'Contemporary' aesthetic. In Britain the leading window glass manufacturer during the 1950s was Pilkington Brothers. They also made opaque textured coloured glass panels for cladding (Muroglass and Armourclad advertisement, top); and thinner rolled patterned glass for bathroom windows and office partitions (Spotlyte advertisement, bottom).*

spotlyte

Spotlyte pattern is composed of small hemispheres on a finely textured background which afford partial obscuration with negligible loss of light. Easily cleaned, adjacent panes do not need matching.

technical details

Light transmission .... 85 per cent.
Thickness .... ¼ in. (26 oz./sq. ft.)
Maximum size .... 100 in. x 48 in.

Chance
• • • • GLASS

the different areas. When planning Farnley Hey in the early 1950s, for example, Peter Womersley conceived an interior that incorporated both open planning and zoning. The result was a house which represents a classic example of 'Contemporary' interior design. The architect's explanation of his initial thought processes when planning the interior of this house, outlined in the *Ideal Home Yearbook*, provides a fascinating commentary:

> In the first place, each one of the separate activities which taken together form the conception of 'home' – eating, sleeping, entertaining, etc – was to be segregated on its own particular floor, requiring no further definition – no walls and screens – to be recognizable as a 'room'. Second, these separate floors were to be arranged, like leaves on a stem, around a central core, which would house all services, pipes and fittings, as well as support the connecting staircase. Finally, all these elements were to be enclosed within a plain heated glass box, whose simplicity would provide a contrast, and yet give coherence to the variety of levels inside.

Ultimately, although the final building did not quite match this description, in spirit the interior was very close to the architect's original, somewhat poetic, conception. It embodied, in a very complete and successful way, the virtues of open planning and zoning, and graphically illustrates the direct benefits that could be achieved by arranging and dividing the house on these lines.

Farnley Hey also provides a classic example of the revolution in interior design brought about by the introduction of large picture windows. This was another new development in interior design of equal significance to open planning, and it was one that the homeowner of the 1950s was actively encouraged to embrace, not only for aesthetic reasons, but for practical reasons as well, as Nelson and Wright pointed out in *Tomorrow's House*: 'Why do most windows have eight to a dozen small panes, when single large sheets of glass are both cheaper and better? (Big, simple glass areas are much easier to clean, far easier to look out of).'

During the 1930s, in both factories and modern houses, the prevailing fashion had been for 'ribbon' windows composed of bands of small or medium-sized panes set at the same level in strips or 'ribbons' around the building. By the 1950s, however, a greater divergence opened up between the type of windows considered appropriate for housing, and those considered suitable for public buildings. While the living room of the private house came to be dominated by the single, large picture window, which sometimes encompassed the length and breadth of the exterior wall, in schools and offices the system of curtain walling became standard practice. This involved the creation of whole walls of flush metal-framed glass panels, or alternatively, panels of transparent or tinted glass alternating with opaque cladding. Sometimes this cladding was also made of coloured or opaque sheet glass or textured glass blocks; sometimes it was in the form of sheet metal.

Glass manufacturers, such as the powerful British St Helens-based firm, Pilkington, played a lead role in the development of architecture from the 1950s onwards, because it was their innovations in glass

Above *Interior of a house at Odden designed by the leading Danish architect of the period, Arne Jacobsen. The floor-to-ceiling windows in the living room of this drum-shaped dwelling give a broad sweeping view of the garden. The light from these windows is strong enough to penetrate into the centre of the circular house, supplemented by additional overhead rooflights.*

Above *The selection of sites that were, in effect, pre-landscaped was an option favoured by some 'Contemporary' architects, including Gordon Drake in this house in California dating from 1946 to 1947. Floor-to-ceiling windows pivot open onto the terrace at the back of the house where mature trees have been left in place.*

Opposite *'Contemporary' houses were often planned so that they would be closely integrated with the natural environment. This highly individual house designed by Buff, Straub and Hensman for Saul Bass in 1958 (Case Study House number 20) was originally designed to accommodate the mature Italian stone pine tree that dominated the site. Sadly, the tree has since had to be cut down.*

technology which paved the way for innovations in design. At the end of the 1950s, Pilkington perfected the technique of producing continuous float glass, for example, thereby increasing both the width and the length of standard-sized sheet glass. Pilkington also experimented in the field of thickened and toughened glass to produce their Armourplate range, suitable for use in doors, and strong enough to be used without a frame. At the same time, the West Midlands firm of Chance Brothers, who were taken over by Pilkington during the 1950s, specialized in the more traditional technique of rolled glass, which was often textured, ribbed or patterned, sometimes in an overtly 'Contemporary' style. In the home, this type of glass, being translucent rather than transparent, was extensively used in bathrooms; while in the work place, it was promoted as being ideally suited for office partitions.

Clear, plain sheet glass was to dominate the aesthetic of the interior of the 'Contemporary' house. To be visually successful, open planning required large quantities of daylight to illuminate the larger spaces that were created through dispensing with interior walls: light had to penetrate further into the interior, and in order to do so it had to be stronger. This was achieved through the installation of larger window areas, particularly picture windows. Fewer but larger windows also had practical advantages as well in terms of maintenance, and economic advantages in terms of financial outlay. It was the sheer quantity of natural light within the 'Contemporary' house that transformed the character of the interior; and even at this early stage in the evolution of the 'Contemporary' house, Nelson and Wright identified the large window as 'modern architecture's most important contribution to house design'.

According to Nelson and Wright, however, prior to the popularization of the 'Contemporary' house in America, windows in modern houses had been installed 'with no regard for light or view'. In addition to the benefit of improved interior lighting, larger windows also allowed the house to be opened up to the landscape. This benefit was recognized as being equally important, whether the immediate environment was a suburban garden, the precious green spaces surrounding an urban housing estate, or a more dramatic open rural landscape. Views of mountains or canyons came to be considered the ideal setting for 'Contemporary' houses in the USA, and were particularly fashionable on the West Coast. Orientation was also important, however, as was the landscaping of the area immediately surrounding the house, as Wolf von Eckardt pointed out in *Mid-Century Architecture in America*: 'Careful orientation... makes the most of existing trees, rocks, and the topography. The design of the garden becomes as important as that of the living room, which, in a sense, it becomes – a place inviting quiet meditation.'

It was for extending the concept of the open plan beyond the physical boundaries of the house itself, and into the surrounding landscape, that Richard Neutra became so famous, following the lead of Frank Lloyd Wright in 1936 at Fallingwater but in a less overtly ostentatious way. Neutra worked with Wright shortly after he first arrived in the USA in 1923, so it is not surprising that he should have been influenced by him, although Neutra's work differs greatly in mood, being less heroic, more serene and understated. Possibly the most stunning example by Neutra of the integration of the house within the

Richard Neutra's Desert House (previous page and top) *built for Edgar Kaufmann in the Colorado Desert in 1946, and the Moore House at Ojai, California, dating from 1952* (opposite and left), *both take full advantage of the serene beauty of the landscape in which they are situated. Low-lying, the buildings do not attempt to compete with the visual power of the mountains, but exert a quiet aura and potency of their own which ensures that they are not dwarfed by the surrounding environment. In spatial terms, both houses are expansive: large, curtain wall windows make them appear almost transparent in places; while from inside, the removal of physical barriers brings the landscape into the interior in a very direct and immediate way.*

landscape was 'Desert House', the house built in 1946 for Edgar Kaufmann in the Colorado Desert. The scale of the windows in which the house was sheathed meant that during the daytime the landscape became an integral living component of the interiors, and at night, throwing out its light, the house acted like a beacon in the mountains. Further elaboration on this house, and on Neutra's techniques in general, is provided in this contemporary commentary by the American architectural writer Cranston Jones in *Architecture Today and Tomorrow*:

> The distinction between the interior and the exterior has been all but abolished by the use of glass, both in mitred corners (an old Wright device to vaporize the traditionally dark corners) and as an all-but-invisible glass curtain wall that slides open at the touch of an electric button. Continuity between interior and exterior is maintained through carrying the same terrazzo flooring without change from living area to patio, so that the house, as such, becomes merely controlled environment caught behind glass between floor and roof.

Richard Neutra's buildings received considerable attention and media exposure during the 1950s both in the USA and abroad, and in the field of domestic architecture he was clearly the most celebrated and influential figure of that time. Although in age and background he fell into the category of first-generation pioneer European Modernist, his arrival in the USA in 1923 meant that by the 1940s and 1950s he was more comfortable and familiar with the American lifestyle than some of the more recently displaced immigrants from Europe. He was particularly well equipped, therefore, to respond to the needs of American clients. From Europe he brought rigour, precision and clarity of vision, but in America he was given the opportunity to develop a more human and poetical form of expression. The spirit of his work remained youthful throughout the post-war period, and his designs for the Case Study House programme in Los Angeles, for example, sit comfortably alongside those of the younger generation of architects who participated in the scheme. His work commanded a high degree of respect among his younger contemporaries, and his ideas and his aesthetics were pivotal to the development of the 'Contemporary' house in America after the war.

The house Neutra designed for Warren Tremaine at Santa Barbara in California in 1947, described by Cranston Jones as 'one of America's great modern residences', was equally successful. In this house as many as possible of the exterior walls were windows, and a great many of these could be removed during times of hot weather. The upper level of the house had a continuous tier of openings, including windows which swung inwards to form a horizontal glass shelf, a system first devised by Neutra to suit the hot climate of the Caribbean. At the lower level, large sections of window could be slid to one side 'like the curtain panels draping them' according to the *Architectural Review* of 1950, so that the perimeter of the house was less clearly defined, but more flexible than in a conventional house with solid walls. Nelson and Wright declared that, 'Living outdoors – and partially outdoors – is one of the major pleasures of owning a modern house.' It was Neutra who, because of his responsiveness to the impact

Top The Bailey House, at Pacific Palisades, Los Angeles, designed by Richard Neutra in 1947–8, has a more suburban setting than the dramatically situated Desert House pictured on the previous pages. Neutra's unique brand of 'Contemporary' architecture nevertheless works equally well in this context.

Above, Opposite and Following Page The highly acclaimed house built by Richard Neutra for Warren Tremaine at Santa Barbara, California, in 1947, with its impressive landscaped garden.
Above In this house Neutra adopted a ploy that he had successfully exploited earlier in the

Desert House – frameless mitred glass joints in the corners of rooms – to allow the maximum amount of light to enter the house, and to provide a completely uninterrupted view of the neighbouring woodland.
Opposite To regulate the amount of sunshine entering the house, adjustable, angled wooden brise soleils were installed.

Above *Two blocks of 'youth dwellings' at Gentofte designed by the Danish architect, Arne Jacobsen, shortly after World War II on behalf of the local council.*

The blocks of flats were carefully orientated on an attractively landscaped site overlooking a lake so that each dwelling enjoyed beautiful views and plenty of sunshine.

of landscape and climate, ensured that this facet of 'Contemporary' house design fulfilled its greatest potential.

Although Neutra is best known for his private houses, like many leading architects of the period he was also extremely interested in and committed to the development of low-cost housing. In his designs for the Channel Heights Housing Project in San Pedro, California, of 1942-4, he introduced in a simplified repeatable form many of the features, including generous windows, that had originally been conceived for the dwellings of private clients. This scheme was of a considerable size and provided housing for 600 families. As a result of these designs, he was later invited by the Los Angeles Housing Authority to put forward proposals for a scheme for a large neighbourhood project to house up to 17,000 people at Elysian Park Heights. This scheme was intended to exploit the setting of a mature well-developed park but it did not come to fruition.

In the building of multiple housing blocks, some of the most enlightened site planning was carried out in Scandinavia, where the importance of the surrounding environment and the need for landscape planning were taken into careful consideration. The blocks of 'youth dwellings' erected in the late 1940s by the local council for young married couples at Gentofte in Denmark, designed by Arne Jacobsen, were a good example. Three blocks were built containing seventy-two apartments, all south-west facing, with their orientation staggered so that every apartment had a clear view of the nearby lake. A garden was created at the edge of the lake by the landscape gardener, Axel Andersen, which incorporated children's playgrounds. The effect of the whole scheme as described in *Architectural Review* in 1950 was one of harmony, and the habitat created for the residents extremely pleasant. Each apartment had beautiful views, through windows large enough to draw the landscape inside, and although the tenants did not have direct access from their apartments to individual gardens, their generous picture windows and balconies proved to be a satisfactory substitute.

This sort of close attention to detail with regard to both site planning and the specifics of interior design was one of the most distinctive features of 1950s' architecture, particularly when the architects concerned were of the calibre of Neutra and Jacobsen. These designers aspired to the very highest standards in both visual and practical terms in an effort to ensure that their clients would be fully satisfied. The well-being of the people who would occupy their buildings was considered of paramount importance and had to be balanced against the impulse of the architect for personal creative expression. Jacobsen and Neutra achieved this balance and hoped that their creativity would foster creativity in their client when it came to the question of decorating and furnishing the house. Fitting out the 'contemporary' house is the subject of the next chapter.

Above *Two views of the Channel Heights Housing Project at San Pedro, California, built during the war (1942–4) as a residential scheme for low-income families, designed by Richard Neutra. The highly successful* work of both Neutra and Jacobsen in the field of low-cost housing during the 1940s and 1950s is a reflection of a much more widespread commitment to this field of architecture at this time.*

Ultimately, the success of any 'Contemporary' interior was dependent on the response of the clients to the domestic environment created for them. In the Bass House, ☞❳ by Buff, Straub and Hensman, (see also page 190) 1958, there was clearly a sympathetic relationship between the architects and the clients.

4. decoration and fittings

'Let our dwelling have no particular "style", but only the imprint of the owner's character. The architect, as producer, creates only half a dwelling; the man who lives in it, the other half.'

Marcel Breuer, New Furniture, ed Gerd Hatje, 1952

Unlike today, when the buyer of a new house is usually presented with a shell and it is the sole responsibility of the new owner to determine the choice of decoration, in the 1950s the architect tended to take a more active role in the design of the interior. There were two clear stages involved in the decoration of a house. First, there were those elements which constituted the fabric of the building or which were, in effect, built-in features, such as floors and certain types of wall finishes (exposed masonry, wooden panelling and tiling, for example); here the architect took the lead. Second, there was the surface decoration, such as paint and wallpaper, and the choice of soft furnishings, all of which were usually selected by the owner. Much as the architect would probably have liked to continue to exert an influence on the interior that he had created

after it had been handed over to the client, as Marcel Breuer pointed out above, it was the character of the new owner which would subsequently determine the nature of the decoration. Breuer's ideas, however, were rooted in the Bauhaus ideals of the pre-war period when Modernist architects had believed that it was still possible to create a 'style without a style'; after the war, while 'Contemporary' architects continued to discourage decoration that was inappropriate to the character of the house, they were conscious that a 'Contemporary' design style had emerged and was there to be exploited.

In 1954 the British architect Colin Penn commented in *Houses of Today*: 'While it is true that the strength, stability and permanence of a house are determined by the structure, the finishes play a hardly less important part.' His remarks reflect the fact that the 1950s was a period when great attention was paid to decorative details, such as surface finishes. As was the case with many 1950s exteriors, texture or, more accurately, the use of a variety of different textures together, was an essential ingredient of the 'Contemporary' interior. Sometimes textures were physical, with a three-dimensional relief; occasionally, they were purely visual, evoked by a flat surface pattern. Both types of texture, real and simulated, were equally important.

Textures incorporated into the interior were often composed of the same materials as the exterior – building materials in fact or forms of masonry – rather than decorating materials. Rough stone and brickwork were frequently used, particularly for chimney breasts, or to create a fireplace surround. According to one commentator, Robert Harling, writing in *The House and Garden Book of Small Houses*, this fashion arose out of necessity rather than choice, because of the need to economize:

> The widespread tendency to let the actual structure of the walls provide the wall finish has arisen from the need to save costs in new buildings and to provide a permanent, easily maintained surface. In this category are to be found fair-faced brickwork, painted bricks and insulation blocks, such as Thermalite, plywood panels and vertical and horizontal match-boarding, as well as sheets of plastic laminate.

Some architects, usually those of the older generation, disapproved of this trend, because they found the rough appearance of these materials unpalatable, and they considered that such untreated surfaces made the interior cold and hostile. Used in a limited way, however, Colin Penn begrudgingly agreed in *Houses of Today* (1954) that such intrusions were acceptable:

> It is sometimes suggested that in order to save money interior plastering should be omitted in favour of bare brickwork. There are several objections to this: the interior face of external walls should not be brickwork but insulation blocks, which have a very unattractive appearance; common bricks are scarcely good enough for interior facing and more expensive ones must be used; the thermal capacity of uncovered brickwork is high and such walls are uncomfortable unless there is an efficient system of continuous central

Expressive and varied surface textures were a distinctive feature of 1950s architecture. Above Peter Womersley's Farnley Hey in West Yorkshire, dating from 1953, combines rough stonework with tongue-and-groove wooden cladding on the outside.

Opposite *In the Bass House in California, designed by Buff, Straub and Hensman in 1958, a variety of textures are used on the interior, including exposed white brickwork on the fireplace, smooth grey quarry tiles on the floor, and warm natural wooden cladding on the walls.*

heating. For these reasons it is very rare that a habitable room is faced entirely with brickwork, but a patch of brickwork on one wall or around a fireplace is quite common.

Among the younger generation of post-war architects there was a genuine interest in texture for its own sake. This was a trend which was also expressed throughout the applied arts during this period. Ultimately, in purely architectural terms, it led to the Brutalist aesthetic of the 1960s, inspired by Le Corbusier, whereby the rough surface of cast concrete was left bare both on the interior and the exterior of buildings. The adoption of this approach in a domestic setting, however, never became widespread, because concrete was used primarily for structural purposes rather than as the main building material, and it was uncommon to find it used other than in strictly limited areas of the domestic interior. In public buildings of an institutional nature, such as schools and halls of residence, and in low-cost public housing in the form of blocks of flats, where economy was often the main factor determining the choice of decorative finish for the interiors, it was employed extensively. However, even in these institutions this was largely a trend associated with the 1960s rather than the 1950s.

Exposed brick or stonework created a quite different effect from that of exposed concrete; its role in the 'Contemporary' house was to act as a foil to the adjacent plastered smooth walls. Visual interest was created by the contrast between the rough and the smooth, and between the finished and the unfinished surfaces. Frequently a combination of up to three or four different finishes were used in a single room, so that each wall or recess contrasted with the next. Most finishes other than paint and wallpaper were composed of natural materials, although plastic laminates were used on occasion as a form of wallcovering, and other types of printed decorative plastic wallcoverings were marketed during the 1950s by firms such as Dunlop and ICI, who were actively experimenting in this field. On the whole, in the living room area natural finishes were considered better because as Robert Harling commented:

> The great value with the natural textures is that most of them will provide a rich, warm-coloured surface, which is, at the same time, sufficiently neutral to provide a good foil for furniture and furnishing.

In the USA, where wood was in plentiful supply, wooden panelling was used extensively as a built-in decorative feature in many 'Contemporary' interiors. A good example of this can be seen in the Case Study house by Charles and Ray Eames discussed earlier. Tongue-and-groove panelling was often traditionally applied to the exterior of houses in both the USA and Scandinavia, not only because of its insulatory properties but also because it created such an attractive finish. This trend also became popular in Britain during the 1950s and 1960s, in spite of the high level of maintenance required in such a damp climate. Known in the UK as matchboarding, wood panelling had also traditionally been used as a form of interior cladding, again because it offered such good insulation, and this tradition was revived

Wooden panelling was often used to line the interior walls of 'Contemporary' houses. Opposite The interior of Case Study House number 8 in Los Angeles, designed by Charles and Ray Eames between 1945 and 1949, which has tongue-and-groove cladding on an area of wall used for the display of paintings by Ray Eames.

Top A distinctive feature of North American interiors was the use of large sheets of veneered plywood as a form of wall-covering. Such panels were also used as the facing material for built-in cupboard units, as seen here in the interior of the Shulman House of 1950 in Los Angeles designed by Raphael Soriano. This interior also includes a

rather more unconventional type of decorative wall finish: cork tiles, which have been extended through from the floor up the walls in the corridor area behind the cupboards. Above Living room of a house at Porvoo in Finland, designed by Bertel Saarnio in 1955, which has a polished wooden floor and wood-panelled walls.

The use of tongue-and-groove wooden cladding on the exterior of 'Contemporary' houses represented a move away from the clinical, white-walled aesthetic of the early Modern Movement to the re-adoption of traditional vernacular building materials.

Above *Particularly sympathetic was the use of redwood cladding on many of Richard Neutra's houses, such as the Treweek House.* Right *Cedar boarding exported from countries such as Canada was widely used for exterior cladding during the 1950s. Here, it is shown applied as the facing material to a house at Kurrajong Heights near Sydney, Australia, designed by Harry Seidler.*

during the 1950s. However, the woods used for cladding on the interior and exterior were usually quite different in appearance, the latter being stained a dark colour to emulate cedar or teak, and the former being generally lighter in colour, often untreated. The Americans favoured redwoods for exterior cladding, but on the whole aimed for something more sophisticated than simple matchboarding on the interior. Often they installed flush plywood panels faced with fine veneers, the emphasis being on the colour and tone of the wood and the pattern of the grain. In Scandinavia, where simpler effects were more common, pine was generally used as the interior finish, usually in the form of tongue-and-groove strips.

As Nelson and Wright correctly observed in *Tomorrow's House*, some of the supposedly new trends emerging in post-war interior design were, in fact, revivals of traditional practices. The value of these traditions had been overlooked during the 1930s when Modernist architecture had been dominated by the uniform clinical aesthetic of the International Style. In a way, therefore, 'Contemporary' architects were re-inventing the wheel in their re-discovery of the virtues of natural materials, as Nelson and Wright observed:

> Some architects have used exterior materials inside the house, and with great success. For example, a brick wall is finished as brick inside as well as out. Similarly, you can have walls of natural stone or wood. These devices are used primarily to give the house unity inside and out that conventional houses seldom have, but in addition they have great decorative effect and the advantage of requiring no maintenance. This is not a new idea; it was used in some of the best of the early Colonial houses.

However, what made 'Contemporary' interiors different from Colonial houses was the context in which these natural materials were used: whereas hitherto the desired effect had been to achieve consistency and uniformity, now the principal aim was to create variety and contrast. Areas of wooden panelling were located adjacent to painted or plastered walls, for example, and rooms or recesses with patterned wallpapers were contrasted with rough stone walls.

The interplay between the plain and patterned, or textured, areas within an interior, or between varying intensities of patterning in different areas of the same room, were considered important design issues during the 1950s, particularly in Britain where printed wallpapers and furnishing fabrics were so popular. During the 1930s, in the 'moderne' house decorated in the Art Deco style, visual contrasts had been established between the main wallpaper and the decorative border, which usually ran along the top or middle of the wall at dado or picture rail level. Because dados and picture rails were both dispensed with during the 1950s in 'Contemporary' houses, borders went completely out of fashion. In their place, new decorative trends in wallcoverings emerged which were better suited to the open-plan interiors of the day. Wallpaper books were often compiled to illustrate how two contrasting wallpapers printed with patterns on a different scale but in the same colourway, could be used on adjacent walls to complement each other. The contrast might be between different walls within a room, different

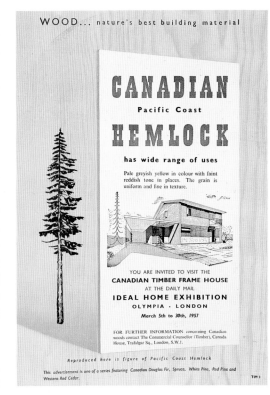

Left *Two advertisements for Canadian woods – Pacific Coast Hemlock and Western Red Cedar – which appeared in* The Architectural Review *in Britain during January and February of 1957. These advertisements were the first in a series for 'nature's best building material', also featuring Douglas Fir, Spruce, White Pine and Red Pine. Wood was being promoted by Canadian timber merchants at this date both as a material for frame construction and also for cladding. The application of wooden cladding to the exterior of 'Contemporary' houses was one of the ways in which modern architecture was 'humanized' in the minds of many people.*

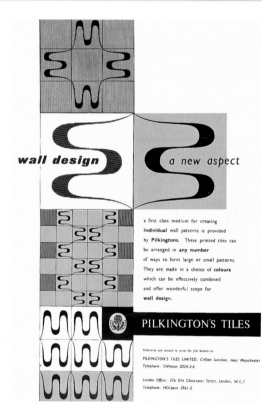

Above *Advertisement for the innovative British wallpaper manufacturer John Line, featuring a stylized 'Contemporary' wallpaper called Carafe, designed by June Lyon for the new London Airport Terminal at Gatwick in 1955. This wallpaper was also commercially available* (see also opposite, top left). Right *Wall tiles produced by the Manchester firm of Pilkington's Tiles, as advertised in* The Architectural Review *in May 1957. This clever printed tile design, which reflected the new taste for abstraction in post-war interior decoration, could be arranged in various ways to produce different patterns.*

rooms within a house, or between the patterns on different types of surfaces, such as walls and soft furnishings. Used strategically in this way, wallpapers could be exploited to evoke subtle shifts of mood within the interior.

Fashions in wallcoverings varied considerably from country to country. In many European countries the walls of a new house would often be painted in white or neutral colours; in Britain, patterned wallpaper was widely used, and in Italy brightly coloured painted surfaces were popular. It was recognized internationally, however, as Robert Harling pointed out, that, 'The walls of a house are much more than structural divisions between voids. Their colour, texture, height, the openings can all play a most important part in the character and apparent size of a room as well as in its comfort.'

Where wallpapers were used, the fashion in the 1950s was for what became known as 'Contemporary' patterns. These were usually abstract, linear or stylized designs produced either by means of roller printing or screen printing. With the latter technique – a process which had become mechanized by the end of the decade – the patterns tended to be bolder, more colourful and on a larger scale. Many wallpaper patterns were not dissimilar in spirit to those being developed concurrently in the field of textiles, and these two areas of pattern design remained closely related throughout the period, although they were generally produced by different manufacturers. Wallpapers, however, tended to be more mechanical in their pattern repeats and less wide-ranging in their use of colour. Designs used in the main living or reception room were often highly sophisticated, and were notable for their use of abstraction influenced by contemporary art. For wallpapers used in the more informal areas of the house, however, more whimsical designs were sometimes chosen, such as the amusing and witty creations of the American designers Ben Rose and Saul Steinberg. Kitchen wallpapers developed their own unique vocabulary which, by today's standards, may seem quirky and kitsch but which at the time was simply intended to be light-hearted and cheerful. Typical designs included brightly coloured themed wallpapers adorned with slices of fruit and vegetables, a trend which originated in the USA but soon spread to other countries such as Britain.

What surprises people most on discovering or rediscovering the interiors of the 1950s is the apparently outrageous and radical use of colour. Colour schemes incorporating bright turquoise, orange and pink, now associated more with the psychedelic era of the mid- to late 1960s, were in fact developed during the latter part of the 1950s. The idea of using bold colour contrasts – particularly primary colours – throughout the interior was a design concept which dates firmly back to the late 1940s, and was widely employed throughout the ensuing decade. Use of strong colour was not, as one might expect, a trend associated exclusively with products designed to appeal to the lower end of the market: in fact, quite the opposite, it was a fashion set by some of the most highly regarded architects and designers of the day, such as Alexander Girard in his textiles for the American firm of Herman Miller. Le Corbusier made startling use of primary colours on the exterior of the Unité d'Habitation in Marseilles; Eero Saarinen made bold colour statements on the interiors and exteriors of some of

Left *Trains*, a children's wallpaper produced in the USA by Piazza Prints in the late 1940s, after a design by the graphic artist, Saul Steinberg. Below *A molecular British wallpaper design inspired by atomic imagery which appeared in the 1959 pattern book, Effects by Heath.*

Two British 'Contemporary' wallpapers from the 1950s. Above *Carafe* designed by June Lyon for John Line, used in the newly opened London Gatwick Airport in 1955, but also particularly suitable for the interior of kitchens or restaurants. Right *Kiddies Town*, a children's wallpaper designed by Jacqueline Groag for John Line.

Two very different British wallpapers from the 1950s showing representational and abstract designs. Below, Near Right *Lincoln*, a themed kitchen wallpaper design which appeared in a pattern book called Byle Onward Decor in 1958–9. Far Right *Cut-out image of an imaginary living room, shown overlaid on top of an abstract wallpaper design from the 1959 pattern book, Effects by Heath. Such cut-outs were produced to show prospective customers the visual effect of different patterns within an interior.*

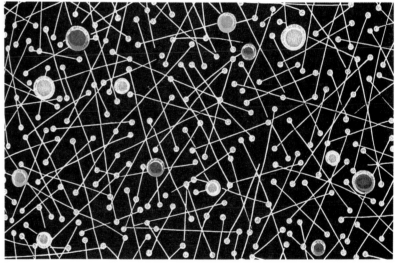

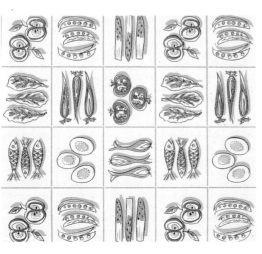

his most important buildings, his *tour de force* being the General Motors' Technical Center in Warren, Michigan; and by the middle of the decade even Marcel Breuer had been prised away from the Modernist practice of producing pristine all-white interiors, when he came to design the Starkey House in Duluth, Minnesota in 1955. Of his 'conversion' he commented: 'White is marvellous! But if you are going to have colour, let's achieve the utmost in effect and contrast. I want the reddest red, the bluest blue, the yellowest yellow. I want the strongest use of colour, the utmost in tension.'

In terms of the public's response, one of the main reasons for this fearless attraction to bright colours was as a reaction against the drab war years. After the war the tide of relief that swept through the West, and the shared sense of liberation, were most naturally expressed through visual exaggeration. Not only were brighter colours adopted, but a greater number of colours were combined together (the mix-and-match idea). 'Harlequin' colour schemes were a natural expression of this new-found freedom, combining brighter tones with a wider range of colours to create a rainbow effect. 'Harlequin' schemes were applied to the full range of domestic accessories, from tableware and glassware to furniture and light fittings. The same principles were also introduced into interior and exterior decoration in order to determine the choice of colours for walls and doors. Some 'harlequin' colour schemes still survive today in the form of the decorative cladding applied to offices, shops and blocks of flats. These show how 'Contemporary' architects extended their decorative colour schemes to encompass both the exterior and the interior of buildings, thereby creating a sense of visual continuity, at the same time as achieving liveliness and variety.

Colour and pattern co-ordination of the type with which we are familiar today were not major preoccupations during the 1950s, although matching fabrics and wallpapers were starting to come on to the market in USA after the war, and in Britain it was possible to buy certain plastic laminates, textiles, wallpapers and ceramics which, although manufactured by different companies, shared the same patterns. The fundamental principles of interior decoration, however, were based not on the aim to co-ordinate colours and patterns, but to create vivid and stimulating contrasts. Such contrasts were by no means arbitrary, however; they were highly considered and took into account colour, texture, pattern and scale. The psychology of colours and patterns played an important role in 1950s design. Dull or dark colours, such as grey or maroon, represented quiet, restful points within a room; conversely, bright or acid colours, such as red, orange or lime green, were intended to be enlivening, and were meant to act as visual highlights within the interior. It was also recognized that rough textures attracted greater attention than smooth surfaces, and that small pattern repeats were retiring, while large-scale pattern repeats were more aggressive. An example of a house in which colour contrasts were used in a particularly creative way was the Case Study house number 9 designed by Charles Eames and Eero Saarinen from 1945 to 1949 with its raised living-room area painted bright orange and its tangerine sofa contrasting with a neutral beige carpet.

The new fashion in 'Contemporary' floor design, however, was for uncarpeted floors. This was partly for aesthetic reasons, but also

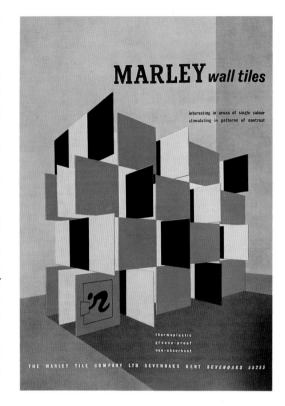

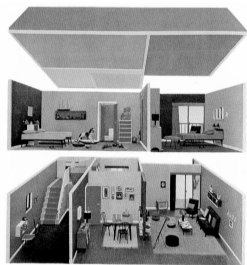

Opposite *Gretel wallpaper designed by Els Calvetti for John Line.*
Top Left *Advertisement for Marley thermoplastic wall tiles which claimed that these tiles were 'interesting in areas of single colour' and 'stimulating in patterns of contrast'. Marley were better known for their floor tiles, an advertisement for which can be seen on page 120.*
Bottom Left *'The joy of painting in Contemporary Colours; it makes your house look more fashionable and up-to-date than ever – and makes you feel years younger as a result!' This advertisement for International Paints, which appeared in the British edition of* House Beautiful *in June 1958, provides a reminder of the distinctive nature of 'Contemporary' colour schemes. Although the effect has been somewhat exaggerated in this advert, often each wall within a British interior was painted in a different colour or covered with a different wallpaper.*
Following Page *The Mirman House in California, designed by Buff, Straub and Hensman in 1958–9, provides a striking illustration of the bold use of colour in the 'Contemporary' interior, including soft furnishings and accessories. Colour photographs taken at the time underline the liveliness and dynamism of the interior design of this period.*

because such floors were hard-wearing, easy to clean and simple to maintain. As Robert Harling explains, after the widespread introduction of central heating after the war, bare floors were no longer considered unpleasantly cold and a new range of potential floor surfaces became available; a development which many architects found very exciting:

> We are only beginning to re-learn the use of the floor as an architectural element... Central heating, especially underfloor heating, has brought back into favour what were once considered hard, cold floors – the handsome terrazzo tiles, slate slabs, random marbles, and glass, ceramic and marble mosaic floors.

Wooden floors of various types – wood block, wood strip, parquet, plywood or veneered ply parquet – were popular for the living room because of the wide range of different grains and colours of wood available. Even lowly chipboard and hardboard could be used in less high-profile rooms, as long as there was no danger of moisture. The widespread use of wooden flooring was hardly surprising in countries with rich supplies of timber, such as Scandinavia and the USA. In Britain, however, the unexpectedly wide range of woods on the market during the 1950s was the direct result of the research carried out by the Timber Development Association during the early years after the war, when wood was in short supply and substitutes for standard materials had to be found. Also, because of the tough sealants that were now available, minimizing the risk of damage, softer, cheaper woods such as pine could be used as substitutes for the more expensive hardwoods.

Synthetic alternatives to natural wood floors included cork tiles and the various forms of vinyl, rubber, thermoplastic and linoleum tiles and sheet flooring that were introduced or re-launched onto the market during the 1950s. Cork produced a soft and warm effect, with the added bonus that it was sound-absorbent, making it specially suitable for children's playrooms and nurseries. Responding to the demand for greater variety, firms such as Robinsons in the UK produced coloured as well as natural cork tiles. The PVC tiles produced by Marley ('Marley De Luxe') and Semastic ('Semflex') were popular in the kitchen because they were hard-wearing and (unlike rubber) grease-resistant, but they were also frequently used in other areas of the house such as halls, corridors, bathrooms and even bedrooms, because they were easy to lay and flexible. Competing with them were the new thermoplastic tiles produced by firms such as Amtico which had the look of marble combined with the quietness and resilience of vinyl.

The established material with which all these new surfaces were competing was linoleum which, as a result of the new marketing initiatives of The Linoleum Manufacturers Association (THELMA) in Britain during the 1950s, was given a new lease of life after the war, in spite of increased competition from the plastics manufacturers. It was advertised as an innovative material by showing how it could be cut and laid in sheet form in customized patterns. Robert Harling, the editor of *The House and Garden Book of Small Houses*, who waxed lyrical on its merits in 1961, was a keen supporter:

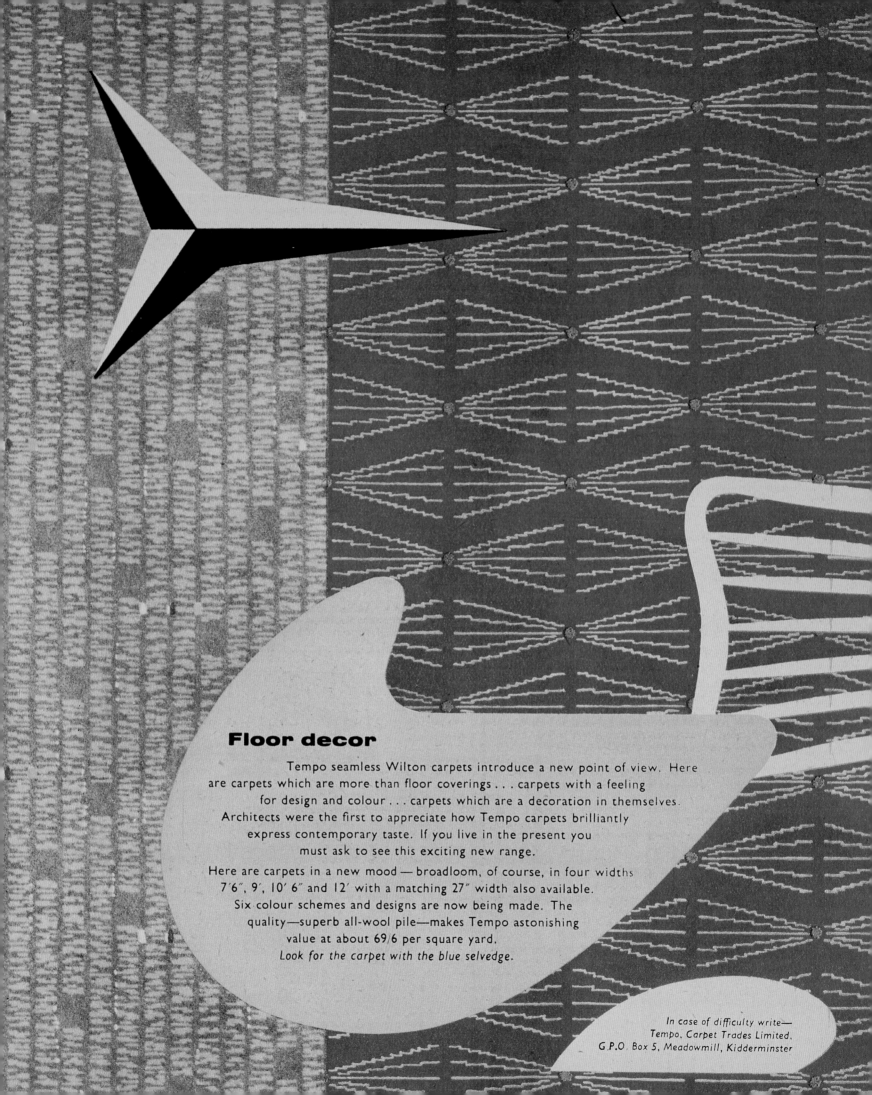

Floor decor

Tempo seamless Wilton carpets introduce a new point of view. Here are carpets which are more than floor coverings . . . carpets with a feeling for design and colour . . . carpets which are a decoration in themselves. Architects were the first to appreciate how Tempo carpets brilliantly express contemporary taste. If you live in the present you must ask to see this exciting new range.

Here are carpets in a new mood — broadloom, of course, in four widths 7′6″, 9′, 10′6″ and 12′ with a matching 27″ width also available. Six colour schemes and designs are now being made. The quality—superb all-wool pile—makes Tempo astonishing value at about 69/6 per square yard.
Look for the carpet with the blue selvedge.

In case of difficulty write—
Tempo, Carpet Trades Limited,
G.P.O. Box 5, Meadowmill, Kidderminster

Lino, for so long the Cinderella of the floor coverings, has come in for a reassessment. A good quality lino is a splendid floor; it is resilient and cold insulating, it can stand up to all the chemicals and greases met in the kitchen. It soon recovers from indentations and is available in a great variety of colours.

Tiles of any material were considered useful in the open-plan interior because, through their arrangement and patterning, they could be used to define different areas of the room. The move from the kitchen to the dining room area, for example, might be indicated by the change from a chequerboard arrangement of alternating light and dark tiles, to the use of single colour tiles emphasizing the marble-like patterning of the material.

If something even more hard-wearing was required – for example, in a hallway or the area of the living room opening onto a paved patio – the architect could choose from a variety of natural and man-made materials. These included traditional glazed ceramic floor tiles, known as quarry tiles; sealed and polished brick or stone; marble, the most expensive but the most durable and sophisticated of floor coverings; and various different types of aggregates – marble, glass mosaic or ceramics mosaic – embedded in cement, usually supplied in tile form. Such floor coverings were particularly popular in Italy, where the climate ensured they remained in use long after they had gone out of fashion in the rest of Europe, because of their effectiveness in cooling the interior. Advertisements from the 1950s reveal that it was Italian companies which were taking advantage of the growth in popularity of these flooring materials in the international market, with the firm of Jaconello playing a leading role, and P Barwin and Edgar Udny acting as major importers in the UK.

In spite of all these new possibilities in floor coverings, carpet remained a popular option in Britain. Unlike the 1930s, when square or rectangular carpet designs with borders and jazzy, abstract geometric patterns were produced, the trend during the 1950s was increasingly for wall-to-wall carpeting. While many carpet manufacturers tended to be rather traditional, some exciting new abstract designs were produced during the 1950s. Among the most adventurous in the UK were those created by established 'Contemporary' textile designers, such as Tibor Reich for I & C Steele & Company and Stockwell Carpets, and Lucienne Day for Tomkinsons. The general trend was away from representation and towards abstraction. However, it was still often the case that the introduction of a patterned carpet into a 'Contemporary' living room resulted in imbalance due to an excess of pattern. For this reason, most of the classic 'Contemporary' interiors of the period had a scattering of rugs on a hard floor, rather than wall-to-wall patterned carpeting.

The 'Contemporary' movement prompted the introduction of a range of striking linear and textural patterns into the British carpet market.
Above Five stylish abstract-patterned carpets featured in Furnishing *magazine in 1957.*
Bottom Left Carpet designed by R Anderson for James Templeton in 1951, based on the molecular structure of Resorcinol, produced under the auspices of the Festival Pattern Group scheme.
Opposite 'Tempo carpets brilliantly express contemporary taste'. Advertisement from House Beautiful, *1957.*

Although the main focus of the 'Contemporary' house was inevitably the living room, which was also invariably the largest room in the house, attention also shifted during the 1950s to the less glamorous service quarters of the house: the kitchen and bathroom.

No matter how traditional or retrogressive the taste of the owners in the matter of architecture and interior decoration, somehow the kitchen was always made the exception to the rule, and fitted out with the most up-to-date equipment and services. However, when it came to installing a kitchen in a 'Contemporary' house, the architect would go further still, revolutionizing not only its equipment but its layout as well. In the USA, the 'Contemporary' kitchen was equipped with services that seemed futuristic compared to those that were generally available in Europe and laid out in an arrangement which, by 1930s standards, was extremely radical and new.

For the busy housewife with a house to run and a family to look after, the kitchen inevitably came to be considered one of the most, if not the most, important room in the house. For this reason, and because, increasingly, it had to serve both as the 'work centre' and the 'social centre' of the home, an increase in size and an upgrading of facilities were justified. Size, however, was a major problem at first because building plots became more expensive and space more limited. This led to the compromise solution of the open-plan interior and in particular, the removal of the wall between the kitchen and the dining room area, and its replacement with a storage-unit type room divider. The three-in-one solution of the large kitchen/dining room/living room, which was adopted internationally after the war as a key feature of the space-conscious 'Contemporary' house, had a lot to offer. Although many commentators of the period openly disapproved of this development because they felt that the 'work centre' should, on principle, be separated from the 'social centre' of the house, it was both a practical and efficient solution. It meant, for example, that if the housewife was busy in the kitchen, she could at the same time keep an eye on the activities of the children in the adjoining rooms. For this reason, too, the location of the kitchen in relation to the garden or outside play area was carefully considered; the kitchen was often given a large window in a prime position overlooking the back garden. Also, as mentioned earlier, it meant that the housewife was less isolated. The new emphasis on the kitchen and its closer relationship with the rest of the house represented an improvement, albeit small, on the situation that formerly prevailed for those whose lot it was to spend their time at home in the role of housewife and mother.

During the 1950s it also came to be recognized that the kitchen need not be a place of tedious drudgery. If equipped with a host of labour-saving devices, it could be treated more as a domestic work-station, the household equivalent of a laboratory or a workshop. For this reason the new technological developments that were being made in the field of kitchen appliances in the USA after the war were described with great relish by Nelson and Wright in *Tomorrow's House* in 1945:

When we think of a kitchen, we think of three items: sink, stove, and refrigerator. The work centre, however, has a lot more than

Opposite and Above
Two views of the kitchen in Case Study House number 21 in Los Angeles, designed by Pierre Koenig in 1958, which was fitted out with the latest in kitchen technology as devised by General Electric, including a combined cooker/dishwasher/sink unit.
Right *Interior of a refrigerator designed by Peter Muller-Munk Associates for Westinghouse, 1954. Companies such as Westinghouse and General Electric excelled at producing ever more sophisticated and technologically advanced new designs for kitchen appliances, which were marketed in the USA as essential prerequisites for the 'Contemporary' dream kitchen. This capacious refrigerator was equipped with a beverage drawer,*

tilting egg racks, snack storage compartments, fruit bins, 'humididrawers' and a 56lb freezer.

merit specified

AS STANDARD EQUIPMENT
... in Arts & Architecture Case Study Houses

Sunbeam MIXMASTER

Sunbeam TOASTER

Sunbeam WAFFLE-BAKER

Sunbeam COFFEEMASTER

Sunbeam IRONMASTER

Sunbeam SHAVEMASTER

Made and guaranteed by SUNBEAM CORPORATION (Formerly Chicago Flexible Shaft Co.)

Previous Page The 'floating' open-plan kitchen of Case Study House number 22 designed by Pierre Koenig in 1959–60, which features two sinks and a cooking range neatly fitted into the tops of the cupboard units. After World War II the USA led the world in the field of domestic gadgetry.
Top The 'merit specified' appliances in the Sunbeam range of 1948, some of which can be seen in the kitchen of Case Study House number 9, the Entenza House of 1945–9 (opposite), along with an enormous refrigerator.
Right By contrast, British product design visibly lagged behind, although one manufacturer of gas cookers, Radiation Ltd, attempted to conjure up an image of modernity in 1956 through the adoption of the range name 'New World'.

three items. It would be wise to plan for possible additions. For one thing, it will almost inevitably have a quick-freeze unit – which will finally be reduced to compact, cabinet size. It will also contain the laundry equipment, which, as we have seen, is also shrinking to manageable proportions. The rapid movement in dish-washing machines, some of which will also dry the dishes... means that more and more people will consider them necessary rather than luxury items. The same is true of that wonderful gadget which disposes of garbage by grinding it up and flushing it away.

Indeed, the entire approach to the equipping of the kitchen became more scientific with the introduction of new technology in kitchen appliances, such as electric food mixers, automatic washing machines, dish-washers, giant-sized fridges and waste disposal units. Brand names for these appliances were to become generic household names (Westinghouse, Hoover, Kenwood and Braun, for example) and, in the USA, the designers of these products attempted to emulate the styling of 'Contemporary' cars and the colour schemes of 'Contemporary' furniture and furnishings.

Cookers were also greatly improved with the introduction of split-level cooking facilities, although this was only in ultra-modern 'Contemporary' houses. All cooking equipment, however, whether operated by gas or electricity, became more streamlined and less cumbersome in operation, with many new refinements such as timers and oven lights. Finally, even the act of cooking was itself elevated to the level of a science – hence the appearance of 'domestic science' as a new subject on the school syllabus – while the management of the home and of household accounting also became known as 'home economics'.

The size of the kitchen itself, however, was tending to be reduced in new houses, which emphasized the need for greater common sense in its design and layout. This led to innovations such as the fitted kitchen, in which a range of co-ordinated units were built in as fixtures around the walls of the kitchen, or sometimes in the form of islands in the middle of the room. In more sophisticated kitchens, all the main mechanical appliances would be built in too, so that everything, including sinks, was set flush at one level and all the surfaces were continuous. This provided more worktop surfaces, bypassed the need for a separate laundry and larder, produced a uniform appearance and increased facilities for the storage of food and utensils. Furthermore, this layout was altogether more practical because everything was readily to hand and more hygienic, because the kitchen was now much easier to keep clean.

In the early days of fitted kitchens, cabinets had to be architect-designed and manufactured to order. Costs were significantly reduced later as standardized parts, such as metal door handles for cupboards which the architect could buy 'off the peg', began to be mass-produced. Later still, some enterprising furniture firms, such as Kandya and Hygena in the UK, began to manufacture standard kitchen units that could be installed by the customer. This eventually led to the situation today where flat-packed units that can be assembled by the customer are produced, in order to reduce costs still further.

The early 1950s saw the advent of the fitted kitchen. Opposite *The Ullman House of 1957, designed by Thornton Abell, with its stylish taps and fitted sink.*

Above *A British version of the American dream kitchen, illustrated* in House Beautiful *in February 1960. Such facilities did not become widespread in Britain until the late 1950s.*

Top and Bottom Right *The capacious two-way cupboards built into the Mirman House in California designed by Buff, Straub and Hensman in 1958–9. These act as a divider between the kitchen and the dining room and, when closed, look like panelling rather than cupboard fronts.*

WRIGHTON KEEPS THE COST   OF DREAMING DOWN

... **TRICITY**

'BUILT-IN' COOKERS IN
COLOURFUL 'CALIFORNIAN'

KITCHENS BY **WRIGHTON**

Above *This 1962
advertisement for
'Californian' fitted kitchens
made by the firm of
Wrighton, marketed as
a package with Tricity
electrical appliances,
provides proof that it
was to the USA that the
British looked for ideas
about their 'dream
kitchens'. The combination*
*of white and primary
colours on the fronts of
the units and drawers is
particularly striking.*
Right *Brightly coloured
and patterned plastic
laminates produced by the
two leading manufacturers,
Formica and Warerite,
were especially popular
for use on kitchen worktops
and tables.*

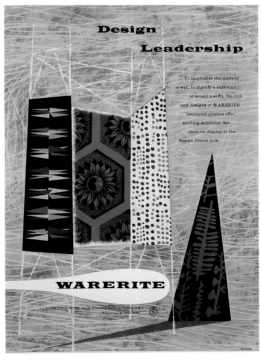

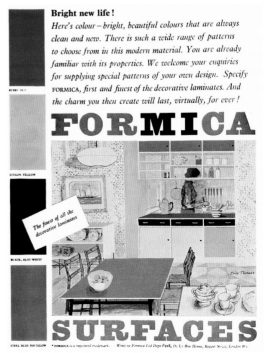

The typical 'Contemporary' fitted kitchen was streamlined in appearance, the walls completely lined with plain, regular-shaped cupboards. Shaped mouldings were avoided in favour of a flush finishes that were easier to clean. Unlike the clinical 1930s Modernist kitchen, which was described by Nelson and Wright as having a 'hospital operating-room atmosphere' with surface decoration almost completely excluded, the 'Contemporary' kitchen had cupboard fronts in attractive natural wood finishes, such as beech, or painted in bright primary colours, such as red, yellow or blue. Kitchen surfaces, including both cupboards and tables, were topped with the new wonder material, plastic laminate, marketed under the tradenames of Warerite or Formica. Such laminates might be plain in colour, in which case they were usually bright, but more often they were decorated with abstract printed patterns in the quirky, linear 'Contemporary' style. In the UK, textural patterns resembling abstracted enlargements of woven fibres were popular. Gaily patterned printed cotton kitchen curtains added another lively decorative element into an already colourful scheme. Wallpapers designed specifically for the kitchen were also fashionable, incorporating food imagery or kitchen implements into their design. Such supplementary decoration, although not strictly necessary, was intended to create a more stimulating and attractive environment in which to carry out domestic chores without diminishing the underlying functionalism of the kitchen.

During the 1950s the kitchen became a cheerful place full of colour and pattern, where many of the latest synthetic materials could be tried out. As discussed earlier, on the floor, for example, were laid the smart new PVC tiles made by firms such as Marley and Semastic, which could be combined and alternated in a variety of different colourways. PVC tiles were quick and easy to lay and with their marble-effect patterning and their solid opaque colouring, they created a positive visual effect on the kitchen floor. Apart from Formica and PVC tiles, other new synthetic materials that came to be widely used in 'Contemporary' kitchens were plasticized vinyl upholstery, often used on kitchen chairs, and vinyl wallpapers, used to combat the effect of condensation caused by cooking. Apart from brightening up the interior with their bold printed patterns and vibrant colours, these synthetic floor, wall and furniture coverings were all alike in being easily washable. Their practical and hygienic qualities made them particularly suitable for use in a kitchen, cleanliness and functionalism being considered essential prerequisites for 'Contemporary' living.

The 'Contemporary' kitchen became a potent symbol of American supremacy in the field of design and manufacturing during the 1950s. Even before such facilities became generally available in Europe, the idea had taken root internationally in the popular imagination. During and immediately after the war, in all the countries directly affected by the hostilities, people had been deprived of all but the most basic kitchen implements and accessories. After the war, therefore, the American dream kitchen became something to aspire to, a symbol of progress and a return to material prosperity. Later, during the Cold War, it was even used by Vice-President Nixon as a weapon in the war of words against the Soviet Union, where consumer goods of this type were not available at this date. During the famous 'kitchen debate'

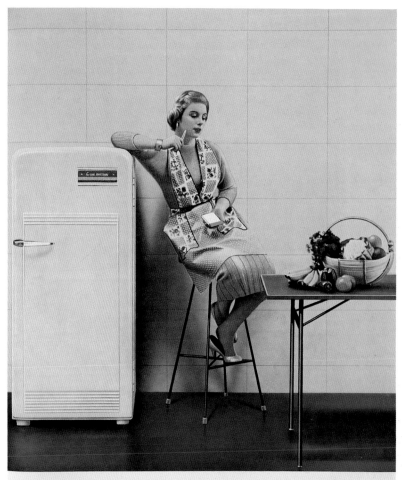

VITROLITE—*made in the interests of better living*

Above *Hygiene was a major consideration in the planning of the 'Contemporary' kitchen. Wipe-down surfaces for cupboard units and walls were considered a great advantage. This advertisement from 1957 draws attention to a new product, Vitrolite opaque glass lining panels, marketed by Pilkington during the 1950s for use in kitchens and bathrooms* (see also page 134).

which took place in Moscow in 1959 between Nixon and President Krushchev in the mock-up of an American suburban house, which formed the centrepiece of a promotional exhibition of American domestic products, Nixon asked Krushchev in front of a hoard of journalists: 'Isn't it better to talk about the relative merits of washing machines than the relative merits of rockets?'

By the end of the 1950s, the 'Contemporary' dream kitchen had become a reality for millions of Americans, and by this date, too, it was becoming more widely available in Europe. Whether it was due to greater restraint, or whether it was simply that they were slow to catch up with the Americans, however, Europeans never achieved quite the same excesses in equipping and decorating the kitchen as did the increasingly materialistic and consumerist Americans.

The 'scientific' approach was also applied to the furnishing and equipping of other service areas of the house, such as the bathroom. Basic bathroom appliances were still chosen primarily for their practicality but the fittings on offer since the war had become more streamlined. Whereas previously such fittings had tended to be rather bulky and monumental, the new fashion was for smaller appliances; baths that were shorter and shallower, for example, and basins supported by wall brackets or chromium-plated steel legs rather than pedestals, many of which adopted the elegant, organic profiles of 'Contemporary' design.

In the UK, a sculptural trend was apparently started by one leading company, after which all the other manufacturers followed suit – one company, Broads, even adopting the name 'Sculptura' for their new range. According to Robert Harling:

> Over the past few years, Adamsez have started a modest revolution in basin and wc design by emphasizing the plastic qualities of clay in flowing, rounded forms. Angles and heavy rims are a hang-over from cast iron models.

The influence of contemporary sculpture on the design of sanitary wares was taken to its furthest extreme in Italy, where the sculptress, Antonia Campi, designed the extruded mushroom-shaped 'Torena' range for Societa Ceramica Italiana di Laveno in 1959. Most designs, however, were more stylized and less literally organic.

The design of other bathroom accessories, such as taps, also became more streamlined at this time, and baths were now offered in new synthetic materials such as fibreglass and perspex, in addition to the standard vitreous china and porcelain enamel. The range of bathroom fittings was also expanded to include the newly fashionable shower, in addition to the traditional bath, washbasin and toilet suite, and bidets, which had hitherto failed to catch on outside mainland Europe, started to be considered as fashionable cosmopolitan design accessories in the UK. In general, greater variety was introduced with the launch of brighter colour ranges for bathroom fittings, and instead of the need to buy individual fittings from different specialist companies, manufacturers were now producing colour co-ordinated suites.

Although the bathroom was a less likely place than the kitchen for the architect to seek to make a design statement, it certainly became

Above *Vitrolite coloured glass cladding, produced by the architectural glass company Pilkington, was promoted during the 1950s as an alternative to ceramic tiles.*
Right *Sinks and other bathroom appliances took on more organic and streamlined shapes during the 1950s, influenced by contemporary sculpture. Previously they had been more angular and bulky. This advertisement for the Lotus sink by Adamsez dates from 1952.*

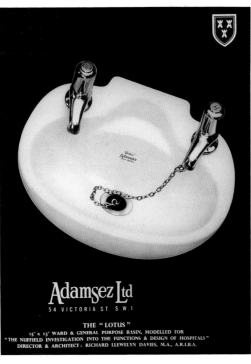

Adamsez Ltd
54 VICTORIA ST. S.W.1

THE "LOTUS"
15' x 13' WARD & GENERAL PURPOSE BASIN, MODELLED FOR
"THE NUFFIELD INVESTIGATION INTO THE FUNCTIONS & DESIGN OF HOSPITALS"
DIRECTOR & ARCHITECT: RICHARD LLEWELYN DAVIES, M.A., A.R.I.B.A.

Left *Small blue Pomona tiles are used as the floor-covering and sink-cladding material in this bathroom designed by architects Smith and Williams c1952. The walls and the shower door are made of Mississippi Coolite sand-blasted glass.*

more stylish during the 1950s to pay attention to details such as fitted basins and built-in cupboard units. The installation of sanitary appliances outside the bathroom proper, such as washbasins in bedrooms and, space permitting, an additional children's toilet on the ground floor off the hall, was another new development.

Developing a taste for 'Contemporary' design was by no means a prerequisite for pursuing an interest in 'Contemporary' technology. Even when the 'Contemporary' style was not to a house-buyer's taste and the client opted instead for a more conservative style of architecture and interior decor, when it came to the question of the basic services, such as heating and plumbing, house-buyers were usually much more adventurous, and almost invariably opted for the ultra-modern rather than the old-fashioned. Since services had to be literally incorporated into the framework of the house, however, it was essential that they be integrated into the design of the structure at the earliest possible stage in the planning process. Complex systems, such as central heating, became part of the invisible 'nervous system' of the house and could no longer be treated as independent structures in the way that chimneys and fireplaces had been. Thus, as the range of integral built-in services expected by the client became more complicated, the 'Contemporary' architect either had to have considerable technical know-how, or was obliged to bring in teams of specialist engineers.

Heating was one of the areas in which major changes were introduced during the 1950s which had a significant effect on domestic habits. Before the war, central heating was considered a luxury in many countries, even where the climate was usually cold, as in the UK. Previously, the stove in the kitchen, or the open fire in the living room, had provided the main sources of heat and, because its beneficial effects were usually confined to one or two rooms within the house, people tended to congregate in these areas. After the war, central heating became much more commonplace, leading to considerable changes in lifestyle as other rooms, such as bedrooms, could be brought into service for daytime activities as well. As houses decreased in size and it became necessary to maximize the use of space, through mixed use it became increasingly important to heat the outlying rooms of the house in order to bring them into twenty-four-hour service.

The traditional method of central heating was in the form of radiators heated by hot water pumped around the house through pipes. Earlier in the century, radiators had been heavy, cast iron apparatus requiring large amounts of space, which were not always particularly effective at radiating heat. It is understandable, therefore, why modern architects were reluctant to incorporate them into their new, streamlined, airy interiors. As lighter, thinner wall-hung pressed steel radiators were developed, however, many 'Contemporary' architects were happy to accept these as an alternative. Even more discreet were the new, long, low skirting radiators. These were thought to distribute heat more evenly than conventional radiators and they could be installed underneath deeper windows. The most discreet of all was the system of hot-water pipes set in grilled ducts in the floor or the wall. These pipes had 'fins' to increase the surface area from which they radiated heat.

Such systems satisfied the demands of the growing number of 'Contemporary' architects who considered any sort of visible intrusion

Above *A small top-lit courtyard with plants and a fountain connects the two bathrooms in Case Study House number 21 in Los Angeles, designed by Pierre Koenig in 1958. The bathrooms themselves are isolated within a central utility core in the middle of the glass-walled house,* along with the gas-fired *water heater and the boiler.* Right *Cascade bath enclosure made of corrugated plastic, designed by Reino Aarnio for the Fiat Metal Manufacturing Company in 1954. Plastic is adopted here as an alternative to glass.*

unacceptable, and who sought instead to install hidden or buried systems. Such systems were not introduced for the sake of novelty alone; it was hoped that they would also be more effective in circulating heat, something that was especially important in the new larger open-plan interiors. Of the many different types of central heating systems on the market during the 1950s, some were frankly experimental, others were more traditional. Examples of different systems included electric heating coils or hot water in plastic tubes embedded in the concrete floor; hot water piped through coils built into the ceiling; and hot air circulated through floor channels and vents. Some systems could be quite complex and sophisticated. One prefabricated hot-air system introduced into Europe from the USA during the 1950s was the Coleman Blend-Air system, which was installed in a series of low-cost houses at Capell-aan-de-ljssel near Rotterdam, by HPC Haan. This consisted of an oil-fired furnace boiler with a blower which sent air rapidly through tubes in the floor to a blender. In the blender this air was mixed with air from the room, which was then released noiselessly back into the interior. In this way, rather than simply pumping out hot dry air, the air from the boiler was tempered by the air from the room. Another hot air system installed in a house in Toronto, by John C Parkin, involved a combination of both radiant and convection heating, with a blanket of warm air being piped under the floor to thin slots under the windows. A rather different system was introduced in the experimental glass house built by Angela and Michael Newberry at Capel, Surrey during the 1950s. According to a contemporary account in Monica Pidgeon's and Theo Crosby's *An Anthology of Houses*, this involved hot water panels embedded in the screed, each panel being 'individually controlled and fully automatic, providing an even draught-free temperature throughout'.

Careful attention was also paid to insulation and new houses often had glass fibre, strawboard or foil-backed plaster-board built into the roof; brick or stone walls were lined on the inside with insulating blocks, and cavity walls were sometimes injected with plastic foam. Houses were deliberately orientated with the main windows facing to the south in order to take advantage of the sun, and where this was impossible, or the winter climate particularly severe, double-glazing was introduced. Unlike previous eras, sound insulation was now considered important, and it was during the 1950s that it became fashionable to install 'acoustic tiles' on ceilings. Also in *An Anthology of Houses* is a contemporary description of a house built by John Winter in Norwich during the 1950s which draws attention to many of these issues, which were, of course, particularly important with regard to open-plan houses:

> The ground floor is centrally heated by hot water pipes embedded in the floor. To keep the heat in, the building was made a compact shape and all surfaces to the outside were highly insulated – Fosalil under the site concrete, double glazing to all principal windows, a foam slag inner skin to the cavity walls and a vermiculite screed on the roof.

New methods of heating the home had a dramatic impact on the structure of the interior: the atmosphere and focus of a room could be

Born Yesterday . . . **already the talk of the town**

THERE ARE THREE TYPES OF WALLSTRIP

Copperad WALLSTRIP is a skirting-board: a skirting-board that heats. Which means that it places the heat where it is most needed—all along the outside walls at the normal source of loss.

It also means that windows can reach to within 12″ of the floorline.

WALLSTRIP allows you the maximum freedom in aesthetic design. No ungainly, heavy equipment is involved. There is nothing to detract from its flowing lines.

For a new building — home, office, school, hall, hospital or institution—WALLSTRIP costs no more than conventional central heating. The cost of skirting-board is, of course, eliminated. Moreover, no special equipment is required ; it can be installed with the ordinary tools of a heating engineer.

If you require further information about WALLSTRIP, we shall be happy to advise you.

Type C—Recommended for most domestic applications, providing mainly convected heat.

Type R—Institutional model of heavy construction, but shallower from wall to front than Type C, providing mainly radiant heat. Smooth surfaces, free of dust-traps, especially suitable for hospitals and other places where hygiene and cleanliness are vital.

Type RC—Again, an institutional model of heavy construction, similar to Type R but providing a combination of radiant and convected heat.

Copperad *Wallstrip*

Warmth from sources — EVERYWHERE

Above *Discreet or hidden heating systems were favoured during the 1950s. One example of a new system which came on the market at this time was the slimline Wallstrip radiator produced by Copperad which ran round the room at skirting board level.*
Left *The Parkray convector fire, which could burn smokeless fuel, was selected by the architect Basil Spence in 1958 for new housing built at Basildon New Town. Note the 'Contemporary' style ball-and-spoke accessories in the hearth and the use of the fireplace as a room divider.*

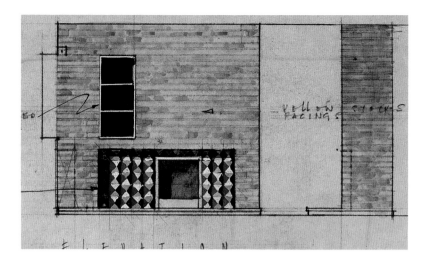

Above *One of several detailed sketches for fireplaces drawn up as possibilities for Roundwood House in Middlesex by the architect Keith Roberts in 1956. This particular design has grey, yellow and white abstract-patterned tiles around the fireplace itself, with the surrounding wall faced in exposed yellow brick. The arrangement is consciously asymmetrical, and recessed into the wall above the fireplace on the left are shelves for the display of ornaments.*
Right *Central heating thermostat designed by Henry Dreyfuss for Honeywell c1954. The circular shape was new at the time.*

Opposite *In the USA a new design phenomenon arose during the 1950s: the 'feature fireplace'. This drew attention to the fireplace as the primary feature within the living room. Well-established by the end of the decade as a design convention, 'feature fireplaces' dating from the early to mid-1960s became* increasingly exaggerated in form as architects gave free range to their imaginations. One of the most astonishing 'feature fireplaces' of the period, dating from as late as 1964, designed by Crites of the architectural partnership Crites and McConnell, is shown opposite.

completely changed by altering the heating source. Furthermore, the act of introducing central heating which distributed the heat through several rooms, rather than of concentrating it in one room, stimulated the development of the open plan. In the longer term, however, although technically inventive, some of these systems proved neither reliable, efficient nor cost-effective, but as post-war architects were experimenting more boldly than perhaps they had ever done before, it is not surprising that their legacy should be a mixed one in terms of technical success.

In spite of the commitment of many architects to technical innovation and experimentation in advanced new heating systems, the psychological attraction of the traditional stove or open fire sometimes proved irresistibly strong. It was not uncommon even in the most technologically sophisticated of houses to find the new and the old combined in the form of a radiant central heating supplemented by a stove or an open fire. This was sometimes necessary in any case with electrically powered central-heating systems dependent on off-peak rates of supply in order to be economical, which often needed topping up towards the end of the day. However, because the direct heating source was now installed largely for decorative rather than functional reasons (although there was no reason, of course, why it could not be both at the same time), more attention began to be paid to its physical appearance and presentation. The position of the fireplace within a room was also given greater consideration by designers. Since one of the distinctive characteristics of 'Contemporary' design was asymmetry, within the main living room it was through the choice of location for the fireplace that this desire for asymmetry was often expressed. Rather than centring it on the main wall, as had formerly been the custom, the fireplace was often now deliberately placed off-centre. It might be located on any interior or exterior wall, or alternatively it might even be completely free-standing.

The secondary role of the fireplace in terms of function was underlined in one of two contrasting ways. The British favoured the subtle, understated approach, saving their more extrovert design statements for other aspects of the interior, such as soft furnishings. British fireplaces surrounds were usually extremely simple, often flush with the wall, and characteristically faced with some sort of masonry, which might be stone, brick or slate. When man-made products such as tiles were used, decorative effects were kept to a minimum: there might be a single repeated printed or relief-moulded pattern on the tiles, but in a limited range of colours or completely monochrome.

This approach was in stark contrast to that of other countries such as Australia and the USA, where the fireplace was often deliberately ostentatious. It was in the USA, for example, that the bizarre phenomenon of the 'feature fireplace' arose. Often free-standing in the manner of a stove, the fireplace was treated as an independent art object, on a par with a piece of modern furniture or sculpture, rather than as part of the physical structure of the building. Often it was located in the centre of the room rather than at the perimeter, and its casing, often metal, was usually intended as an artistic statement, and was often overtly sculptural in form, sometimes strongly organic. It is hard to believe, expressive though they were, that many of these fireplaces

functioned very effectively, but as the heat from them was usually supplementary to the main system, this did not appear to matter. It is significant, however, that some of the most extravagant feature fireplaces were developed in relatively mild climates, such as California and New South Wales. In Britain, although the fireplace was developed as a design feature, in view of the climate, it was certainly expected to function. Similarly, when it came to the question of furniture (the subject of the next chapter), the British attached greater importance to practicality and comfort, and less to eye-catching design.

During the 1950s and early 1960s 'Contemporary' fireplaces came in all shapes, colours and sizes. The theatrical 'feature fireplace', which became all the rage in the USA, provided the architect with an opportunity for an unashamed flight of fancy.

Opposite *Like the example on the previous page, this free-standing fireplace, designed by William Pereira and Associates in 1963, has the aerodynamic form of an up-ended rocket.*

Above *By comparison, this circular fireplace, designed for a house in Phoenix, Arizona by Blaine Drake in 1950, is more restrained, although still assertively modern and unconventional.*

5. furniture and furnishings

'Just because of the variety of possibilities... every interior designer and every customer should be aware of his responsibility to furnish a home with taste and modesty. Neither an overcrowding of effects nor a pure functionalism is the right solution.'

Gerd Hatje, New Furniture (1952)

A genuinely 'Contemporary' house demanded equally 'Contemporary' furnishings in order to project confidently the all-important feeling of modernity of the post-war period. An open-plan interior alone was no guarantee of success if the furniture inside it was heavy and unsympathetic, or if the furnishing fabrics were flowery and retrogressive. To create a 'Contemporary' interior a complete new scheme was required that encompassed soft furnishings such as curtains, rugs and upholstery, as well as the furniture itself. Also vital were the details of minor domestic accessories, such as wastepaper bins, magazine racks and light fittings, as well as the choice of tableware and decorative ornaments.

During the 1950s a revolution took place in the field of domestic design. The modern became mainstream and the 'Contemporary' style began to influence the appearance not only of expensive and exclusive items, such as art glass and silverware, but also low-priced mass-produced everyday goods, such as earthenware crockery and printed rayon curtains. This meant that, even for those who were not fortunate enough to live in a newly-built 'Contemporary' house, modern furniture and furnishings were still accessible, enabling them to create a 'Contemporary' look in a house dating from an earlier period.

This new 'variety of possibilities', as Gerd Hatje recognized, presented a marvellous opportunity for the public, but there was also a danger that consumers might be overwhelmed by the choice of goods on offer. What Hatje was hoping would happen was that a balance would be achieved between the austerity of 1930s Modernism and the over-abundance of the post-war boom. What finally emerged as the 'Contemporary' style, however, represented a mixture of these two elements – high ideals and mass-market compromise – but it is this very combination of high-minded principles tempered by democratic impulses that makes the style so fascinating.

Central to the success of the 'Contemporary' interior was the choice of modern furniture. During the 1930s, cantilevered chairs with tubular steel or bent laminated wood frames rather than wooden legs had looked comfortable in the spacious Modernist interiors of the day, but after the war such furniture, even though it was still relatively up-to-date, was already too large and heavy-looking for the more compact living spaces that were now being created. To create houses that were really in tune with 'Contemporary' living, the architect had to install furniture of a new, lightweight, pared-down style. This could happen only if designers and manufacturers recognized that the whole basis of interior design had changed and that, henceforth, their furniture must accommodate these changes. In his 1952 survey of *New Furniture*, Gerd Hatje pointed to the trend in modern architecture:

> ...to give up the idea of the home as a collection of rooms serving definite purposes. The conception of architecture as a social manifestation exercises a strong influence upon furniture production. The new form of dwelling, which combines rooms serving more than one purpose, demands durable furniture which is easy to move.

This meant that furniture had to be more flexible, both in its potential application and in its methods of construction. One way of satisfying the need for furniture that was 'easy to move', for example, was to make it more lightweight; and one method of adapting to 'rooms serving more than one purpose' was to produce furniture that had a number of different functions. It was by responding to such 'social' pressures that 'Contemporary' furniture began to evolve during the late 1940s and early 1950s. Although aesthetics were important too, it was functional and technical considerations that determined the future course of development for modern furniture after the war.

The key word which keeps being reiterated in the introduction to *New Furniture* is 'light'. Of 'Contemporary' chairs Hatje writes; 'The demand for lightness in optical effect, lightest possible weight and

Below The Superleggera *chair designed by Gio Ponti for the Italian manufacturer, Cassina, in 1957. In English the name of the chair means 'super-light', which is an accurate description of what must be one of the lightest chairs ever produced.*

Above Cover of the British magazine House Beautiful *from February 1958, illustrating chairs designed by Charles Eames for Herman Miller which, after proving popular in the USA during the early 1950s, were subsequently promoted in Europe.*
Opposite Furniture and furnishings by two leading Danish designers. The three chairs at the top were designed by Arne Jacobsen for Fritz Hansen between 1951 and 1955, while Verner Panton was the designer of the table, the wire Cone chair of 1958 manufactured by Plus-Linje, and the abstract-patterned rug of 1960 produced by Unika-Vaev.*

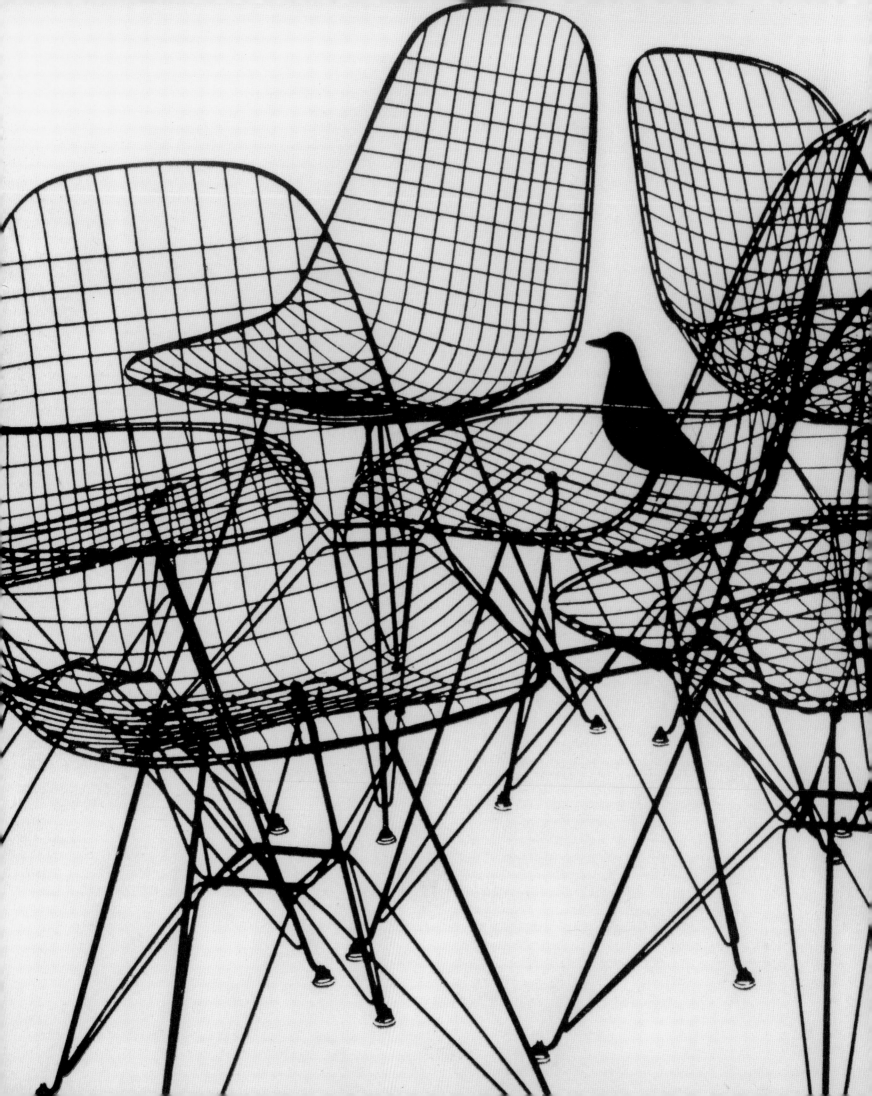

greatest possible resistance to wear, are best fulfilled by metal frames with their great bearing capacity and stability, for which relatively little material is required.' Similarly, of tables, 'the demands for lightness and elegance of form, adaptability to use and durability, have caused designers to give up traditional forms. The heaviness of the top and legs gave way to lightness. Light steel tubing or slender wooden legs, which often are attached slantwise to secure a firm stand, are the formal expression of this conception.' And of cabinets he says, 'single cabinets... are mostly constructed of light but very firm frames and panels of wood or plastics. These cabinets combine lightness with stability.' Lightness was considered an essential quality of all types of 'Contemporary' furniture, and it was this feature which differentiated it from pre-war furniture. In the 1930s designers, such as Finnish architect Alvar Aalto, had begun this lightening process by making furniture more malleable but at this date they were still much hampered by technology. With the benefit of the breakthroughs in plywood technology that had been made during the war, it seemed as though almost anything was possible, and this acted as a great stimulus for visual and technical experimentation amongst the new generation of designers.

One of the reasons why the furniture industry was able to adapt its output to suit the requirements of 'Contemporary' architecture after the war was because of the direct involvement of so many leading architects in this field of design. This had an appreciable knock-on effect on the quality of the furniture in production during the 1950s, some of the most influential designs of the period being those created by architects such as Charles Eames for Herman Miller and Eero Saarinen for Knoll in the USA, Arne Jacobsen for Fritz Hansen in Denmark and Gio Ponti for Cassina in Italy. It was also during the 1950s that the new specialist profession of furniture designer was consolidated, with the emergence of important figures such as Robin Day working with Hille in the UK, Hans Wegner working with Johannes Hansen and Fritz Hansen in Denmark, and Ilmari Tapiovaara working with Asko and several other companies in Finland. This reflected the fact that furniture design was now being treated with the seriousness it deserved, and was recognized as a specialist form of design engineering.

This was also the case in the field of lighting, with the emergence of specialist designers such as Gino Sarfatti for Arteluce in Italy, Poul Henningsen for Louis Poulsen in Denmark and Lisa Johansson-Pape for Stockmann in Finland. As with furniture design, the lighting industry also benefited from the creative involvement of such leading architects as George Nelson for Howard Miller in the USA, Arne Jacobsen for Louis Poulsen in Denmark, and the husband-and-wife team of John and Sylvia Reid, working with Rotaflex and George Forrest in the UK. Individuals from other artistic disciplines, such as sculpture, added significantly to the development of a 'Contemporary' aesthetic, the most important contribution being Isamu Noguchi with his organic-shaped lantern-like paper lampshades.

The best furniture and lighting of the 1950s satisfied the joint, but sometimes conflicting, demands of function and creativity: it looked good and worked well at the same time. Designers successfully harnessed the new materials and the new technology but instead of

Opposite Cover of The Architectural Review *from June 1952, featuring a cluster of wire chairs designed by Charles Eames for Herman Miller. These chairs were supplied with detachable upholstered covers which could be removed for cleaning. According to the original caption for this striking image, 'The cover shows several specimens... undressed, so to speak.'*

The two leading furniture designers of the day in Britain and the USA respectively were Robin Day working for Hille in the UK, and Charles Eames, who had an equally long and fruitful relationship with the American manufacturer Herman Miller.

Top The innovative moulded plywood chairs and tables designed by Eames during the mid-1940s and produced from 1946.
Left Robin Day shown with his wife, Lucienne, a leading freelance textile designer, featured in an advertisement for Smirnoff Vodka. Robin Day's adjustable reclining armchair is illustrated (left), while two of Lucienne Day's printed cotton textiles for Heal's Fabrics are shown in the background. The fact that the Days were chosen by a leading drinks manufacturer to promote their product during the mid-1950s is an indication of the 'superstar' status of the couple at this date. In the USA, Charles Eames and his artist wife, Ray, attracted similar media attention.*

The 1950s was an out-standingly creative decade for the design of lighting. Below *Range of organically shaped plastic-coated Bubble lamps designed by George Nelson for Howard Miller from 1952.* Bottom *Advertisements for two British manufacturers of 'Contemporary' light-fittings: Falks (left) featuring a design from 1954 by J M Barnicot; and Rotaflex (right), the most innovative British lighting firm of the decade, whose principal designers were the architects John and Sylvia Reid.*

Right *Hanging lamps designed in Finland by Lisa Johansson-Pape for the Helsinki department store, Stockmann.* Below Right *A metal standard lamp designed by the Swedish-born Los Angeles-based architect, Greta Magnusson Grossman, as seen in one of the Case Study Houses.* Opposite *Danish pendant lamps by two internationally renowned companies, Louis Poulsen and Le Klint. The pleated paper lampshades of Le Klint (bottom right), produced from 1944 onwards, were* designed by the father and son team of Kaare and Esben Klint. The three metal lampshades are all manufactured by Louis Poulsen, and include the PH5 of 1958 (top right), and the PH Kontrast of 1957 (top left), both designed by Poul Henningsen, as well as the dome-shaped AJ lamp of 1959 (bottom left) designed by Arne Jacobsen.*

Technical innovations revolutionized the furniture industry during the 1940s and 1950s.

Opposite *Four covers from the Italian architecture and design magazine* Domus *from 1955–7, featuring foam rubber upholstered chairs made by Arflex, a subsidiary of the tyre manufacturer Pirelli.*

Top Left *The lounge and dining chair versions of the famous moulded plywood furniture of Charles Eames, manufactured by Herman Miller from 1946.*

Bottom Left *Publicity shot for the Herman Miller Company dating from the mid-1960s showing two different ranges of furniture designed by Charles Eames in 1952. One set has moulded plastic seats strengthened by fibreglass; the other range is made from steel wire. Both sets were available on a wide variety of alternative bases, examples of which are shown here, including wheeled pedestals, wire-frames, steel rod and wooden rockers.*

Below *Cut-away cross-section through the upholstery of the Luciano armchair of 1957 designed by Giancarlo de Carlo for Arflex, showing the use of Pirelli rubber webbing to support the foam rubber upholstery.*

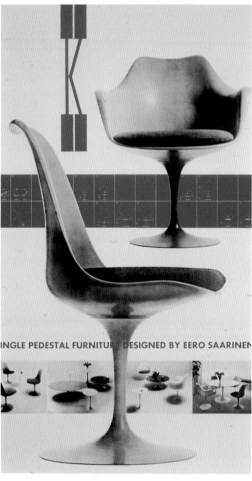

The main American rivals to the Herman Miller Company in the field of 'Contemporary' furniture were Knoll. Knoll achieved renown for their innovative new furniture designs by leading architects and artists of the day, for their functional office furniture designed in-house, and for putting back into production some classic Modernist chair designs from the 1930s by Mies van der Rohe and Marcel Breuer. Above An interior furnished by Knoll with Mies van der Rohe's Barcelona chairs and steel bar framed furniture designed by Florence Knoll. Right Advertisement for the Pedestal or Tulip range of plastic shell furniture designed by Eero Saarinen in 1956, which dispensed with the conventional four chair legs in favour of a single 'stem'.
Opposite The sculptor Harry Bertoia's Diamond armchairs for Knoll (1952), seen in the Jones House of 1955 designed by Quincy Jones and Frederick Emmons in Los Angeles.

INGLE PEDESTAL FURNITURE DESIGNED BY EERO SAARINEN

trying to emulate the design solutions of earlier generations, they exploited this technology to evolve new answers to previously insurmountable problems. For example, although furniture was becoming lighter in weight and slighter in size, it was still expected to be durable. The materials, therefore, had to be very strong and physically robust, and the methods of construction had to be more reliable. Steel rod construction largely replaced tubular steel as a form of framework for seat and carcase furniture, because the gauge of the metal was so much narrower, although chair and cabinet legs were sometimes made of turned wood tapering to the foot. Thinner moulded plywoods, strengthened by improved glues, replaced solid woods and thicker laminated woods for panels, seats and seat backs. In the manufacture of upholstered furniture, synthetic foam rubber cushions supported by Pirelli rubber webbing were widely adopted, replacing heavier materials such as horsehair, metal springs and feather cushions. With new developments in the technology of polymers (another field in which Charles Eames played a key role), it became possible to mould the actual shell of the chair from plastic, which was strengthened and given body and texture by fibreglass. This shell, produced in a range of colours in an attractive organic shape, could be left in its natural state without any further treatment, or alternatively it could be padded with foam rubber and then upholstered.

Although the idealistic philosophy of the Arts and Crafts Movement of the late nineteenth and early twentieth centuries was now considered of little relevance – especially in highly industrialized societies under pressure to mass produce furniture at affordable prices – this is not to imply that 'Contemporary' furniture rejected the need for fine craftsmanship. There was considerable skill, for example, in harnessing technology so that it produced results of an acceptably high standard, and even with factory-made goods there was often a considerable amount of work carried out by hand that was not necessarily evident in the finished product. During the 1950s there were two distinct aesthetics in furniture design which, although apparently opposed, were sometimes combined in a single design. These were the industrial aesthetic, largely associated with the USA, which involved the use of man-made materials, such as metals and plastics, in designs which appeared to have been made largely by machines rather than by hand; and the handicraft aesthetic associated with Scandinavia, where items were made from natural materials, such as wood, and appeared to have been made by hand rather than by machine. Appearances could be misleading, however, and sometimes work that appeared to have been carried out by machine was found, on closer inspection, to have been carried out by hand; and vice versa. A good example of the former is the wire 'Diamond' chair designed by Harry Bertoia for Knoll; examples of the latter are provided by many of the furniture designs by Arne Jacobsen and Hans Wegner mass-produced in the Danish factory of Fritz Hansen.

Furniture being an expensive and bulky commodity to export, it was often the case that a large part of the output was produced for the home market. In the 1950s, however, all three Scandinavian design superpowers – Finland, Denmark and Sweden – recognizing that their own populations were relatively small and that the home market was

One of the leading furniture-manufacturing nations of the 1950s was Denmark. The firm of Fritz Hansen dominated the market in the field of mass-production, and the chair designs by the architect Arne Jacobsen were exported all over the world. Many of Jacobsen's designs became instant classics and are still in production today, looking as modern as ever. The pictures on these pages are all recent publicity photographs, and although the upholstery materials and the paint colours have changed since the 1950s, the basic designs are still the same after forty years. *Below A swarm of* Ant *chairs dating from 1952.* Far Left *Butterfly chair from the Series 7 range dating from 1955.* Middle Left *Egg chair dating from 1958.* Near Left *Swan chair dating from 1958.*

Demountability and stackability were major considerations in the design of chairs after World War II. Flat-packing was particularly important for furniture intended for export in order to keep transport costs down, particularly on low-cost products.

Right *The Ax chair designed by Peter Hvidt and O Mølgaard Nielsen for Fritz Hansen in 1950, seen here flat-packed for export.*

Below Left *A stack of moulded plastic shell DSX chairs designed by Charles Eames for Herman Miller in 1952.*

Far Right *Ilmari Tapiovaara's Domus chair, also known as the Stax chair, produced in Finland by Asko from 1947. This chair could be transported flat-packed, and was produced under licence by various manufacturers in different countries, including Knoll in the USA.*

not large enough to support their manufacturing capability, turned actively towards exports. Two ways round the transportation problem included the development of 'knock-down' furniture that could be flat-packed and then erected by the retailer, and the establishment of a system of licensing so that a company's products could be made abroad by other firms on payment of a commission. Both these solutions were employed by the Finnish firm of Asko for Ilmari Tapiovaara's 'Domus' chair, a basic plywood stacking chair also known as the 'Finnchair' or 'Stax' chair. This was exported to some countries in kit form, and in others, such as the UK, it was manufactured under licence.

Changing social behaviour also influenced the development of 'Contemporary' furniture. In the dining room, for example, the sideboard was becoming an endangered species. Increasing informality in dining habits meant that a young couple setting up home would no longer necessarily possess two sets of crockery, one of earthenware for everyday use, the other of china for special occasions. Instead they would probably just have one all-purpose set, which needed less storage space. The amount of ornamental glassware in the average home also declined, and after the war solid silver or silver-plated cutlery, which required regular polishing for its upkeep, also rapidly came to be considered obsolete in many households. It was replaced by low-maintenance stainless steel cutlery, stored to hand for everyday use in the kitchen drawer rather than in the dining room. These changes in social habits sounded the death knell for the old-fashioned, heavy, space-consuming sideboard. In Britain, where old habits died hard, those sideboards that did survive were usually longer, lower and leaner. Often they were located in the living room rather than the dining room where they were used to house hi-fi equipment or cocktails rather than fine china.

In the open-plan house the multi-functional room divider was often favoured in place of the heavy, traditional sideboard. Such room dividers were often designed so that there was easy access to cupboards via sliding or hinged two-way doors from both the kitchen and dining room sides of the unit. Another type of room divider might be installed between the dining and recreation areas of an open-plan living room, or a 'storage-wall' system, of the type developed in the USA by George Nelson, might be set against a long wall in the living room. This type of flexible storage unit, whether free-standing or wall-mounted, could be used to store books, records and even the record player itself. Decorative features, such as the incorporation of coloured or patterned panels, sometimes plywood painted bright primary colours, or printed plastic laminates in 'Contemporary' patterns, added welcome new elements of colour and pattern into the living room.

The advantage of room dividers, and other types of flexible storage systems or unit furniture, was that they could be built up in blocks to whatever scale was required, in a variety of combinations to suit the rooms in which they were located. Sometimes various component parts were also designed to serve an independent purpose, such as the slatted bases of cupboard units which could also be used as a bench for seating or as an occasional table. As the practicality of such multi-functional furniture became more widely acknowledged, the concept of knock-down unit furniture purchased in kit form began to take off.

Top *A range of free-standing, modular storage units and room dividers designed by Charles Eames for Herman Miller from 1949, which were suitable for use both in the office and the home.*

Above *Comprehensive Storage System, a flexible, demountable 'storagewall' system designed in 1959 by George Nelson for Herman Miller. The poles on which the cupboards and shelves are hung can* be altered in height, and are 'sprung' between the floor and the ceiling. Nelson's moulded plastic swagged-leg chair of 1958 for Herman Miller is seen on the left.

Although the 'Contemporary' interior had a more democratic layout than was common before the war, there were still vestiges of status divisions between different areas of the house, which were reflected in the choice of furniture. In the informal setting of the kitchen, for example, dining furniture was usually quite basic and might take the form of a patterned Formica-topped table with a set of metal legged vinyl-covered chairs. If a 'breakfast bar' in the form of a work surface or counter had been installed, seating arrangements were more informal still and would usually involve simple bar stools, often made of black-enamelled steel rod with padded vinyl-covered seats. By contrast, in the more formal setting of a separate dining room, there was likely to be a more substantial and expensive 'Contemporary' dining room suite, composed of a solid wooden table and chairs. These might be made of teak or some other expensive hardwood, and would probably originate either from the workshop of a craftsman cabinetmaker, usually Danish, or from a prestigious New York or London manufacturer or retailer, such as Vladimir Kagan or Heal's.

Falling half-way between these two extremes was the semi-informality of the open-plan living room/dining room. Here, a new design solution was called for, the answer to which came in the form of high quality mass-production: tables and chairs made of metal and wood, usually plywood, well-designed but moderate in price. Suppliers of furniture in this category included Herman Miller in the USA and Fritz Hansen in Denmark, while in the UK firms such as Kandya and Race Furniture produced cheap and cheerful equivalents.

In the 'Contemporary' living room, furniture was mostly composed of individual easy chairs, as sofas now became much less common. Space was at a premium, thus the traditional, bulky and overstuffed British three-piece suite was viewed with disapproval by 'Contemporary' architects. The attention of designers, therefore, turned to the task of creating comfortable but elegant and modern armchairs. Successful solutions were the organic all-embracing 'Womb' chair of Eero Saarinen for Knoll, and the comfortable wood- or metal-framed upholstered armchairs with teak armrests widely produced in Sweden and Denmark. Woven upholstery fabrics were often very bright due to the advances made in dye technology; sometimes these were combined with interesting textural effects achieved through experimentation with different combinations of yarn.

Because of its innovative shapes, colours and materials, 'Contemporary' furniture played a dynamic role in the 1950s interior. It was certainly much less ponderous and bulky than standard 1930s furniture. Significantly, too, there was also less of it; the 'Contemporary' interior represented the antithesis of clutter, which meant cutting down to a minimum the amount of furniture within each room. Pressure on space meant that each item had to have a specific purpose: nothing was to be superfluous. In addition to the main seat furniture, however, there might be a limited number of other small items of furniture in the living room, such as occasional tables, magazine racks, wastepaper bins and lampstands, as well as examples of the new electrical appliances that were now populating the post-war interior, such as television sets and hi-fi systems. In fact, it was in this area of design – smaller-scale domestic accessories – that the

Southern California became a hot-house for 'Contemporary' design after World War II, and the Case Study House programme, initiated by the Los Angeles-based Arts and Architecture magazine in 1945, provided an ideal vehicle for promoting innovative new furniture and accessories fabricated in local workshops.
Above and Right Bent steel rod framed furniture designed by Dorothy Schindle in 1955, reflecting the spindly and attenuated design aesthetic popular in both furniture and sculpture of the period.
Opposite Steel bar framed furniture by Hendrik Van Keppel and Taylor Green in the house designed for Max and Rita Lawrence, the co-founders of the Los Angeles ceramics

firm, Architectural Pottery. Examples of some of the monumental plant-holders made by the Architectural Pottery are also shown in this interior.

'Contemporary' style was first widely adopted. Even in households not otherwise receptive to modern design, you might find, for example, a 'Contemporary'-style wire-rod tripod plant holder in the hall or a Formica-topped coffee table in the living room so that, one way or another, 'Contemporary' design penetrated even the most reactionary homes.

A plethora of new firms sprang up to satisfy the market for these accessories. In the UK there was Hiscock Appleby, who manufactured steel-rod and painted wooden ball accessories inspired by ball-and-spoke molecular models; in Denmark, Dansk Design produced a range of well-designed 'Scandinavian Modern' products, such as turned wooden candlesticks for the American market; on the West Coast of America, the Architectural Pottery supplied a range of large-scale jardinières; and in Italy, the idiosyncratic designer Piero Fornasetti created exotic, highly decorated and surreal household items, including umbrella stands, screens and wastepaper bins.

Apart from furniture, the single most important element of the 'Contemporary' interior was soft furnishings in the form of carpets, curtains, and furniture upholstery. The degree of emphasis laid upon these elements varied from country to country. In the UK, with its renowned textile industry and its long history of achievement in the field of pattern design, textiles were usually prominently displayed, particularly in the form of printed cottons. In Scandinavia, although textiles, especially woven textiles, were considered a vitally important element of the interior, they were often used in a deliberately understated way; and in the USA, although soft furnishings of many different sorts were widely appreciated, they tended to be used rather sparingly. On an international level, surprisingly little communication took place between textile manufacturers in different countries, a situation which fostered the continuing independence of native traditions.

A creative crossover did take place, however, between the fine and applied arts during the 1950s, as many leading textile designers were overtly influenced by developments in contemporary painting, and several important artists were commissioned to produce textile designs for leading manufacturers. This, combined with the injection of colour and vitality into post-war textile design and the growing flexibility that arose from the introduction of newly mechanized techniques of screen-printing, meant that furnishing fabrics took on a new lease of life during the 1950s.

The fashion for the newly popular 'Contemporary' style was particularly evident in the confident use of abstraction in printed textiles. This was expressed in many different guises ranging from playful linear patterns with a strong graphic quality, particularly appropriate for the reduced scale of many post-war domestic interiors; to bolder, more brightly coloured and energetic designs, which required a longer drop in a larger room to be shown to best advantage; and striking, overtly painterly patterns, often commissioned directly from artists, with even larger scale repeats, designed for use in the dramatic setting of spacious public interiors. At all these levels, there was a trickle-down effect in terms of the influence of leading fabric designers and manufacturers of the day on goods designed and manufactured for the middle and lower ends of the market where, for example, cheaper fabrics, such as rayon

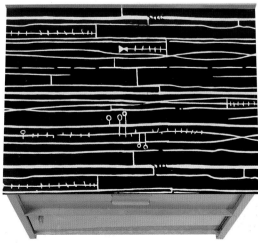

Above *Flat at Viceroy Court, London, converted by Higgins and Ney, featured in* The Architects' Journal *in October 1954 as an example of how to make an old-fashioned interior look 'Contemporary'.*
Far Left *Television with birch cabinet and wrought iron base, designed in the USA c1954 by the Motorola Design Department.*

Left *Small cupboard/chest of drawer unit viewed from above, with blue painted door, varnished wooden drawers and patterned plastic laminate top. The unit was produced in 1957 by the British firm of Kandya; the pattern on the laminate, called Linear, was originally designed by Lucienne Day as a fabric for Heal's c1954.*

Opposite *Fall, designed
by Lucienne Day for
Edinburgh Weavers, UK.
Day, the leading British
textile designer of the
1950s, worked freelance
for a number of companies,
including Edinburgh
Weavers, Liberty, British
Celanese and Heal's.
Right* Foliate Heads, *designed by John Piper for
David Whitehead, 1953.
During the 1950s the
Lancashire firm of David
Whitehead put into
production a whole range
of fabrics designed by
British artists and
sculptors, including John
Piper, Henry Moore,
Louis Le Brocquy and
Eduardo Paolozzi.*

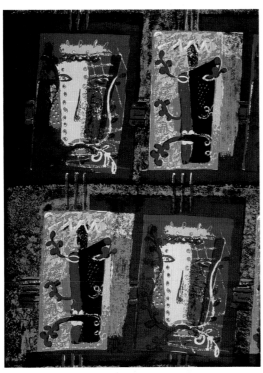

*Printed furnishing fabrics
provided pattern designers
of the 1950s with one
of the richest fields of
opportunity for creative
design. Much excellent
work was carried out in
Britain during this
period, particularly by
Heal's Fabrics and David
Whitehead, the two
outstanding firms of the
period, who employed
a wide range of talented
freelance designers and
artists, as well as
encouraging their own
in-house staff.
Below* Pottery fabric
designed by Stig Lindberg
for Nordiska Kompaniet,
Sweden, 1947.

*Lindberg was a ceramic
designer who worked for
the Swedish firm of
Gustavsberg. The shapes
and patterns of the vessels
pictured on this printed
textile are similar to
his ceramic designs.*

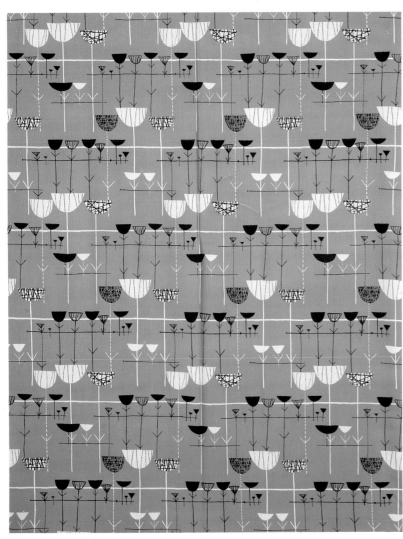

Left *Roller-printed rayon
fabric designed by Marian
Mahler for David
Whitehead, 1952, inspired
by Lucienne Day's famous
Calyx design for Heal's
dating from 1951 (see* also back cover*), which
set the tone for
'Contemporary' pattern
design in Britain for the
rest of the decade. Mahler's
modestly priced fabric was
aimed at the lower end of* the market while the higher
priced screen-printed artist-
designed range of textiles
also produced by David
Whitehead was aimed at
a wealthier middle class
audience.

Although Britain was pre-eminent in the field of furnishing fabrics, textile design flourished in many different countries. The fabrics produced during the 1950s were very wide-ranging and reflected the taste and character of the countries in question, but abstraction was a dominant feature internationally.
Right *Keys*, designed by Ruth Adler for Adler/Schnee, USA, c1954. This design, printed on haircloth, is based on patterns derived from abstracted key shapes.

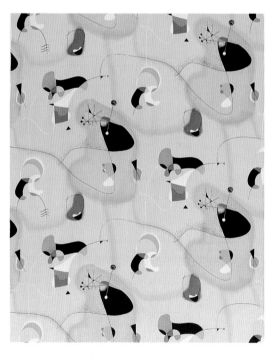

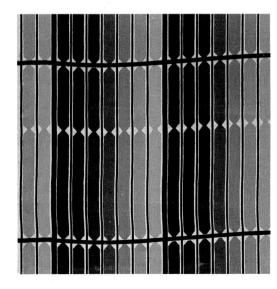

Above *Kites and Mites*, designed by Paul McCobb for L Anton Maix, USA, c1954. Many of the designs produced in the USA during the 1950s had witty or punning titles such as this. The 'mites' of the title are the small children flying the kites.

The Italians produced some of the most vibrant and exotic textile designs of the period.
Above *Ormeggio*, designed by Enrico Paulucci for M I T A di M A Ponis, c1954.
Opposite *Spago*, designed by Gigi Tessari for J S A Busto Arsizio, 1957.
Following Page *Citrus* designed by Maija Isola for Printex, Finland, 1956. Printex went on to become the well-known firm of Marimekko. This design heralds the bold large-scale abstract designs that dominated the early 1960s.

Left *Windy Way*, designed by Astrid Sampe for Nordiska Kompaniet, Sweden, 1954. Sampe, the leading Swedish textile designer of the period, was head of textile design at the department store Nordiska Kompaniet.

Above *Espace*, designed by Elsbeth Kupferoth for Pausa A C Mechnische Weberei, Germany, c1954. This pattern, by the leading German textile designer of the period, reflects the influence of the Spanish artist Joan Miró.

Tibor   stockwell   Stevens

DAVID WHITEHEAD FABRICS

D. Whitehead Ltd. Higher Mill Rawtenstall Lancs

Above *This advertisement is a joint promotion from 1953 for a rug and various textural furnishing fabrics by the British designer/ manufacturer Tibor Reich. The Avocado curtain is a Tibor Textureprint; the Caribbean rug is manufactured by Stockwell Carpets; and the chair, designed by Ronald Long for R S Stevens, is upholstered with a woven fabric called Mesh, produced by Reich's own company.* Right *Advertisement for David Whitehead Fabrics from December 1952, showing chairs designed by Robin Day for Hille in the foreground, and a screen-printed fabric designed by Jacqueline Groag draped behind.*

rather than linen, and lookalike variants of the more expensive and exclusive designs were produced.

Although pattern design in general, and textile pattern design in particular, were in a buoyant state in the UK during the 1950s, elsewhere patterned textiles were still used quite sparingly in many 'Contemporary' interiors. When furnishing fabrics were used, however, it was a tribute to the quality of the textile design of this period that they were treated not just as another design feature, but as an artistic statement in their own right. They were rarely used to create a neutral background: they usually played a dynamic and assertive role within the interior.

As discussed in the previous chapter, carpets played a much less prominent role in the 'Contemporary' interior than many of the newly adopted hard floor coverings such as cork or vinyl tiles. The fashion in Scandinavia and the USA during the 1950s was to scatter woollen rugs on a polished wooden floor. These rugs were not meant to be attention grabbers, however: their patterns and colours were generally quite muted and restrained, nor were they expected to compete with the more strident printed curtain fabrics, nor with the often acid colours of woven upholstery fabrics. Although by no means dull, the 'Contemporary' rug exerted its influence in a more subtle way. Many of the best rugs of the 1950s, made of woven or tufted wool, were produced in Scandinavia. Rug patterns were very different from wallpaper and curtain patterns, being more contemplative and less busy. Colours were often limited to two or three, and patterns were simpler and more schematic than those adopted for furnishing fabrics. Often their visual appeal was in the new textural element; they introduced into the interior a variety of contrasting textures being one of the distinctive characteristics of 'Contemporary' architecture and design.

To embrace the 'Contemporary' style completely meant a new look for tableware and ornaments as well. During World War II, the production of china and glassware had been low on the agenda and, in some countries, such as the UK, government restrictions had banned the production of all decorated wares other than those for export for up to seven years after the war. By the early 1950s, therefore, there was a huge demand for tableware of any sort, but especially for colourful and gaily patterned ceramics to enliven the home. Shortly after the war, a number of manufacturers had emerged in each country to take advantage of this new market, and in doing so they revolutionized the hitherto tradition-bound ceramics industry.

There were many innovations in the ceramics industry during the 1950s, including the introduction of more fluid organic tableware shapes influenced by contemporary sculpture; the development of 'Contemporary' patterns of a stylized or abstract nature, a greater range of colours and a wider selection of techniques of decoration. These incorporated mechanical techniques, such as screen-printing, direct-printing and aerograph-spraying, and the revival of hand decorating techniques, such as freehand painting and sponged decoration. Gone were the colourful but now dated 'jazz' patterns of the 1930s, applied using the technique of overglaze enamel painting, which made the surface of the pots prone to damage; gone, too, were the angular geometric shapes that were the popular accompaniment to these

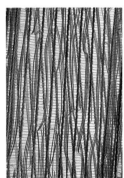

Top *Surrey woven furnishing fabric, designed by Marianne Straub for Warner Fabrics in 1951 as part of the Festival Pattern Group scheme. The brief of the designers involved in this project was to create patterns for a range of mass-produced applied arts based on crystallography diagrams. This particular pattern is based on the molecular structure of afwillite.*

Although the brightly coloured and boldly patterned printed cotton furnishing fabrics of the 1950s were undoubtedly very vibrant, they were not to everyone's taste. Some people preferred more subtle or subdued effects, and opted instead for duller or more neutral colours, and for woven fabrics where the interest was in the complexity of the weave rather than in the two-dimensional surface pattern.

Left *Woven woollen rug produced by Danish Carpets c1957 with an unusual abstract pattern.*
Above Left and Right *Two imaginative woven textiles which exploit both natural and synthetic fibres, designed by the American Jack Lenor Larsen for his own company. On the left, Limelight, from 1953 which combines saran, modacrylic and rayon; on the right, Jason, of 1956 which blends cotton, nylon, viscose, goat hair and mylar.*

patterns, but which were impractical for everyday use. Finally, came the rejection by many consumers of the traditional floral patterns on bone china or porcelain, richly decorated in enamels and gilding, which now looked incongruous in the 'Contemporary' home.

The impetus for many of these changes was provided by Scandinavian and the American designers. Most notable were Stig Lindberg of Gustavsberg in Sweden, and Russel Wright and Eva Zeisel working for US firms such as the Steubenville Pottery Company, the Iroquois China Company, Castleton China, Hall China and the Red Wing Pottery. These designers originated and developed the organic trend in tableware, creating fluid plastic sculptural forms which looked equally good, if not better, in their undecorated state as they did when decorated with printed patterns. A good compromise, therefore, was to use monochrome glazes on individual pieces, but to offer 'mix-and-match' sets composed of pieces decorated in a variety of colours. The informality of this arrangement, pioneered by Russel Wright in his 'American Modern' service before the war, greatly appealed to the American market, and also caught on internationally. Similar ideas were also introduced by Kaj Franck at the Arabia factory in Finland shortly after the war. These services were both functional and beautiful: they looked good, but they were also highly satisfactory in terms of storage and stacking.

The Scandinavian glass industry was also in a particularly buoyant state after the war, and its designers took the lead in developing a range of 'Contemporary' glassware that would complement the new ceramic tablewares being produced by their colleagues in the pottery industry. Their glassware was extremely elegant and shapely, reliant for its impact on shape or colour rather than surface decoration. As in ceramic tableware, organically inspired plastic forms predominated. The Scandinavians were also known throughout the world for their outstandingly beautiful and original art glass, which was often found on display in 1950s homes, adding the final touch to the sophisticated 'Contemporary' interior. Finnish, Danish and Swedish ceramics, glass and furniture were considered the height of chic both in Europe and the USA during the 1950s, and it was during this period that a clearly defined 'Scandinavian Modern' aesthetic emerged, which was such a vital ingredient of the 'Contemporary' style.

'Contemporary' ceramics were characterized by organic shapes and abstract patterns. Jessie Tait, the resident pattern designer at Midwinter, was extremely successful in adapting ideas originating in fabric design to the decoration of three-dimensional surfaces.
Top Primavera coffee set by Midwinter with a pattern by Jessie Tait dating from 1954 shown on the Stylecraft shape.

Above Savanna tableware designed by Jessie Tait for the Fashion shape launched in 1955. The Staffordshire-based firm of Midwinter was the most innovative ceramics factory in Britain during the 1950s. The colours they used were applied under the glaze, and were therefore highly resistant to wear and tear, a good marketing characteristic. Savanna, with its use of bright yellow colouring

and its bold all-over abstract pattern, typifies the 'Contemporary' idiom in pattern design.
Right Blue Fire teapot and casserole, designed by Hertha Bengtson for the Swedish firm Rorstrand in 1949. The high, looped handles and curvilinear outline of this service reflect the prevailing influence of organic sculptural forms on tableware at this date.

'fantasia'
A fresh treatment
of the fashionable
black and white theme

The range of colours used on ceramic tableware during the 1950s was highly distinctive, as was the way in which areas of pattern and colour were juxtaposed on different surfaces.

Above *The concept of 'mix and match' tableware* as demonstrated by the *Kilta tableware range designed by Kaj Franck, produced in Finland by Arabia from 1948 onwards. Consumers were able to build up a service of their choice from a range of pieces decorated with complementary* monochrome glazes.

Top Right *Fantasia tableware designed in 1959 by Harold Bennett for the British firm Burgess and Leigh. In this service, black and white glazed surfaces contrast with areas of printed pattern. The pattern itself depicts* vases and bowls in the 'Contemporary' style.

Bottom Right *Chequers plate designed by Terence Conran for Midwinter in 1957 using a pattern originally produced as a printed furnishing fabric for David Whitehead in 1951.*

During the 1950s 'Scandinavian Modern' design took the world by storm, and the Finns, the Swedes and the Danes regularly carried off the honours at the prestigious Milan Triennale exhibitions. Scandinavian glass was the ultimate in domestic chic, and Swedish designers in particular excelled at producing both everyday table glass and ornamental art glass. The Swedish firm of

Orrefors achieved international renown, and a sample of their stylish products from this period is shown on this page.
Above Left *Group of Prydnadsglas drinking glasses designed by Nils Landberg, 1960.*
Above Right *Water jug and wine glasses for everyday use, also designed by Nils Landberg, 1950.*
Near Right *Kraka vase designed by Sven Palmqvist, 1955.*

This vase contains a mesh of tiny bubbles captured within a layer of coloured underlay glass.
Far Right *Orange Tulip glass designed by Nils Landberg in 1957. Landberg designed a series of these extravagant glasses, the stems of which were extremely narrow and attenuated.*

Above *Kantarelli vases designed by Tapio Wirkkala for the Finnish firm of Iittala in 1947, inspired by the shape of chanterelle mushrooms.*
Far Left *Looped bowl designed by Paul Kedelv for Flygsfors in Sweden, 1957.*
Near Left *Bowl designed by Sven Palmqvist for Orrefors in Sweden, dating from early 1950s, infused with red underlay.*

Aerial view of part of the Roehampton ☞ Estate completed during 1956–7, designed by London County Council's Architects Department. Re-housing families who had lost their homes during the Blitz was one of the top priorities for the authorities in London after World War II.

6. society goes 'contemporary'

'Our new architecture is an architecture of democracy, in which every building has a contribution to make to its owner and the community in the complex urban design of the twentieth-century life. The new client of this new architecture is the ordinary citizen.'

Philip Will, Mid-Century Architecture in America (1961)

One of the reasons for the ready acceptance of 'Contemporary' architecture by the wider community after the war was its rapid adoption internationally as the prevailing style of public architecture. As Wolf von Eckardt pointed out in *Mid-Century Architecture in America* in 1961, 'even those who still prefer "traditional" at home accept "modern" as the appropriate architecture for the schools of their children, their places of business, and – a little more reluctantly – for their churches and temples.' Because of the physical havoc wreaked by World War II post-war building programmes in Britain and mainland Europe were on a massive scale. For architects and city planners this represented a remarkable opportunity to reshape whole communities. Not only was there the chance to

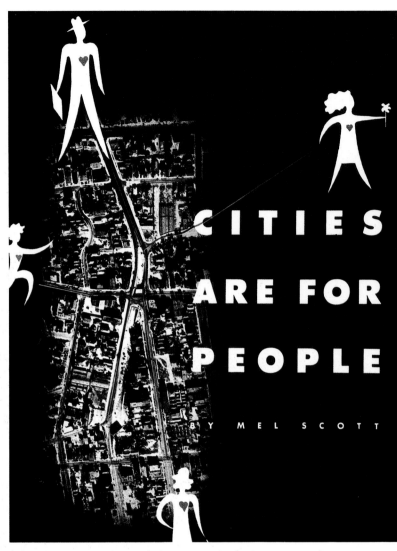

Above *Town and city planning became a major issue during the 1940s. In 1942 Mel Scott published a report called* Cities Are For People *(the cover of which is seen here), containing proposals regarding the future development of Los Angeles.* Right *The cover of the Official Guide to the Festival of Britain. The impressive exhibition pavilions temporarily erected on the South Bank in London in 1951, provided many visitors with their first introduction to 'Contemporary' architecture.*

develop potentially innovative low-cost housing schemes, but also to erect new public buildings such as schools, universities, and churches, shops and sports stadia, offices, factories, transport terminals and airports. In countries such as the UK, where there had been considerable resistance to modern architecture before the war, many of the old prejudices evaporated when it was recognized that only 'Contemporary' architecture could tackle projects of this scale. According to GE Kidder Smith in *The New Architecture of Europe*: 'the "new" architecture that thus arose has had a powerful effect in introducing contemporary architectural concepts to a very broad range of the British public.' On the basis of this breakthrough, he confidently announced in 1962 that 'Modern architecture has arrived.'

Meanwhile, in the USA, rapid economic expansion, combined with the post-war baby boom, triggered off ambitious building programmes to house the increased population, and then to provide these communities with local and regional services. The duty of architects to serve the community as a whole, rather than simply to satisfy the needs of individual clients, was an attitude that was being actively fostered by the American Institute of Architects (AIA) at this time. However, it was also recognized that local and central government had a primary role to play, and that it was the responsibility of each individual within the community to take part in the current debate. Philip Will, president of the AIA, in his foreword to *Mid-Century Architecture in America*, used the phrase 'an architecture of democracy' to describe this three-way relationship. Whether public buildings served a commercial or a social purpose, they were all being built for public usage and therefore although the nominal client might be the local authority or a private company, the real clients were the people who would actually use the building, whether as service providers or as customers.

However, with racial discrimination still rife in many parts of the USA throughout the 1950s, and with the memory of McCarthyism still vivid at this time, the assertion that the USA was a country in which there could be 'an architecture of democracy' was perhaps somewhat debatable. It was only a democratic society for those people whom the community chose to enfranchise, and throughout this period whole groups remained effectively disenfranchised because of their race, religion or political beliefs. Very few American architects had the courage to challenge the situation, although the Austrian-born Richard Neutra was a notable exception, perhaps because he still considered himself an outsider. His comments in *The Decorative Art Studio Yearbook* (1951-2) on the the prevailing attitudes of the time and the nature of 'Americanism' are of special interest, all the more so for being written in an ironic vein:

Ours is a time when American and un-American attitudes are widely discussed. And so we should like to state three points of Un-Americanism to set us off properly from the foreigners who try to build. First of all, it is – in normal times – very Un-American to have any shortage of materials. Second, a lack of equipment is very Un-American. Rather, we have all the gadgets in the world, from those for bulldozing the hills and bullying the landscape, to those for electrically grinding the garbage and flushing it out of our miracle kitchens. And third, of course, it is very Un-American not to be financed, not to have means.

Neutra was conscious that there were many 'foreigners' on American soil who were not fully accepted by the society in which they lived; and also that there were many in the USA who were not 'financed', who lacked the means to pay for adequate housing, never mind 'gadgets' or 'miracle kitchens'. During the 1950s, he was one of the few architects working in the USA who spoke out forcefully about social issues such as poverty, and who showed himself to be committed in the fullest sense to 'an architecture of democracy'. In his speculative work Neutra also addressed the larger question of planning, a subject which passionately interested him as he felt it was fundamental to the future, not just of America, but of the world. Aware of the USA's growing isolation, which had arisen largely because of its wealth in relation to other countries after the war, he was anxious that Americans should endeavour to see themselves as part of a larger world community, and take responsibility for their actions on an international level:

> Our architects and planners ought to keep an eye on the rest of the world, on its economic, social, psychological aspects, or else we become foreigners on the planet, while we busily pay off that miracle kitchen of tomorrow. The tomorrow will less probably be ploughed under by hydrogen bombs if we cautiously learn to see ourselves, our cities, our houses, our modes of living, our aspirations and also our shortcoming as somehow related to the rest of the world.

In the materialistic USA, Neutra was somewhat isolated in his views, but in impoverished Europe he would have found many like-minded professionals during the early post-war years. In the UK, for example, a wave of socialist idealism swept through the country in the immediate aftermath of the war. A reformist Labour government was elected to power in 1945, which then swiftly established a comprehensive and impressive welfare state system, that was to be much admired abroad. Thus, here, the state, through the agency of local government, took an active role in the provision of both housing and community services, taking an interventionist role in town planning, as well as taking the lead in erecting large numbers of schools. British achievement in housing and education was singled out for particular praise by GE Kidder Smith in his survey of post-war European architecture:

Top and Above *The provision of social facilities within newly developing or expanding communities was recognized as an important factor in the success of such schemes.* Above *Two views of the Eagle Rock Community Centre designed by Richard Neutra in 1954.*

> Government architecture in most of the world (including the US) sides with a common norm of little distinction; in England, however, its achievements have often been superb. Indeed the London County Council's architectural staff has produced some of the finest housing and the finest schools in Europe, and much famous provincial work (the Hertfordshire and Middlesex schools, for example) can also be attributed to Government architects.

The scale of the housing problem in and around London after the war was enormous: there was pressure on local authorities to build in excess

Above *Aerial photograph taken in 1958 of the Roehampton Estate designed by the Architects Department of London County Council. Many such large local authority housing schemes were built in Britain during the 1950s, although this was one of the most highly praised at the time. Built on a beautiful wooded site overlooking Richmond Park it consists of a variety of different brick-faced housing types, including the 'point' blocks seen in the foreground and the Le Corbusier-inspired concrete 'slab' blocks in the distance.*
Opposite *Interior of a flat on the Roehampton Estate. The chair and the curtain in the living room are both from the London department store Heal's.*
Right *Advertisement for Inertol enamel masonry paints, illustrated in use on the balconies of the Churchill Gardens Housing Estate at Pimlico in London, designed by Powell and Moya in 1951. Colour, whether in the form of cladding or paintwork, was recognized as an essential ingredient of 'Contemporary' architecture.*
Far Right *This black-and-white photograph of the same building produces a very different impression by contrast with the advert.*

Top and Above *Two views of the centre of Harlow New Town (chief architect and planner Frederick Gibberd) built from 1957 onwards. Note the use of decorative coloured cladding to add visual interest to the building fronts over the shops, and the imposing striped ball-and-spoke clock, intended to provide a focus for the square. This type of pedestrianized mall became the model for many redevelopment schemes in towns and cities throughout Britain during the 1950s and 1960s.*

of 7,000 dwellings each year. Of the housing schemes which Kidder Smith singled out for particular praise, some are well-known, such as the Roehampton Estate (London SW15) designed by the Architects Department of London County Council; others, now somewhat under-rated, are the Churchill Gardens Development in Pimlico (London SW1) by Powell and Moya; the Holford Square Estate (London WC1) by Skinner, Bailey and Lubetkin; housing in Bethnal Green (London E2) by Denys Lasdun and Partners; and Harlow New Town, in Essex, for which Frederick Gibberd acted as the chief architect-planner.

New Towns were a uniquely English phenomenon, which attracted much interest abroad during the 1950s. What distinguished them from other housing developments of the time, particularly those in the USA, was that, being physically distanced from the urban centres whose overspill populations they were built to house, they were not sprawling suburbs of existing cities, but independent self-contained towns. In the words of the admiring Kidder Smith:

> The New Towns, although they were originated in an effort to get people out of the clutch of the great cities, primarily Greater London, are not dormitory satellites, but self-contained cities, complete with their own offices and industries, and their own recreational facilities.

In contemporary discussions of public housing initiatives, the other country invariably mentioned alongside Britain was Sweden which had already become well known for its thoughtful and sensitive approach to the provision of low-cost housing during the 1930s, although at this date the initiative was being taken not by local authorities, but by the communities themselves through the agency of co-operative building societies. The achievements of these organizations were singled out for particular praise in 1945 by Nelson and Wright in *Tomorrow's House*. One of the distinguishing features of the Swedish programme was the inclusion of integral healthcare and childcare facilities within each apartment block, which were freely available to every tenant regardless of wealth.

The other outstanding achievement of the Swedes after the war was in city planning, the success of which was underpinned by an enlightened policy of land acquisition by city councils, such as Stockholm, during the early part of the century. This enabled local authorities to extend their boundaries in a considered rather than an arbitrary way in later years when the need arose. One of the most successful developments of the early post-war period was Vällingby, for which the chief-planner was the distinguished architect Sven Markelius, working with the Stockholm Town Planning Office. Kidder Smith described this development in evocative and highly charged terms:

> The new 'town section' – not satellite city – in west Stockholm has more lessons to offer the cities of our times than any other development yet built. It shows to a beautiful degree how the suburbs that increasingly envelop the world's cities can be well-planned, park-like viable centres, and not haphazard accretions strangled in transportation, mired in shopping, and frantic for enough schools

Above *The carefully planned pedestrianized town centre of Vällingby (chief planner Sven Markelius and the Stockholm Town Planning Office), a new urban development built on the outskirts of Stockholm during 1953–9 which received universal acclaim at the time. Of particular note in this view are the attractive fountain paddling pools, the mosaic designs on the pavements, the quirky ball-and-spoke* street lighting, and the openness of the square. Left *An artist's impression by Kenneth Brown of signage in the centre of Stevenage New Town (chief architect Leonard Vincent), from* The Architectural Review, *August 1957. This sketch emphasises once again the dynamic role of colour in 'Contemporary' architecture, and its positive effect on civic and commercial buildings.*

Tapiola Garden City (chief architect Aarne Ervi) was the Finnish equivalent of Sweden's Vällingby, built five miles to the west of Helsinki, and described by G E Kidder Smith in 1961 as 'one of the finer suburban developments in Europe'. Constructed from 1956 onwards on a 640-acre forest site, the development was initiated by Heikki von Hertzen in collaboration with a special housing foundation, supported by various trade unions and social welfare organizations. All the houses are built on a very human scale and throughout the scheme suburban buildings are closely integrated with the natural environment.

Above and Right *The designers of the terraced housing shown here, dating from 1959, were the talented husband-and-wife team of Heikki and Kaija Siren.*

Above, Left and Right *Two views of the interior of one of the houses at Tapiola Garden City in Finland designed by Heikki and Kaija Siren, the exterior of which are shown on the opposite page. The design aesthetic is functional and somewhat minimalist, with extensive use of tiling on the floors and exposed brickwork on the walls. The lithe spiral staircase provides an elegant focal point within the first-floor living room.*

Right *Row of terraced houses at the Bellavista seaside development at Klampenborg near Copenhagen, designed by Arne Jacobsen in 1949. Built of yellow brick, black tiles and wood, this group of fourteen houses was a model small-scale development of its time.*

Particularly significant was the abandonment of the flat-roofed aesthetic of the pre-war Modern Movement in favour of asymmetrical pitched roofs. This gives the roofscape of these terraced houses a dynamic and expressive rhythm.

and public facilities. Every road, every building location, every need for Vällingby's 23,000 inhabitants was minutely planned before ground was broken. It is the embodiment of Sweden's intimate relationship between architecture and the land on which it stands. Virtually all the major decisions in the moulding of Vällingby were good ones: strict preservation of the landscape and trees; free planning in space with fingers of green everywhere; separation of pedestrian and motor traffic; direct railway to the centre of the city; full cultural and entertainment facilities; a great variety of housing types; one central plant for heat and power.

Vällingby embodied in real terms many of the ideals and aspirations of architects and city planners of the post-war period in relation to the community. It was acclaimed worldwide, and acted as a model and a point of reference for future developments internationally. As city planners were to discover, however, building a successful 'Contemporary' community which fulfilled all the needs of the inhabitants, and at the same time matched the material resources available, was one of the most difficult challenges they faced and one with an extremely high failure rate. As Vällingby demonstrated so effectively, a 'Contemporary' community was not just a housing estate, it was a network of carefully considered and interrelated social facilities designed to meet the specific needs of the inhabitants. It was not necessary for the architecture of individual buildings to be highly distinctive, but it was essential that, as a group, these buildings satisfied the domestic, occupational, educational, medical, recreational and transport needs of the people they were built to serve.

Three recent views of Le Corbusier's Unité d'Habitation near Marseilles, completed in 1952, incorporating within one huge block a wide range of different apartment types, as well as various commercial and social amenities intended to make the Unité's residents virtually self-sufficient.
Opposite *As Le Corbusier intended, the concrete walls dividing the balconies of each apartment are still painted in white and primary colours so that the block as a whole is ablaze with colour.*

A community housing initiative of a different type which also received widespread attention during the 1950s was Le Corbusier's Unité d'Habitation near Marseilles. Although only one Unité was ever built on this site, it was originally intended as the first of six blocks which together would have formed a larger and less isolated community. Each Unité, in addition to providing accommodation, was designed to cater for the basic social needs of the people who lived within it, including shopping (an open street was created mid-way up the building), education (a school was incorporated into the design) and recreation (a gymnasium, meeting room and sculpture playground were all built on the roof). All in all, it consisted of 337 apartments of twenty-three different types – from one-room bedsits to large family flats – designed to accommodate 1,600 people. As is well known, however, the built-in services offered by the Unité were never fully accepted by its residents. Le Corbusier failed, for example, to reform people's shopping habits, and as this was so fundamental to the building-up of a sense of community within such a large housing development, the idealistic aims of the project were never fully realized.

Top *The roof, with its organic flaring 'funnel', takes the form of a fantastical sculpture garden intended as a playground for children.*

Above *Vividly coloured stained glass is also used for decorative purposes within the building.*

Le Corbusier was by no means alone amongst architects of the day in choosing to concern himself with the problem of low-cost housing, but few came up with such radical solutions. Many more would have tackled such schemes had they been given the chance to build, but opportunities to become involved in high-quality non-speculative housing developments were surprisingly few outside the UK and Scandinavia during the 1950s. This was a source of embarrassment to most socially committed

architects who recognized that their talents were not being put to the fullest use if they were limited to designing houses for wealthy middle-class clients. This was one of the major attractions, therefore, of working for a local authority, and the reason why, at this date, high-calibre architects were attracted to work with enlightened local authorities such as London County Council and Stockholm City Council.

Many architects were conscious, even before the war, that they should be devoting their energies to the problem of housing larger numbers of people. In the discussion of modern architecture that took place in books and magazines, however, attention tended to be focused on individual private houses or on high-profile commissions for commercial buildings. This situation was lamented before the war by Yorke when he observed, by way of apology, in the introduction to *The Modern House*:

> This book concerns the individual villa type of house; and though the author does not pretend that the building of villas is a good or even a possible solution to the problem of housing the people, he does believe that until land is so controlled that flats can be planned in proper relation to neighbourhoods and to open space the major-ity of people will continue to want to live in detached or semi-detached houses, and it is important that the relation of the small house to modern architecture and to the modern social system be appreciated.

The main inhibiting factor that Yorke identified – the acquisition of suitable land for such large scale projects – was one which the Swedes had been able to surmount at Vällingby because the local council had had the foresight to acquire the necessary land in advance. In the UK after the war, the situation was somewhat different. The severity of the housing shortage in bomb-damaged London meant that the County Council had to acquire as much land as possible on the outskirts of the capital, in order to build new estates such as that at Roehampton. This in turn gave architects the spur they needed to tackle the problem of low-cost housing seriously.

Some countries, such as Italy, Australia and the USA, erected a considerable amount of housing very quickly after the war, either in the form of high-rise apartment blocks in urban areas, or estates of detached houses in the suburbs, but it was often poorly planned. Furthermore, when this development was initiated by a private devel-oper for commercial gain, rather than by a local authority or a government agency, essential support services commensurate with the scale of the new developments were not automatically provided. Sometimes, communities were left stranded with no shops, no health-care provision and even, in some cases, no adequate roads. In the UK, local authorities tried to address all these issues at the planning stage. This in itself was no guarantee of success, but without it projects were doomed to suffer the uncertainty of fickle and unreliable market forces.

Although much of the speculative housing built in the UK after the war was as poorly planned and inadequately serviced as in other parts of the world, there was one notable exception in the work of Eric Lyons for the Span Development Group. Span housing, was aimed at the

Opposite *Cité de l'Abreuvoir housing estate at Paris-Bobigny*, designed by Émile Aillaud, and completed in 1959. Originally the towers were painted a much lighter colour so the effect would have been rather different. In designing these idiosyn-cratic cylindrical towers Aillaud was reacting against the established Modern Movement bias towards strictly rectilinear buildings. The block seen on the far left is one of several which are three-pointed. Other blocks built on this estate, and on another development

designed by Aillaud the same year at Paris-Pantin called *Cité des Courtilières*, are long and sinuous, running in an extended curvilinear snake-like form-ation for up to a kilometre. Top *An example of one of the numerous modest, low-cost terraced housing schemes designed by Eric Lyons and built by the Span Development Group in London during the 1950s and 1960s. These houses form part of a development called The Hall at Blackheath in London dating from 1959. The vertical tile-hanging at first-floor level is a*

distinctive Span characteristic, later adopted as a somewhat hackneyed formula by many local authorities in the UK on new council houses built during the 1960s. Above *The interior of a Span house which, although small, shows how Lyons made the most of limited space by incorporating the principles of open planning and picture windows into his design.*

Above *Templewood School, Welwyn Garden City, designed by Hertfordshire County Council Architects Department under C H Aslin, built on a modular system using an 8¼ft/ 2.5m grid and standard-ized prefabricated components. As a result of the adoption of this modular system of building, a total of one hundred schools were built in the county of Hertfordshire alone between 1946 and 1955.*

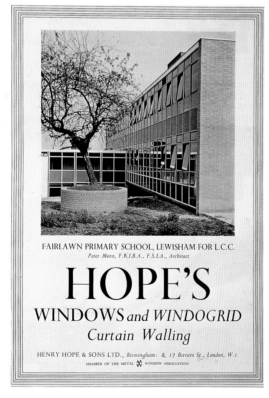

FAIRLAWN PRIMARY SCHOOL, LEWISHAM FOR L.C.C.
Peter Moro, F.R.I.B.A., F.S.I.A., Architect

HOPE'S
WINDOWS and WINDOGRID
Curtain Walling

HENRY HOPE & SONS LTD., Birmingham: & 17 Berners St., London, W.1
MEMBER OF THE METAL ✠ WINDOW ASSOCIATION

Above *Curtain-wall cladding systems were widely adopted during the 1950s for both schools and offices. This advertise-ment for Hope's Windows from May 1958 illustrates the Windowgrid* *cladding system in use at Fairlawn Primary School at Lewisham in London, designed by Peter Moro. Brightly coloured panels such as these were commonly used on school buildings at this time.*

enlightened but impoverished middle classes, and mostly built during the 1950s and 1960s in desirable but as yet undeveloped parts of London, such as Blackheath, in the form of low-rise flats, terraces and maisonettes. Generally no higher than three storeys and set in attrac-tively landscaped communal gardens, these modest flats were compact and well-proportioned, designed to maximize the use of limited space. Span housing was very popular as it provided high-quality accommo-dation at a modest price in pleasant surroundings close to the city centre. In spite of the fact that these dwellings were uncompromisingly modern in appearance, with flat roofs and open-plan interiors, they demonstrated even to the most conservative clients that well-designed 'Contemporary' homes could be synonymous with comfort and convenience.

Before the war very few commissions for public buildings had been awarded to architects of the Modern Movement, although the Modernist aesthetic had been deemed acceptable for purely functional buildings, such as factories. Modernism, albeit mostly in the guise of the more lightweight 'moderne' style, had also influenced the appear-ance of buildings associated with leisure and entertainment during the 1930s, such as hotels, cinemas and seaside pavilions. However, the majority of 'serious' public buildings commissioned by the state during the interwar years were in a somewhat ponderous classical style, clas-sicism being the still dominant aesthetic of officialdom. After the war this changed, however, as governments, universities, local authorities and private companies internationally began to commission buildings in the 'Contemporary' style.

One of the reasons for this change of direction was the psychologi-cal impact of the war. There was now a conscious desire to leave the past behind, and little incentive simply to reproduce what had gone before. Victorian architecture was by now widely discredited and was manifestly unsuitable for providing the revamped services that society needed. Moreover, as with housing, people were now more responsive to modernity, having become tired of shabbiness and buildings that appeared to be old-fashioned. During the 1950s society wanted to look to the future, not to dwell on the past.

In many countries, after housing, because of the post-war baby boom, the highest priority for local authorities was to build new schools. Of the 1,200 schools in London before the war, for example, only fifty remained undamaged in 1945. In the UK the pressure to provide new facilities quickly meant that local authorities had to evolve new approaches to the design of school buildings. This led to the devel-opment of new systems of standardization and prefabrication. A modular system was developed in Hertfordshire which proved highly effective and adaptable. Although component parts were standardized, the system could be put together in a variety of combinations to produce visually varied results. As a result of such innovations, more schools were built more quickly in the UK during the early post-war period than at any other time before or since.

Changes to the education system and its infrastructure were, in any case, long overdue. In the UK the majority of schools in use during the 1930s had been built during the nineteenth century. Often they were grim and prison-like in appearance, such an environment serving

Left *Exterior of Aboyne Lodge Primary School at St Albans built by Hertfordshire County Council Architects Department under C H Aslin during 1951–2. Although built using a standardized modular system, each of the new schools built in Hertfordshire has its own identity.*

Above *Interior of a classroom at Aboyne Lodge. Note the lightness and airiness of the classroom as a result of the plentiful windows, and note also the abandonment of old-fashioned desks in favour of a new and more flexible system of half-hexagonal tables.*

Arne Jacobsen's yellow brick Munkegård School at Gentofte near Copenhagen, completed in 1956, designed for 1000 children aged between seven and sixteen.

Above *The aerial view shows the grid layout of the building: the classrooms all run east to west, while the corridors run north to south.*

Right *Interior view showing one of the well-lit classrooms, illuminated by two tiers of south-facing windows. Each classroom looks out onto a courtyard, and each courtyard is paved with a different surface and contains a work of art.*

to foster and perpetuate a sometimes repressive regime. Old methods of teaching were now going out of fashion with the introduction of more liberal ideas about education and child psychology. Even before the war concerns about the state of the nation's schools, particularly in inner-city areas had arisen because of a heightened awareness of the need to raise standards of healthcare, not only by diet but through exposure to light, fresh air and exercise. As a result, the new schools that were built after the war were radically different.

Such trends were international. New schools built as far afield as Denmark and the USA shared a common philosophy, which was reflected in a new aesthetic. What was striking about 'Contemporary' schools was the quality of light – in some cases of transparency – throughout the building or the building complex. Victorian and Edwardian school buildings had usually been concentrated in one solid block, with high brick walls enclosing the playground. 'Contemporary' schools were generally low-rise (the educational equivalent of a bungalow), sometimes constructed in self-contained but inter-connecting units spread over a large area, and usually surrounded by a generous allocation of playing fields. Even in inner-city areas attempts were made to locate schools on green field sites. The institutions themselves were also more outward-looking, literally as well as metaphorically. There were windows everywhere, not just in the classrooms, but in corridors and stairwells, assembly rooms, dining rooms, gymnasiums and laboratories. This gave schools a new feeling of openness, engendering a more positive attitude towards education. According to Wolf von Eckardt, commenting on developments in the USA: 'School buildings, rather than being places to confine children for the ordeal of getting an education, have themselves become tools of teaching.'

The layout of school buildings and their inter-relationship was considered all-important. In Denmark, Arne Jacobsen's Munkegard School at Gentofte, near Copenhagen, described by Kidder Smith as 'the finest secondary school in Europe', is a striking example of an innovative layout as a reflection of the new ethos in teaching. Designed as a grid of alternating classrooms and playgrounds, it was arranged so that each classroom looked out on to a courtyard, each paved and landscaped in a different way to avoid monotony, and each adorned with a work of art. Smallness of scale was considered important. Although many schools were larger, therefore, classes were generally smaller, despite population size being on the increase. The large classes that still prevailed in Britain were much disapproved of in the USA, for example.

Jacobsen was by no means alone in seeking to make art an integral part of the design within his school at Munkegard. During the 1950s it was believed that school buildings, although essentially functional, should seek to foster creativity, and for this reason both art and decorative art were acknowledged as important elements within the educational environment. In the UK, although art might take the form of a lithograph on the classroom wall or a piece of modern sculpture in the grounds, it was more likely to be incorporated as a tile panel on an exterior wall or as a mural in the entrance hall. Such decorative art elements were frequently integrated within the fabric of the building, whether in the form of imaginative brickwork on the exterior, mosaic

After World War II schools were increasingly regarded as places of mental stimulation rather than repression. This was reflected in the more open layouts adopted at this time, and the importance attached to the placing of works of art and decorative art features, such as murals, within school buildings.

Top *Tile panel at a secondary school at Muswell Hill in London, designed in the mid-1950s by Richard Sheppard and Partners. Tile panels were ideal for schools because they created 'instant' works of art at a modest cost.*

Above *Swirling abstract glass mosaic design by Philip Suffolk on the wall of a stairwell at a girls' comprehensive school in Putney designed by Powell and Moya, completed in 1955. Purpose-designed features such as this were more expensive because they involved bringing in an artist from outside.*

decoration on a stairwell, or an abstract arrangement of coloured cladding on the outside of the building, alternating with curtain-wall windows. Attention to detail was also a characteristic of many American schools of the period, as Wolf von Eckardt noted at the time: 'Ingenious use of materials, contrast, and colour are applied to making the places of learning cheerful and attractive as well as functional. Some of these schools even venture into a judicious and economical use of art work.'

In Britain, schools built during the 1950s in the 'Contemporary' style can often be detected by their curved organic components, such as wavy canopies or vaulted roofs, complementing a rectilinear structure. Such features represented a growing international trend towards a more sculptural form of expression in public buildings, particularly those making use of concrete. This kind of embellishment and detailing created considerable variety of visual effect within individual schools. In the UK there was variety, too, even between schools in the same area built by the same local authority using the same modular system, although recognizable patterns were also evident.

Later, a similar approach was adopted in new hospitals of the period, where the need for functionalism had to be balanced against the need to create a positive and life-affirming environment. Once again, as with houses and schools, there was a clear difference between the pre-war and the post-war aesthetic, as pointed out by Wolf von Eckardt:

> The earlier tendency was to incorporate into spotless health factories all the advances in medical knowledge and technology with the greatest possible efficiency and aseptic polish. In the fifties our hospitals and clinical facilities took efficiency for granted and again, concentrated on liveability, on charm and cheer as an indispensable psychological incentive to healing and convalescence.

After the war the provision of further education was significantly extended in many countries, a trend that continued into the 1960s with the consolidation of the idea of campus-based institutions set in green field sites with spacious landscaped surroundings such as York. In the UK, the trend towards expansion also affected the development of established academic institutions, particularly the nineteenth century so-called 'red brick' universities, such as Manchester, which sought to increase their intake of students during the 1950s by erecting new halls of residence and faculty buildings. Also keen to expand were the Oxbridge colleges. The acclaimed St Catherine's College in Oxford designed by Arne Jacobsen was just one result of this programme of expansion, although by the mid-1960s so much new building had taken place in Cambridge that a whole book, *New Cambridge Architecture* by Nicholas Taylor, was devoted exclusively to this subject.

The 1950s also marked a period of growth for specialized educational institutions such as colleges of technology. In the USA, several leading figures from the European Modern Movement played an important role in this area, starting in the late 1930s with Alvar Aalto's curvilinear dormitory buildings of 1939 at Massachusetts Institute of Technology (MIT) followed by the extensive involvement of Mies van der Rohe at the Illinois Institute of Technology between 1939 and

Opposite The curvilinear dormitories of Alvar Aalto's Everett Moore Baker House at Massachusetts Institute of Technology, of 1947–9. The walls are faced with rough brick, and this, combined with their strongly organic shape, *set Aalto apart from the prevailing trend in the USA at that time towards minimalist rectilinear college buildings, such as those of Mies van der Rohe at the Illinois Institute of Technology (see following page).*

Top and Left
St Catherine's College, Oxford, designed by Arne Jacobsen in the late 1950s, completed in 1964, represents a rare example of a leading international architect working in Britain during the early post-war period. St Catherine's is a highly accomplished and sophisticated building which set new standards in the design of residential, social and educational facilities for higher education, and confidently asserted its modernity in the historic university city of Oxford in the face of overwhelming tradition. The strictly geometric rectilinearity of the building is counterbalanced by the overtly curvilinear furniture. All the furniture and lighting within the college was designed by Jacobsen, resulting in a strong organic unity.

Below and Opposite
Two views of Eero Saarinen's Morse and Stile Colleges at Yale University, of 1958–61. The approach adopted by Saarinen at Yale was very different to that of Mies van der Rohe at Illinois (right and below), especially his choice of such a rich and unusual rough textured stone and concrete finish as the facing material for his buildings. In his design for this complex, however, Saarinen was aiming to create an impression reminiscent of an Italian hill town. The site includes interior courtyards, terraces and paths, therefore, as well as the buildings themselves.

Mies van der Rohe spent many years during and after World War II designing buildings – eighteen in all – for the new campus at the Illinois Institute of Technology, where he took up the post of Director of Architecture in 1938, retiring in 1958. The site is laid out on a 24ft by 24ft (7.3m by 7.3m) grid, and the buildings are strictly modular, constructed of steel, glass and buff-coloured brick.

Top Right *Carmen Hall, a classic rectilinear Miesian building.*
Bottom Right *Crown Hall, housing the Department of Architecture and Planning, completed in 1955. It is the largest building on the campus, and is basically composed of one column-free main room measuring 120ft by 220ft (36.6m by 67m) with a 20ft (6m) ceiling.*

1958. The architect Walter Gropius, meanwhile, was commissioned to design a new Graduate Centre at Harvard where he was teaching in 1949-50, and Eero Saarinen was invited to design a variety of college buildings in many different parts of the country including the Kresge Chapel and Auditorium at MIT (1953-6), the Law School at Chicago (1956-60), and the Ezra Stiles and Morse Colleges at Yale (1958-62). During the 1950s expanding campuses also provided Saarinen with a string of projects for residential accommodation, including women's dormitories at Drake University in Iowa, the University of Chicago and the University of Pennsylvania.

Whereas in the context of education an overtly creative approach to architecture was often encouraged in the design of office buildings, aesthetic considerations were generally considered of less importance. Here an increasingly anonymous, run-of-the-mill, functionalist aesthetic prevailed internationally during the 1950s, dominated by high-rise skyscrapers clad with curtain-wall window systems. Offices came to be considered as similar to factories; that is, places where productivity and efficiency were primary considerations. In this context it appeared to make sense to pursue the idea of form following function to its logical conclusion. After the war, although the idea that the house should be considered as a 'machine for living in' had gone out of fashion, the idea of the office as a 'machine for working in' was gaining ground, especially in the larger corporations. This caused many companies to rethink their approach to the housing of their workforce. Clear lines of communication were recognized as essential, for example, and it was thought that these could be significantly improved by altering the layout of the office. Instead of a warren of tiny cubicles, therefore, offices became large and open-plan, partly in order to maximize the use of space, but largely to improve efficiency through the operation of a different style of administration and management.

Corporate headquarters, especially in the USA, were usually conceived on a somewhat grander scale and tended to be planned in one of two different ways, either as high-rise or low-rise, depending on the space restrictions of the site. The high-rise approach was embodied in the soaring skyscraper, typified by Lever House of 1951-2 by Skidmore, Owings and Merrill (SOM) in the centre of New York, and by the Pirelli Building by Ponti, Nervi and Associates in the centre of Milan (1958-61). Low-rise developments, on the other hand, were spread over a large area, usually on a green field site, as with Eero Saarinen's General Motors Technical Center at Warren, Michigan (1951-7), or the expansive new headquarters for the Connecticut General Insurance Company, near Hartford, Connecticut designed by SOM (1954-7). In both types of developments, especially in the USA, these confidently modern buildings, with their forceful and uncompromisingly 'Contemporary' interiors, were an expression of the newly developed corporate ethos of the clients for whom they were built. Physical expansion, whether upwards or outwards, signalled not only the wealth and commercial well-being of the company at the time of the development, but was also a symbol of future aspirations and an expression of power and possession.

Commercial clients varied in the degree to which they were prepared to consider the well-being of their workforce, or the requirements of the

Above The tapering contours of the Pirelli Building in Milan, designed by Ponti, Nervi and Associates and built between 1958 and 1961. Ponti was opposed to the rigid rectilinear post and

beam construction methods and curtain-wall cladding systems popular in the USA at this date, which he considered unimaginative.

Top Eero Saarinen, who designed the General Motors Technical Center at Warren, Michigan between 1951 and 1957, was one of the few architects of the period who was able to work with equal confidence in both an expressive-organic and a modular-rectilinear idiom. The dome in the distance houses the company's styling auditorium.

Opposite Curtain-wall cladding system used to create a glass tower: Lever House in New York designed by Gordon Bunshaft for Skidmore, Owings and Merrill in 1951–2. This photograph is taken from underneath the recessed entrance to another famous glass tower, the Seagram Building designed by Mies van der Rohe and Philip Johnson in 1958. Now that every major city in the world is dominated by skyscrapers, it is easy to forget how imposing such buldings appeared when they were first erected after World War II.

Top and Above *Eero Saarinen's Styling Division building at the General Motors Technical Center at Warren, Michigan, built between 1951 and 1957. It was while working on the General Motors project that Saarinen resolved many of the technical details which made curtain wall* systems commercially viable. The interior of the building was as sophisticated as the exterior, and reflected Saarinen's minute attention to detail.
Opposite *When commercial clients were receptive, architects often took the opportunity to incorporate works of art into their* buildings. The sculptor Harry Bertoia, for example, was commissioned by Gordon Bunshaft of Skidmore, Owings and Merrill to create a giant welded screen for the mezzanine of the Manufacturers Trust Company's Fifth Avenue Branch in New York in 1954.

inhabitants of the district in which they chose to erect their buildings. According to Sherban Cantacuzino in *Great Modern Architecture*, one of the reasons for the success of Lever House in New York was because, 'A co-operative client was persuaded to sacrifice the best part of his valuable site in Park Avenue and to set it aside, as open space, for the use of the public in the street.' The author continued, 'In the sheer glass tower, occupying only one quarter of the site and set with its short end facing the main street, we have perhaps the first elegant use of curtain walling, expressing the self-sufficient nature of the air-conditioned and artificially-lighted glass cage.' The use of curtain walling in itself, therefore, did not necessarily imply blandness and anonymity: it could be used to project detachment, but it could also be chic and 'elegant', as in the works of SOM and Mies van der Rohe. In spite of superficial similarities there was a huge gulf between the originators of this aesthetic and their many lesser imitators.

The difference lay primarily in attention to detail, both visual and technical, and the most outstanding architects of the period were all distinguished by their single-minded rigour in this respect. It was essential, for example, to ensure that what was projected in terms of materials or structure really worked. This could only be done by rigorous testing beforehand; it was also essential that the architect should see each project through to completion, with an insistence throughout on the highest standards of workmanship in the execution of the building. Sensitivity to human needs was also extremely important if a building was to be successful in practice as well as in theory.

Eero Saarinen, one of the most successful architects of the 1950s, combined many of these qualities. Although very much interested in individual expression, he was also concerned to exploit the latest advances in technology and engineering in order to bring to perfection modular building systems and curtain walling suitable for large-scale offices. At the same time he recognized that office buildings were for people, individuals who required both physical comfort and visual stimulation to perform well for their employers. Attention to detail and creative expression were an essential part of his approach to the design of public buildings, therefore, and for him art was not something to be confined to the home. Of his aims for the General Motors Technical Center he is quoted in the book *Eero Saarinen On His Work*: 'Our intention was threefold: to provide the best possible facilities for industrial research; to create a unified, beautiful and human environment; and to find an appropriate architectural expression.'

In his choice of building materials Saarinen sometimes drew inspiration from the products of the client company itself: this was the case in both the headquarters for the firm of Deere and Company and at the General Motors Technical Center. Of the latter the architect commented, 'the design is based on steel – the metal of the automobile. Like the automobile itself, the buildings are essentially put together, as on an assembly line, out of mass-produced units.' Architects of this calibre, who could apply their talents to such a wide range of public buildings, from airports to churches to embassies, demonstrated the strengths and the flexibility of the 'Contemporary' style, and showed that it could be equally successful when applied to small-scale and large-scale projects.

Corporate power bases of the type designed by Saarinen during the 1950s were usually constructed on a modular grid-like plan and required a new style of 'Contemporary' office furniture to equip them. This was provided by emergent firms such as Knoll Associates and Herman Miller in the USA, and by revitalized older firms such as Hille in Britain and Cassina in Italy. Of the four, Knoll, headed by Hans and Florence Knoll, was the most progressive in office furniture design, and it was Florence Knoll herself who took the lead in developing the square-section steel-bar framed furniture that was to become synonymous with the international corporate aesthetic of the post-war period. This was a construction technique that was applied to both carcase furniture, such as desks and cabinets, and seat furniture. Knoll Associates, who by the end of the decade had expanded to become Knoll International, also became well known during the 1950s for putting back into production some of the classic 1930s designs of the Modern Movement, such as the Barcelona chair by Mies van der Rohe, which was often to be seen in the lobbies of corporate buildings during the 1950s and 60s.

It is interesting to note that while the architecture of offices adopted the rigorous geometric planning associated with factory design, a significant number of newly constructed factories abandoned geometry in favour of more fluid, sculptural forms. This growing interest in organic sculptural expression ran parallel to the pursuit of rigorous geometry in public buildings of the period, particularly those requiring large vaulted shell structures such as market halls, sports arenas, airports, train and bus terminals, factories and warehouses. Although curvilinear forms had formed an essential ingredient of Alvar Aalto's architecture before the war, Aalto's organic impulse was mainly expressed in undulating walls rather than in roof structures. It is for the latter that the 1950s will primarily be remembered, however, especially the remarkable profiles of Eero Saarinen's airports and Pier Luigi Nervi's Olympic stadia in Rome, although Frank Lloyd Wright, going against the trend as usual, made one of the most dramatic statements of all in his outwardly spiralling walls for the Guggenheim Museum in New York.

During the course of the 1950s the influence of sculpture began to be seen on an increasingly wide range of public buildings, such as churches, art galleries, auditoria and finally, in government buildings in the new cities of Brasilia (chief architect Oscar Niemeyer, from 1956) and Chandigarh (chief architect, Le Corbusier, from 1950). In retrospect, this new plasticity of form stands out as one of the most unusual and original characteristics of 'Contemporary' architecture. It was by no means just an aberration or an offshoot from the mainstream, but reflected the centrality of the visual arts to all forms of creative expression during the 1950s, from the design of wallpapers to *haute couture*. Its importance was underlined by the fact that, by the end of the decade, it had been accepted and embraced not only by the younger members of the profession, but also by some of the leading figures from the Modern Movement, notably Le Corbusier and Marcel Breuer. In 1963 in *Space, Time and Architecture*, Sigfried Giedion reflected:

That architecture is approaching sculpture and sculpture architecture is no deviation from the development of contemporary architecture...

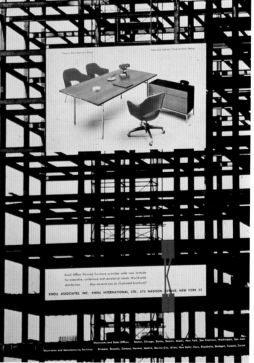

Opposite and Top *The Union Carbide building, dating from 1960, was one of four glass towers built in New York by Skidmore, Owings and Merrill during the first fifteen years after World War II. The interiors, with their luxurious Barcelona chairs, their modern art and their smart office furniture by Knoll, typify the new aesthetic of corporate North America during the post-war era.* Left *It is hardly surprising that the furniture used in modern American office buildings during the 1950s should complement the architecture itself, when in some cases it was designed by the same people. Eero Saarinen worked closely with Knoll throughout the decade, for example, and his chairs are seen in this advertisement, along with examples of the steel bar framed tables and desks designed by Florence Knoll.*

Alongside the rectilinear buildings that were being erected in many cities during the first fifteen years after World War II, there was an emergent movement in 'Contemporary' architecture that favoured organic curvilinear expression and shell structures.

Top Left *Parabolic arches, cantilevered canopies, and wave-like roof structures were all 'in' during the 1950s, and all three are combined in this airport terminal building at Renfrew near Glasgow, designed by Rowand Anderson, Kininmonth and Paul.*

Near Left *Frank Lloyd Wright's design for the Guggenheim Museum in New York, completed in 1959, was blatantly organic and sculptural, thereby associating the form of the structure of the building with its function as an art gallery.*

Far Left *Rubber factory at Brymawr in South Wales designed by the Architects Co-operative Partnership, completed in 1951, showing the wavy canopies of the Drug Room.*

Opposite *The impressive reinforced concrete roof of a London Transport Bus Depot built at Stockwell in 1953, designed by Adie, Button and Partners.*

Industrial buildings were regarded as a creative challenge by architects during the 1950s. *Above Arne Jacobsen's Carl Christenson Motor Works, a cylinder-boring plant at Aalborg in Denmark completed in 1956, shows just how elegant and beautiful* a factory building can be. It is constructed from reinforced concrete faced with brick, with steel and glass partitions on the interior. Were it not for the metal stack to the right, this building might quite easily be mistaken for a church.

Right *Pier Luigi Nervi combined the talents of the engineer with the creativity of the artist: the pattern of the strengthened radiating ribs moulded into the concrete ceiling in his Gatti Wool Factory in Rome of 1951–3 follow the isostatic lines of stress calculated for this structure.*

During the first phase of the present development painting stood in the foreground. Now, in the second phase, it is sculpture.

This trend was widely acknowledged by other critics at the time. Speaking of the buildings of Pier Luigi Nervi, one of the leading exponents of this style, Ada Louise Huxtable wrote in 1960 that:

They... demonstrate the radical change in aesthetic vision characteristic of all of the arts of our time. Today, painting, sculpture, architecture, and the arts of design pursue weightlessness, forms in tension, and dynamic plastic expression, rather than the solidity and classic balance admired by earlier generations. A sympathy for solidity was natural in a world of brick on brick and stone on stone; a preoccupation with lightness, dematerialization and dynamic forms in equilibrium is natural in a world of spider-strong steel, thin shell concrete, and amorphous plastics that invite new principles of construction and manufacture and the use of stimulating new shapes. New materials, new purposes, and new forms go hand in hand.

What gave architects the freedom to develop this new aesthetic and to experiment with form in such a bold way were the technical advances made in the fabrication and application of reinforced concrete. The strength and flexibility of reinforced concrete, rather than its aesthetic potential, was what originally influenced its development as a building material, first in skyscrapers and bridges during the late nineteenth and early twentieth century, and later in factories and warehouses. Even during the 1950s it was in industrial buildings that concrete was often used most fearlessly, some of the best examples being the Brynmawr Rubber Factory in South Wales (completed in 1951) by the Architects Co-Partnership in conjuncton with Ove Arup, and the many ingenious designs by Nervi in Italy, such as his Government Salt Warehouses at Tortona (1950-51), his Tobacco Factory and Warehouses at Bologna (1951-2 and 1954), and the Gatti Wool Factory in Rome (1951-3).

For Nervi, the experimental work he carried out for the Italian Government during the 1930s and 40s on the construction of huge concrete framed air hangars proved invaluable in suggesting new ways in which reinforced concrete could be used, not only for structural walls, but also to create vaulted roofs that could span huge distances without support. Nervi united artistic brilliance with engineering genius, and with this combination of talents demonstrated that functional architecture need never be graceless, nor modern materials an excuse for poor artistic expression. In fact, quite the reverse: with a thorough knowledge of the technical properties of reinforced concrete, he showed that it could be a graceful and poetic medium.

Ultimately Brutalism became the dominant aesthetic of the 1960s, but it was by no means the only logical development of the use of concrete: there were real alternatives, as Le Corbusier discovered in his chapel of Notre Dame-du-Haut at Ronchamp in France. Church buildings in general were another rich area for architectural experimentation during the 1950s, and Le Corbusier's work at Ronchamp should be

Building with concrete was seen as an heroic enterprise during the 1950s.
Top *Interior of Tobacco Factory at Bologna designed by Pier Luigi Nervi in 1951–2. The reinforced concrete ceiling was created in large sections in situ by pouring concrete from above onto re-usable 'ferrocemento' formers raised on scaffolding.*

Above *Advertisement for the British Reinforced Concrete Engineering Company, featuring one of the two pit-head winding* towers at the Rothes Colliery built at Thornton in Fifeshire, Scotland in 1956, designed by Egon Riss.

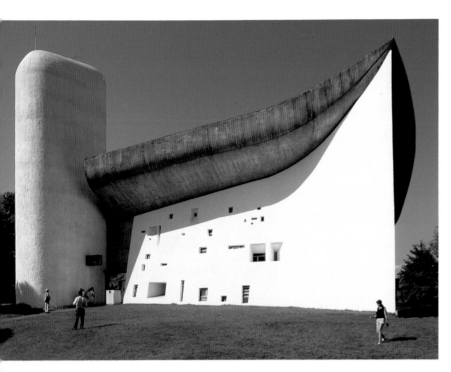

Top and Above *Two views of Le Corbusier's Chapel of Notre Dame-du-Haut at Ronchamp, completed in 1955. The exterior is dominated by the massive sculptural* *presence of its organic concrete roof. Inside, the tiny stained glass windows, deeply recessed into the thick fortress-like wall, glow like gems in the dark.*

seen within this wider context. Homes, schools and the workplace were, of course, the top priorities for building reconstruction and development after the war, but spiritual needs were also recognized as important. The traumas of the recent war meant that the reconstruction of devastated churches and cathedrals was often charged with symbolic significance, as with the re-building of Coventry Cathedral in England. However, what made the 'Contemporary' church so different in feeling from those which had been built before the war was the impact of the revival of the Liturgical Movement on the design of ecclesiastical buildings. This point is strongly emphasized in the book, *Modern Churches of the World* (1965), by Robert Maguire and Keith Murray:

> The Liturgical Movement has rediscovered the essential creative significance of the liturgy as the source of renewal of the life and teaching of the Church. This reformation is having its influence over a wide spectrum of the Church – Orthodox, Roman Catholics, Anglicans, Presbyterians, Methodists, Baptists, Lutherans and Calvinists... The Liturgical Movement has shown the intimate connection between liturgy and architecture. When architecture becomes a matter of style, the relationship between client and architect is of little consequence. But once the architect recognises that a building fulfils a practical and symbolic function in the life of a community then this relationship becomes crucial.

After the war, determined efforts were made to encourage closer communion between the clergy and the congregation, and to remove the sense of remoteness that had hitherto prevailed. This was achieved by altering the physical layout of the church so that the congregation could become more directly involved in the service. Sometimes this meant that churches were conceived almost or completely in the round. Invariably, even in Catholic churches, it meant stripping away the physical evidence of pomp and ceremony in church interiors, providing a purer and less cluttered environment in which to focus on worship.

Judged from this standpoint, many of the best post-war churches were built in West Germany, where specialist church architects such as Rudolf Schwarz achieved a high level of refinement as a result of sustained work in this field over a number of years. There was a deliberate and uncompromising severity and austerity about the interiors of many 'Contemporary' churches in Europe and Scandinavia during the 1950s, as if architects felt the need to purge their buildings of any hint of stylistic excess that might be interpreted as impure. This is not to suggest that decorative elements were excluded altogether, however, or that 'Contemporary' churches eschewed ornament in a puritanical way as being evidence of moral degeneration and sinfulness; nevertheless, what little decoration there was tended to be charged with special meaning and intensity. Being such a sensitive area, designing a church was no easy matter, as Wolf von Eckardt pointed out:

> The challenge of designing a place of worship is greater than any other. There are the complex functional needs of the church or synagogue: the need to accommodate large congregations on important holidays without making the much smaller number of faithful

Above and Left *Some of the most beautiful understated churches of the period were built in Scandinavia. This Cemetery Chapel at Tampere in Finland, designed by Viljo Revell in 1960–1, is created from a reinforced concrete parabolic shell, with the concrete left exposed on both exterior and the interior. The simple unadorned interior has curtain wall windows on both sides overlooking quiet meditative courtyards containing pools of water.*

Above *Chapel at Otaniemi Technical University in Finland* designed by the husband-and-wife team of Kaija and Heikki Siren, built during 1956–7. The installation of a glass curtain wall at the end of the church, so that the trees behind form the backdrop to the altar, was a stroke of genius. The altar itself, together with the font and the pulpit, are made of slender steel bar frame construction so that they do not block the view.

Right *Cemetery Chapel at Imatra in Finland* designed by Jaakko Kontio and Kalle Raike, dating from 1961–2. The two triangular gable windows provide the only source of natural light in the chapel. The glazing bars in these windows repeat the theme of diagonals expressed in the shape of the roof, which was made deliberately steep at the request of the client so that snow would not accumulate on it.

on ordinary Sundays feel lost; the need to accommodate meaningful liturgy and tradition without clinging to meaningless conventions; the need to express the religious outlook of the congregation which may desire withdrawal or world-openness. There is also the vague but sometimes insistent demand of some congregations that 'a church look like a church'.

The majority of British churches of the 1950s failed to meet these criteria and, with the exception of Coventry Cathedral, few achieved the same intensity of vision as their counterparts in mainland Europe and Scandinavia. This was largely because of the reactionary nature of the Church of England, and its conservatism in the choice of designs for new buildings. This lack of direction, in turn, had an effect on the level of church attendance in Britain, which went into decline after the war. According to Kidder Smith, writing in 1961, 'There are more fine new churches around Basel or Cologne than in the whole of the United Kingdom. To flip through *Sixty Post-War Churches* (Incorporated Church Building Society, London, 1957) will make even the most devout an agnostic.'

There were also major differences in the approaches to modern church-building in the USA, which reflected not only the greater affluence of the latter by contrast with Europe, but also a bolder and more self-confident ecclesiastical vision. Often American architects tackled the design of churches in an overtly emotive way in an attempt to inspire devotion in the congregation by evoking awe. One way of producing an awe-inspiring effect was to situate the church in a dramatic location, perched on the edge of a cliff, for example, as with the Chapel of the Holy Cross in Sedona, Arizona, designed by Anshen and Allen. Another way was to create a deliberately exaggerated shape, and some of the more extreme American 'Contemporary' churches were considered audacious, even disrespectful, by European standards. In spite of the ecclesiastical criticisms levelled against these somewhat flashy buildings, however, they were undoubtedly successful when judged purely on their technical and aesthetic merits. Victor Lundy's first Unitarian Church at Westport, Connecticut (1960) was one such example: the sculptural expression of the soaring, concave timber roof being a rather self-conscious attempt to embody the idea of spirituality in physical form; a non-church-goer's idea of what church-goers needed to inspire them to devotion. At the same time, it was undoubtedly a remarkable physical structure.

As with other public buildings, such as sports stadia and airport terminals, churches reflected the widely held view that 'Contemporary' architecture was ideally suited to artistic, and particularly sculptural, expression. It was this organic, sculptural form of architecture, limited almost exclusively to public buildings rather than private dwellings, which produced some of the most memorable and structurally ambitious buildings of the 1950s. In this field the public accepted the most radical and futuristic interpretations of the 'Contemporary' style, and architects were allowed the most scope for experimentation. Not surprisingly, therefore, because of the importance of technical expertise in architecture at this type, some of the most interesting buildings of the early post-war period were those in which structural engineers took a lead role.

Top *Eero Saarinen's cylindrical brick-faced Kresge Chapel at Massachusetts Institute of Technology, dating from 1953–6, is yet another 'Contemporary' church which flies in the face of tradition.*
Bottom *The altar in Kresge Chapel made of white marble, is lit by a window from above. The light from this window also illuminates a shimmering suspended golden screen created by the sculptor, Harry Bertoia.*

Judged by European and Scandinavian standards, some churches built in the USA during the 1950s were theatrical and flashy. Opinion was divided, however: for some people, the visual attention demanded by these structures undermined their spiritual purpose; for others, the drama of the building served to heighten their spiritual experience. Above *Chapel of the Holy Cross at Sedona, Arizona, designed by Anshen and Allen. Built from concrete in an extremely dramatic but* harsh setting, some would say that this church is more like a tomb than a place of worship. It recalls the visual effect of the Pyramids in the barren desert setting of Egypt. Right *Philip Johnson's expressive New Harmony Shrine in Indiana, dating from 1960, marked his abandonment of the minimalist aesthetic of Mies van der Rohe, and his adoption instead of what he called 'eclectic traditionalism', a search for new inspiration in the architecture of other countries and past centuries.*

Opposite *First Presbyterian Church at Stamford, Connecticut, designed by Wallace Harrison in 1959, (structural engineer Felix Samuely). This was Harrison's attempt to create a modern church with the richness of colour and effect seen in Gothic cathedrals. In it concrete slabs and lattices create a framework for the suspension of fragments of glass originating from Chartres Cathedral.*

Above and Right
*Exterior and interior views
of Lambert-St Louis
Airport Terminal designed
by Minoru Yamasaki
in 1956, highlighting
its elegant concrete vault
construction.*

*The installation of
windows in the arches
of the vaults results in a
remarkably open and airy
interior. From the outside
the building has a dynamic
and sprightly quality.*

The three outstanding architect-engineers in the field of public buildings in the 1950s were Pier Luigi Nervi in Italy, Felix Candela in Mexico and Eduardo Torroja in Spain, all of whom devoted their careers to the research and development of reinforced concrete. Although there was nothing new about the basic materials – steel and concrete – what was different was the way in which they were combined, and the mathematical precision with which load bearings and stresses were calculated. Because of the certainty of greater accuracy and control, the material could be treated more ambitiously. This had a knock-on effect on the aesthetic of the buildings that were proposed as Wolf von Eckhardt described in Mid-Century Architecture in America:

> Completely new forms and shapes and the spanning of large spaces without columns or other interior obstructions have been made possible by a major breakthrough from the age-old structure of compressive strength to a new structure of tension... Based on mathematical calculations of stress and tension, engineering pioneers... have broken the tyranny of cubical forms by developing what might be called shell construction. In this method, walls and roof, support and load, framework and ornament are one as in the egg... Other shapes which derive their strength from form rather than mass are the saddle-back hyperbolic paraboloid and crimped triangles... But thin flexible skins are possible only when it [concrete] is reinforced with steel wires. 'Steel,' writes Torroja, 'gives tenacity to stone. Concrete gives mass to steel. Combined they will resist tension in accordance with the existing network of stresses' to reach out and span space of fantastic proportions.

Felix Candela in his Los Manantiales Restaurant in Mexico City (1958), and Minoru Yamasaki in his Lambert-St Louis Airport (1956) in the USA, both exploited this potential to the full, as did Eero Saarinen in his design for Dulles International Airport in Washington DC (1957-62).

Undoubtedly the greatest achievements of the decade in the use of reinforced concrete, however, were those of Pier Luigi Nervi. By his own admission Nervi had a love affair with the material which he described admiringly in *Architecture Today and Tomorrow* by Cranston Jones as 'the finest construction material man has found to this day'. What distinguished him from his contemporaries, the majority of whom had a background solely in architecture rather than engineering, was that Nervi had a deeper understanding of how concrete really worked, and thus of how it could most effectively be used. With knowledge came greater respect for the material itself, and an insistence on the highest standards of execution. For Nervi, concrete was a craftsman's material – not a cheap substitute for brick or stone, but a medium with its own distinctive character, and thus its own range of expression. Nervi was aware, however, that the in-depth knowledge of the engineer was not in itself a guarantee of success:

> It is obvious that engineering and the mental make-up produced by engineering training do not suffice to create architecture. But it is just as obvious that without the realizing techniques of engineering

Top and Above Perhaps the most astonishing airport building ever created, Eero Saarinen's TWA Terminal at Kennedy Airport, completed in 1961, is strongly organic both on the exterior and the interior. From the outside, as has often been said, it resembles a swooping bird coming in to land with its wings outstretched; from the inside, it is perhaps even more fantastical, and the biological overtones are even more exaggerated.

Following Page Dulles Airport at Washington, DC, the last major design of Eero Saarinen before his premature death in 1961, completed posthumously in 1962. The asymmetrical wave-like concave concrete roof is suspended across a span of 150ft (45.7m) by outward-leaning concrete

ribs. The planes do not draw up to the terminal: instead, specially designed 'mobile lounges' transport passengers from the building to the runway. There is, therefore, no need for endless pedestrian corridors.

Pier Luigi Nervi was the most talented structural engineer of his age.

His achievements using reinforced concrete, or 'ferro-cemento' as he called his particular version of this material, are still unrivalled today.

Above *The Palazzo del Lavoro at Turin, dating from 1961, combines massive concrete columns with exposed radiating steel girders. Even when moving away from total reliance on his favoured material, concrete, Nervi produces a startling and original design.*

Right *Detail of the angular concrete pilasters supporting the dome of the Palazzo dello Sport, the larger of Nervi's two Olympic 'sports palaces', designed in collaboration*

with Marcello Piacentini and built in 1959–60.

Far Right *The ceiling of the Palazzetto dello Sport, the small 'sports palace',*

built during 1958–9 for the 1960 Rome Olympics, designed by Nervi in collaboration with Annibale Vitellozzi.

This spectacular ceiling was constructed using prefabricated components.

any architectural conception is as non-existent as an unwritten poem in the mind of the poet.

It was because of the rigorous technical standards he demanded that his buildings were so successful, and not purely, Nervi would argue, because of sculptural considerations: 'In any building aesthetic perfection derives from technical perfection. Beauty does not come from decorative effects but from structural coherence'.

After his structural experiments with air hangars for the Italian government during the war, Nervi spent several years carrying out intensive research into the properties of concrete, investigating how its strength could be further improved. This led to the development of 'ferro-cemento', a fine concrete mortar strengthened by layers of steel mesh and rods – a material which could be cast remarkably thinly without losing any of its strength. The ability to create pre-cast components, combined with the fact that with the new material less cement was actually needed, meant that when competing for contracts Nervi was able to under-cut his rivals, while still offering a much higher quality product. As a guarantee of quality, Nervi established his own construction company to carry out the engineering work on the projects he had designed.

His first major project after the war was the Turin Exhibition Hall of 1948-9. When it was completed its vast size and airiness caused a sensation, especially when it was revealed that the whole building had been erected in the space of eight months. The key to Nervi's success was not in endeavouring to be consciously artistic, but in allowing the form of the building to evolve out of the functional requirements of the structure, expressed through the most suitable materials. He also wished to attain purity of expression through economy of materials and labour because, in his view: 'In the absence of taste, economy is the best incentive for art.' The buildings for which Nervi became world famous were his three sports stadia designed for the 1960 Olympics in Rome. In these buildings he employed distinctive ribbed basketwork roof structures made of prefabricated reinforced concrete. Two of these stadia (the larger Palazzo and the smaller Palazzetto dello Sport) were covered domes; the third (the Flaminio Stadium) was an oval-shaped open arena, built to seat 46,000, with cantilevered canopies projecting over the spectators. The two domed stadia had elegantly patterned ribbed ceilings, the smaller with Y-shaped supports carrying the exterior dome. Spanning 194 ft/59 m, the Palazzetto was the first of the three stadia to be built and was hailed at the time as a modern-day Pantheon. The interiors were notable for being completely column-free.

During the 1950s various communities around the world benefited greatly from the services of a number of remarkable architects such as Nervi, visionaries of towering intellect and ability who were of sufficient stature to rise to the enormous challenges facing society. Others, although undoubtedly talented, were less successful in overcoming practical problems, whether technical or financial. One architect who fell into this category was Oscar Niemeyer, the highly creative and ambitious architect of Brasilia, whose grand schemes were never fully realized, however, because they brought about the economic collapse of the country before building work was completed.

Brasilia was a warning to society of the dangers inherent in allowing architecture to overreach itself. Perhaps as a result of the tragic lesson of Brasilia, the general trend by the early 1960s was away from a reliance on the heroic individual to growing dependence on collaboration and a team approach when tackling large-scale projects. As Sigfried Giedion noted in *Space, Time and Architecture* in 1963:

> It would be a complete misunderstanding to suppose that contemporary architecture has been evolved by a few isolated geniuses. Vigorous artists, creative spirits strong enough to push beyond the dominant conventions – without these, of course, nothing could have been achieved. But contemporary architecture is no longer dependent upon a few individuals; it has its roots deep in the life of our day. It grows more and more anonymous: innumerable workers in every part of the world contribute to its nourishment and progress.

Wolf von Eckardt summarized the shared aims of 'Contemporary' architects in relation to the community when he wrote in his introduction to *Mid Century Architecture in America*:

> The tension generated by this interplay of the forces of individuality and creativity and the forces for conformity and for law and order are the mainspring of our inner life, the staff of our mental health. It is not one or the other which sustains the human spirit. Both are essential. Perhaps it is now time for our planners, architects, and their critics also to come around to this view – that unchecked individuality in architecture will ruin us as surely as monotony if it isn't subjected to order. We need the balance.

Eckardt's perceptive comments and advice are as relevant today as they were thirty years ago. Indeed, there are many valuable lessons to be learnt from the aspirations and achievements of architects and designers working in the 'Contemporary' idiom during the 1950s in the domain of both public and private architecture, which is why the period warrants closer attention and deserves greater respect.

The consumer society of the early 1960s: as standards of living rose, so public expectations grew. It was inevitable that this would ☞ eventually result in an anti-materialist reaction, which was what happened in many western countries during the late 1960s.

From the early post-war period until the early 1960s, there had been a ferment of activity in the field of construction and manufacturing. Not only were huge quantities of consumer goods being produced in ever more technically and aesthetically sophisticated designs, but an enormous amount of new housing had been built and new public and commercial buildings erected, the majority in the 'Contemporary' style. The boom was not just one of quantity, however, although the sheer scale and variety of what was produced was significant; it also represented a flowering of artistic activity in the field of architecture and design. Cranston Jones summed up the position very evocatively when he wrote in *Architecture Today and Tomorrow* in 1961:

> Flux, flow, change are dominant characteristics of mid-twentieth century life. Our landscape is now identified by twelve-lane highways that bulldoze through mountains, forests, and the hearts of cities. Urban tracts are poured into place almost overnight, while stately residential avenues are declared obsolescent within two generations. It is a restless, explosive age, and architecture, which is called upon to give form and expression to this continuing revolution, is in itself in a highly dynamic state of evolution.

The 1950s was a time of great hope and optimism, and also a time of significant and quickening change. Many exciting and unusual new design ideas were taken up by manufacturers and rapidly put into production; and a remarkable number of inspired architectural projects came to fruition, often with extraordinary speed. For talented and go-ahead architects and designers there were great opportunities during this period to see their ideas realized: clients and manufacturers had money to invest, and the public welcomed fresh ideas and were less prone to cling blindly to tradition. This was also the halcyon period of virtually full employment, and although wages in many countries were still low, most people did have more money in their pockets and, not surprisingly, were actively seeking material goods on which to spend it. By 1963, however, Sigfried Giedion had detected a change of mood:

> At the moment a certain confusion exists in contemporary architecture, as in painting; a kind of pause, even a kind of exhaustion. Everyone is aware of it. Fatigue is normally accompanied by uncertainty, what to do and where to go. Fatigue is the mother of indecision, opening the door to escapism, to superficialities of all kinds.

This feeling of exhaustion experienced by the architectural profession was an inevitable reaction against the frenzy of building activity that had been taking place since the war. Fired by the need to rehouse the population and to create new cities, towns and suburbs, architects and designers had been working in top gear for over fifteen years, with little time, it seemed, to pause and reflect on what was happening. By the early 1960s some were feeling burnt out, and out of their tiredness arose doubts and confusion. In 1953 the future had seemed so certain, and the way forward clear, but ten years later some architects had visibly begun to flag: it was time to take stock and review the situation.

In his new introduction to the revised 1963 edition of *Space, Time and Architecture*, Giedion voiced his hopes and fears for architecture in the 1960s, and endeavoured to identify the factors that were now playing a part in determining the future course of architecture. In the twenty years since its first publication, the geographical spread of modern architecture had broadened and it had become truly international. Not only were many of the pioneers of the European Modern Movement now active in the USA, but there had also been a flowering of native talent in North America itself. In Northern Europe, inspired by the achievements of Alvar Aalto during the 1930s, there had been a powerful surge of creativity in Finland, Denmark and Sweden from which had emerged the distinctive Scandinavian Modern design aesthetic of the 1950s. In Central Europe, Italy, newly freed from fascist dictatorship, had undergone a renaissance in the field of architecture and the applied arts. These, then, were the new design superpowers of the early 1950s.

The map of global activity became even more extensive during the course of the 1950s, however, as modern architecture became a truly 'International Style'. This was the name given to Modern Movement architecture during the 1930s by appreciative American admirers in the USA such as Philip Johnson, although at this time 'international' had simply meant selected parts of Europe and the USA. By the early

1960s, the Iron Curtain had been erected between Eastern and Western Europe, but global frontiers in other parts of the world were being eroded. Not only were leading European and North American architects working much further afield on major projects in Asia and the Middle East – Le Corbusier in Chandigarh, Edward Stone in Delhi and Walter Gropius in Baghdad, for example – but other countries, hitherto considered outside the mainstream of the Modern Movement, also began to create new identities for themselves. Japan, for example, buoyed up by Western aid after the war, developed at a phenomenal rate, resulting in the explosion of cities such as Tokyo, and the emergence of a school of talented, Le Corbusier-inspired, native architects headed by Kenzo Tange. In South America there were exciting developments in Mexico, led by the work of the Spanish-born Felix Candela; and in Brazil, as has been seen, Le Corbusier's protegé, Oscar Niemeyer, was appointed as the principal architect of the new capital city of Brasilia. During the 1930s young architects in these countries had looked to Europe for their inspiration but, by the late 1950s, they found that American and European architects were now marvelling over the achievements of their former disciples. The wheel had turned full circle and, as Giedion pointed out in 1963: 'contemporary architecture has become enriched, both in architecture and urbanism, by contributions from other countries from the rims of Western civilization, first from Finland and Brazil, lately from Japan.'

Although Giedion acknowledged the growing internationalism of architecture in the early 1960s to be a positive influence, internationalism was, at the same time, partly responsible for the disorientation that he had identified amongst architects working in the USA and Europe. While attention had been focused on the established architectural centres, a certain intensity of vision had been sustained, but now, as attention shifted to Asia, South America and elsewhere, this vision was less clear.

The future of 'Contemporary' architecture was by no means entirely in the hands of the protagonists themselves however: there were many external factors, including social trends, which were clearly beyond their direct control. As standards of living had risen during the 1950s, public expectations had risen also and this, ironically, was ultimately one of the reasons leading to the demise of the 'Contemporary' style. Although 'Contemporary' architecture was by no means austere, it did originally embody an element of restraint, which had arisen partly in response to the need to make the most of limited resources after the war. As a result, houses and apartments had become smaller than they had been before the war; building techniques had become less elaborate; and interiors had been furnished in a more modest way. As Western society became more affluent during the late 1950s and early 1960s, however, the demand for consumer goods grew, putting pressure on these ideals. It was hard to uphold a restrained approach to interior decoration in the face of growing consumer choice and mounting commercial pressure.

During the intense consumer boom of the early post-war period, manufacturers misguidedly came to believe that the market for their products would continue to grow indefinitely. Under these circumstances, since a levelling out of sales and profits was considered unacceptable, they engineered the concept of built-in obsolescence in order to maintain a turnover in the sales of their products. Consequently, fashion came increasingly to dominate the mass market, resulting in the introduction of novelty for its own sake. It was inevitable after the excesses of the consumer boom of the late 1950s and early 1960s that a reaction would eventually set in, and indeed this is what began to happen during the mid- to late 1960s. By the 1970s, with growing worldwide economic instability, rising unemployment and mounting inflation, the consumerist bubble had clearly burst. As a result, there was mounting public uncertainty about architecture and design: with less confidence in the future, people sought security in the past, leading to stylistic retrogression.

There were other reasons for the demise of the 'Contemporary' style, however, apart from economic factors. During the 1950s, as we have seen, 'Contemporary' design had become so popular in both the public and the domestic sectors that, by the early 1960s, it was no longer an expression of the avant-garde but of the establishment. This was clearly the case in the public sphere where instead of the watered-down classicism of the 1930s, new public buildings were usually treated as an aesthetic challenge, an opportunity to make a bold architectural statement in the 'Contemporary' style. This was also true to a large extent in the domestic sphere, where many new houses were built in the 'Contemporary' style, rather than, as previously, in a pastiche of an earlier design idiom. This was a source of considerable pride within the architectural profession at the time, as Wolf von Eckardt noted in 1961: 'If our architecture expresses the spirit of our times, our best churches and temples, our best houses, offices, schools, and other buildings, give cause for optimism.'

In the case of individually designed private houses, especially those where the architect worked closely with the client, the trend towards modernity proved to be an almost unqualified success. In the field of low-cost high-density public housing, however, where resources were more limited and pressure upon space was greater, the 'Contemporary' approach met with a mixed response. Unfortunately, it was in this field as the second generation of tower blocks began to be erected, designed by lesser architects than those who had created the originals, that some of the worst technical and aesthetic blunders were committed. Sadly, Britain, which had once led the way forward, now headed the decline. This coincided with a period when British local authorities and developers became over-confident about their ability to erect schemes on an increasingly large scale. Part of the difficulty arose from lack of central control, which allowed the greed of developers, the unscrupulousness of builders and the penny-pinching of local authorities to determine the level at which building standards were set. The larger the schemes – and during the 1960s housing and office developments grew enormously both in size and scale – the more gargantuan were the problems that resulted from their failure. This was also the case in many other European countries.

The resulting crisis of public confidence was perfectly understandable. Many of the grand Modernist theories about social engineering simply had not worked in practice. Furthermore, with the growth in unemployment and the increase in poverty-related social problems such as crime and drug abuse during the 1970s, the physical environment of many of the poorer housing estates served to exacerbate the situation. Because tenants felt increasingly isolated and there was little sense of community, they began to put the blame on the actual buildings. Physical problems with the structure of the buildings themselves, compounded by poor maintenance, added to the misery of life in a badly designed tower block. In Britain it is the legacy of problems associated with these second- or third-generation 'Contemporary' housing developments (mostly dating from the 1960s rather than the 1950s) that has given modern architecture such a bad name. The net result of this, however, is that twentieth-century architecture as a whole, including many worthy initiatives from the 1950s, has been seriously undervalued or unfairly abused in recent years.

In the wake of the disillusionment that set in during the 1970s, it is hard to recapture that sense of enthusiastic idealism in early post-war Europe. Today, it is easy to forget that during the 1950s, in the aftermath of the recent war, people had been quite content to allow themselves to be liberated from the past. It was only as the idealism of the period began to turn obviously sour during the second half of the 1960s that people began to react so fiercely against the 'Contemporary' style, as a reflection of this idealism. It is interesting to consider, therefore, what turned them against the idea, not just of the 'Contemporary' style of the 1950s, but of any sort of contemporary style *per se,* and what made people revert once again in the 1970s and 1980s to the ideals of the Cape Cod dream cottage and the half-timbered Tudorbethan villa that they had left behind during the 1930s.

One of the reasons why much post-war architecture has been so vilified must be the fact that the materials from which many public buildings were constructed have weathered so badly. This is particularly true of concrete. What architects and builders of the time had failed to appreciate was that to obtain the best results from using concrete, this material, like any other, had to be treated with respect for its inherent properties and qualities. And, like other materials, it required basic maintenance. Concrete was not a material from which successful results could be obtained without the necessary technical expertise and, as many architects were to learn, with hindsight, any cutting of corners could have a disastrous effect.

The mounting public disapproval of the 'Contemporary' style during the 1960s and 1970s was not, however, simply a matter of the rejection of modern materials. Changes of taste were important, but the rejection ultimately centred on ideas as well as aesthetics. As Giedion noted, 'Architecture is a highly complex activity; it works in the boundary area halfway between the regions of aesthetic feeling and practical doing. But this is just the reason why we look to it to give us the kind of surroundings that will express the life of our period.' During the 1950s the meanings and resonances carried by the 'Contemporary' style were the unselfconscious expression of a post-war *Zeitgeist.* The prevailing feeling was one of optimism: there was a firm belief that a better future was in store, and boundless confidence in the ability of scientific and technological progress to improve the standard of living and quality of life. During the 1960s, under the darkening cloud of the Cold War it became more difficult to maintain such

certainties. Consequently, the stylistic expression embodied in the design and architecture of the period began to seem much less straightforward, and the results were more confused and divided. Although during the 1960s modern design still prevailed, there was no longer the single, unified, internationally recognizable 'Contemporary' style, that there had been during the 1950s.

During the late 1960s a reaction set in as people began to question the idea of modernity as the way forward. This way of thinking began to influence not just the younger generation, but also those people who had set up home in the 1950s and who had initially embraced 'Contemporary' design with such relish. During the early post-war period, buoyed up by the endorsement given by the establishment and by the media to the 'Contemporary' style, the general public had built up the confidence to select the modern instead of the traditional. Now, however, they suffered a crisis of confidence as they saw both the aesthetics and ideals of this formative period of their lives being rejected. This caused many people to question their allegiance, and ultimately to abandon it in favour of something supposedly more socially acceptable. Thus, in Britain during the 1970s, came the revival of the neo-Georgian style of architecture, and a return to favour of all things Victorian, heralded in the interior design world by the rise of the firm of Laura Ashley. This led in the 1980s to the popularization of the pseudo-country house style, as the inhabitants of urban districts and suburbia began to express a hankering for life on a grander scale, ill-suited though this was to the size of their dwellings. The pattern was similar in other Western countries as people sought to escape from the present in an overly idealized view of the past. Eventually the public came so far along this path that they completely forgot that the idea of a 'Contemporary' style – an aesthetic reflecting the present rather than the past – had ever been conceivable.

Could there ever be a return to a 'Contemporary' style? In an age in which the eclectic raiding of historical ornament has been officially condoned both by the architectural fraternity, in the form of Post-Modernism, and by the general public, egged on by a cynical marketing campaign conducted by leading manufacturers of home furnishings, there seems little hope in the near future that a new 'Contemporary' style could emerge. Today, there is so little faith in the creativity of the present, and so great a reliance on pillaging the creativity of the past (and more recently of Third World cultures) that a change of direction seems highly unlikely.

Ironically, even 1950s design itself has been revived recently as a form of historical pastiche. To date, however, this revival has been largely restricted to American kitsch, the excesses of which have been further exaggerated by the selective memory inherent in design retrospection. The fact that kitsch – the down-market offshoot of the more high-brow 'Contemporary' style – has been taken up and popularized by today's youth does not, in itself, give reason for hope. The interest that this fad demonstrates is very superficial, and it has not fostered an understanding of the basic principles underlying the idea of a 'Contemporary' style, without which the original phenomenon cannot be appreciated. The current fascination for the 1950s largely reflects the stagnant condition of present-day manufacturing, which no longer

has the confidence to move forward, and is more than ever reliant on producing rehashes of the past.

Viewed in this light, the current resurgence of interest in 1950s design is largely evidence of the fact that manufacturing is now in an even deeper rut than it was in the 1970s, when revivalism first began to divert design from its natural forward course. A genuine 'Contemporary' style for the 1990s would be something completely new and original. Such was the impact of 'Contemporary' design when it first emerged after the war; at its height it was nothing less than the spontaneous expression of a feeling of creative and social liberation and represented a genuinely radical and revolutionary solution to the problems facing modern society.

The administrative core of Brasilia, the new capital of Brazil, was designed and built at lightning speed from 1956 to 1960. The chief planner for the city was Lucio Costa, while Oscar Niemeyer, a talented Brazilian disciple of Le Corbusier, was appointed as chief architect, and was responsible for the majority of the principal government buildings.
Opposite One of two rows of government buildings housing the various ministerial departments. The centre of Brasilia contains a striking mixture of organic and rectilinear architecture.
Above The Congress Buildings: the Secretariat is housed in the twin towers of the block to the right; the Chamber of the Lower House is located inside the sculptural cup-shaped building in the centre.
In October 1960, a mere six months after the Brazilian government had officially taken up residence in the new capital, it was revealed that the money with which the city had been built had largely originated from foreign loans, and the country was now saddled with debts on a colossal scale. Although undoubtedly impressive, therefore, the architectural achievements of Brasilia were overshadowed by the revelation that this incredibly ambitious project had brought the country to the verge of economic collapse.

glossary

Art Deco
Derived from the title of an epoch-making international exhibition held in Paris in 1925 called ·L'Éxposition des Arts Décoratifs et Industriels Modernes, this term was coined retrospectively to describe the style popular in Europe during the so-called Jazz Age from the mid-1920s to the late 1930s. Art Deco, which was described as *moderne* at the time, was inspired by the angular shapes and patterns of Cubism, but was frowned upon by the Modernists because of its apparent levity.

ball-and-spoke structures
Forms loosely based on scientific models of molecular structures composed of wooden or plastic balls connected by metal spokes or rods. Ball-and-spoke structures reflected the keen public interest in atomic imagery after World War II, and were very popular in Britain for furniture legs and the frames of household accessories such as magazine racks and plant stands.

Bauhaus
The legendary progressive German school of architecture and design founded by Walter Gropius in Weimar in 1919. The birthplace of the European Modern Movement, the Bauhaus included not only Gropius, but also Marcel Breuer and Ludwig Mies van der Rohe among its staff, and many teachers and pupils from the school played a major role as practitioners of and propagandists for *Modernism* in the USA both before and after World War II. In 1925 it transferred to Dessau, and in 1928 it moved to Berlin, before being closed by the Nazis in 1933.

Brutalism
Somewhat emotive term coined during the late 1950s to describe the use of exposed concrete in public buildings after World War II, a trend which gained much wider currency during the 1960s. Brutalist architects such as Le Corbusier and Kenzo Tange left the concrete exposed on both the exterior and the interior of their buildings, and did not even attempt to disguise the marks made by the planks of wood used as shutters in the casting process.

cantilevered
A technique used in buildings so that one of the upper floors projects horizontally out from the main exterior wall without any visible means of support. Normally achieved through the use of *reinforced concrete*. The term cantilevered is also used in the field of furniture to describe the type of chairs developed during the 1930s with no back legs, the back of the seat being supported by the strength of the curved tubular steel or laminated wood frame.

Case Study Houses
One-off experimental houses usually intended as prototypes for larger scale production, often sponsored by magazines of architecture or design, or by the manufacturer of a particular building product for promotional purposes. The most famous Case Study houses of the post-war period were those initiated in Los Angeles by *Arts and Architecture* magazine.

Cape Cod cottage style
Stylistically retrogressive houses popular in the USA during the 1920s and 1930s, modelled loosely on the type of New England cottages associated with Cape Cod, Massachusetts, adorned with pitched roofs and *tongue-and-groove cladding*. The nostalgic Cape Cod cottage style epitomized the popular ideal of the American dream house, but was strongly disapproved of by the Modernists. Its equivalent in Britain at the time was the *Tudorbethan style* suburban villa.

cladding
Thin layer of material used as surface infill between the main *post and beam* structural supports utilized in the construction of modern public buildings. Cladding materials adopted during the 1950s included glass in the form of *curtain walls*, and various different types of sheet metal. Later, prefabricated concrete panels were also widely used.

curtain wall
Walls made up almost entirely of windows. In a house, curtain walls take the form of large panes of glass replacing one or several walls of a room; in an office block, curtain-wall cladding involves encasing the framework of the building in a membrane of windows, thereby creating a glass tower.

eclecticism
Term used in the USA during the 1920s and 1930s to describe the over-reliance by commercial architects of the day on a wide range of historical revival sources for the adornment of domestic buildings. Examples of eclecticism include the *Cape Cod cottage style*, the Colonial style and the Spanish Colonial style.

Festival style
The name given to the style of modern architecture and design launched at, and afterwards associated with, the Festival of Britain, held on London's South Bank in 1951. The Royal Festival Hall provides a lasting reminder of the Festival style, while Ernest Race's Antelope chairs, designed as public seating for the Festival, characterize the light-hearted and somewhat whimsical nature of the genre.

fibreglass
Glass in fibrous form: a new material exploited during the 1950s both as a woven textile used for furnishing fabrics, and as a textured base material used to give substance and strength to moulded plastic seat furniture. Later also used for insulation in roofs and cavity walls.

foam rubber
Lightweight airy synthetic material produced as a by-product of the rubber industry. The introduction of foam rubber into the furniture industry after World War II revolutionized the method by which chairs and settees were upholstered, replacing springs and horsehair. The use of foam rubber was pioneered by the Italian furniture firm, Arflex, whose parent company was the car tyre manufacturer, Pirelli.

Formica
One of the trade names used to promote the new range of coloured and patterned plastic laminates which came on the market after World War II, Formica was widely adopted as the generic name for this product during the 1950s. Used extensively in kitchens and for table tops, plastic laminates similar to Formica were also produced in Britain by the firm of Warerite.

functionalism
Practical concept closely allied with the Modern Movement, whereby the success of a product or building was judged by its suitability for the task in hand, or, in the words of the British Design and Industries Association, its 'Fitness for Purpose'. Such thinking still had a strong influence on the work of architects and designers practising during the 1950s.

harlequin colour scheme
Multi-coloured or rainbow schemes favoured during the 1950s by manufacturers of ceramic, glass or plastic tableware and accessories. In a coffee set, for example, each saucer in the set might be glazed in a different colour. Closely allied to the concept of 'mix and match', whereby consumers could choose the precise colour 'combos' of their household goods from a wide range. Harlequin or Fiesta colour schemes were also applied to furniture, lighting and interior decoration.

International Style
Term first used by the American architect Philip Johnson in 1932 as the title for an exhibition held at the Museum of Modern Art in New York illustrating the work of the pioneer European Modern Movement architects during the 1920s. Called the International Style because it was thought to be a neutral style – a style without a style – and therefore equally applicable to any country.

kitsch
Term coined retrospectively to describe some of the more crass commercial mass-market developments in domestic design that took place during the later 1950s, arising out of the consumer boom and the explosion of popular culture towards the end of the decade. Sometimes mistakenly applied to designs that are simply innocently self-referential, such as kitchen wallpapers printed with patterns of fruit and vegetables.

mezzanine
Part-room or balcony inserted at a level mid-way between two main floors when the room below has a double height ceiling. A new feature introduced into both domestic architecture and public buildings during the 1950s.

moderne
Now usually referred to as Art Deco, moderne was the adjective actually used during the 1930s to describe the type of fashionable modern styling, such as *streamlining*, widely adopted in popular commercial architecture and design of the period. Moderne buildings and products had a superficial veneer of modernity, whereas Modernist design was deeply rooted in the concept of *functionalism*.

Modernism
A revolutionary new design movement which gathered strength during the first half of the twentieth century, introducing into architecture the concept of 'a style without a style', and shaking off the trammels of stylistic *eclecticism* and historical revivalism. Modernism represented design pared down to the bone. At its core was a belief in the centrality of functionalism, and a suspicion of ornament for its own sake because it served no obvious purpose. Hence the comment by Mies van der Rohe, 'Less is more'.

modular construction
A type of construction technique based on the idea of building using repeatable units of the same size. Applied during the late 1940s and 1950s to the design of schools and public housing with a view to achieving economies through mass-production and prefabrication.

New Towns
Influential British Government planning policy introduced immediately after World War II to tackle the housing shortage in the capital by establishing independent new population centres outside the boundaries of the city. Two of the earliest New Towns were Harlow in Essex and Stevenage in Hertfordshire. During the 1960s and 1970s New Towns were also developed in other areas of Britain.

open plan
Buildings with a minimum of interior walls and more flexible room divisions. A *Modernist* concept formulated during the 1920s and 1930s by the French architect, Le Corbusier, which was widely applied to the interior design of houses and the layout of offices during the 1950s and 1960s. Open planning was intended to make the most of limited space by 'freeing' the plan of buildings so that they were no longer partitioned into box-like cubicles.

organic
Adjective used to describe the new curvilinear sculptural aesthetic which made such a strong impact on the forms of 1950s architecture and design, from the roof of Eero Saarinen's bird-like TWA Airport Terminal in New York to the shapes of Scandinavian art glass. Organic design developed as a direct result of the influence of the biomorphic abstract sculpture of artists such as Jean Arp and Henry Moore during the 1930s.

post-and-beam construction
Method of building in which a grid-like framework of vertical posts and horizontal beams are first erected, then the walls are created with lightweight cladding. For office and apartment blocks the posts and beams were usually made from steel or reinforced concrete; for houses they were usually either steel or wood.

prefabrication
Type of construction relying on building components which have been wholly or partly pre-assembled in advance, sometimes off-site. The main types of prefabrication which evolved during the 1950s involved steel frames and pre-cast concrete ribs, blocks and panels.

rayon
British trade name for a synthetic yarn widely used during the 1950s as a substitute for more expensive natural furnishing fabric materials such as linen and cotton.

reinforced concrete
Concrete in which steel rods, bars or mesh have been embedded during the casting process. This combination of steel and concrete is still recognized as one of the strongest and most reliable building materials in engineering terms.

ribbon windows
Bands of small elongated rectangular windows running in a ribbon formation around the walls of factories and houses built during the 1930s. Ribbon windows, which were usually metal framed and set several panes deep, led ultimately to the *curtain wall cladding* systems of the 1950s.

room divider
An item of storage furniture, partly enclosed, which acted as a substitute wall within an *open plan* room, indicating the unofficial divisions between areas with different functions, such as the kitchen and the dining room.

Scandinavian Modern style
A distinctive new aesthetic that emerged in Finland, Denmark, Sweden and Norway during the late 1940s, which combined the clean lines and functionalism of *Modernism* with natural materials and high-quality craftsmanship. Scandinavian Modern design was sophisticated without being elitist and was characterized by fluid, elegant *organic* shapes.

shell structure
Large domed or arched roofs unsupported except at the perimeter, usually made of *reinforced concrete*, characteristically *organic* and curvilinear in form. Created during the 1950s for a wide range of industrial buildings such as airports, bus terminals, factories and sports stadia.

stackable
Refers to tableware designed to stack neatly and economically, thereby reducing the amount of space required for kitchen storage. Also, refers to chairs designed to be stacked when not in use.

steel decking
An American term used to describe ribbed sheet steel, described in Britain as corrugated iron. Primarily used as a roofing material, the folding of the metal increases its strength.

steel frame construction
Buildings constructed using a framework of steel *posts and beams*, often prefabricated and used as an alternative to *reinforced concrete*. Some architects, such as Craig Ellwood, left the steel frame exposed on both the interior and the exterior of their buildings, an aesthetic revived by high-tech architects of the 1970s and 1980s.

steel rod
Solid narrow gauge rods of steel, circular in cross section and bent to shape, used for the structural framework and legs of chairs, tables, sideboards and innumerable household accessories, such as plant stands and coat racks. Often exploited in Britain in the form of molecular *ball and spoke structures*.

storagewall system
A modular unit-based system of flexible multi-purpose domestic storage, mainly composed of cupboards and open shelves, but also incorporating features such as desk flaps and gramophone decks. Storagewall systems replaced traditional cupboards, dressers and sideboards in *open plan* living rooms, and could be either free-standing, in the form of room dividers, or literally built against a wall.

streamlining
The widespread adoption from the 1930s onwards of a type of *moderne* design styling taken from aerodynamic forms, such as planes, ships and sports cars. Streamlined domestic products, such as refrigerators, had rounded corners and were often decorated with a chromium-plated metal trim. Streamlined buildings were often funnel-shaped, reminiscent of ocean liners. Streamlining was associated with luxury and affluence and remained popular in the USA throughout the 1950s.

tongue and groove
A simple system of wooden panelling involving narrow vertical planks interlocking at the edges so that the projecting 'tongue' of one plank fits into the indented 'groove' of the next. Traditionally used as a form of insulation, and widely adopted during the 1950s as a form of *cladding* on the exterior of houses, and for decoration in Scandinavian interiors.

Tudorbethan style
Retrogressive eclectic architectural style popular in Britain during the 1920s and 1930s which combined fanciful elements of Tudor and Elizabethan buildings with the standard characteristics of modern brick-built suburban dwellings.

vinyl
A type of plastic widely exploited during the 1950s, which could be used both as a flooring material in the form of PVC in place of traditional linoleum, and as a wipe-clean plastic-coated upholstery fabric on kitchen chairs. Plasticized vinyl treatments were also applied to wallpapers during the 1950s to make them grease-proof and washable.

zoning
Type of domestic layout adopted in the USA during the 1950s whereby rooms intended for socializing and making noise were grouped together in one area of the house, and rooms intended for study and sleeping were physically isolated in another area. Zoned houses were usually single storey and tended to be designed with distinct wings or branches in an L or X formation.

collections of interest

The following museum collections and archives contain significant examples of 1950s design. As these collections are not always necessarily on view, however, it is essential to contact the organizations beforehand in order to check on current displays and access arrangements. Postal addresses are also given below.

Australia
Powerhouse Museum, Sydney, (general decorative arts)
   PO Box K346, Haymarket, NSW 2000

Canada
Musée des Arts Décoratifs, Montreal (general decorative arts)
   c/o David Hanks and Associates
   200 Park Avenue South, New York, USA

Denmark
Holmegaard Museum, Fensmark (glass)
   Holmegaards Glasvaerker, Fensmark, DK-4700, Naestved
Museum of Decorative Art, Copenhagen (general decorative arts)
   Det Danske Kunstindustrimuseum, Bredgade 68, 1260 Copenhagen K

Finland
Arabia Museum, Helsinki (ceramics)
   Hämeentie 135, SF-00560 Helsinki
Finnish Glass Museum, Riihimäki (glass)
   Suomen Lasimuseo, Tehtaankatu 23, Riihimäki
Iittala Glass Museum, Iittala (glass)
   Iittala Lasimuseo, Hackman Iittala Oy, SF-14500 Iittala
Museum of Applied Arts, Helsinki (general decorative arts)
   Taideteollisumuseo, Korkeavuorenkatu 32A, SF-00130 Helsinki

France
Centre Georges Pompidou, Paris (general decorative arts)
   F75191 Paris Cedex 04

Germany
Kunstgewerbemuseum, Berlin (general decorative arts)
   Tiergartenstrasse 6, D-1000 Berlin 30
Vitra Design Museum, Weil am Rhein (furniture)
   Charles Eames Strasse 1, D-7858 Weil-am-Rhein

Italy
Murano Glass Museum, Venice (glass)
   Casa Goldoni, Palazzo Mocenigo, Murano, Venice
Museo della Ceramica, Laveno Mombello (ceramics)
   Civica Raccolta di Terraglia, Palazzo Perabo, 21014,
   Laveno Mombello
Museo Internazionale delle Ceramiche, Faenza (ceramics)
   Via Campidori 2, 48018 Faenza

Sweden
Archive for Swedish Design, Kalmar (textiles)
   Kalmar Konstmuseum, Slöttsvagen 1D, 392 33 Kalmar
Gustavsberg Museum, Gustavsberg (ceramics)
   Gustavsberg Porslin, Box 310, 13400 Gustavsberg
Nationalmuseum, Stockholm (general decorative arts)
   Box 16176, S-10324 Stockholm

Orrefors Glass Museum, Orrefors (glass)
   Orrefors Glasbruk, S-380 40 Orrefors, Småland
Växjö Glass Museum, Växjö (glass),
   Smålands Museum, Box 102, 351 04 Växjö, Småland

UK
Broadfield House Glass Museum, Kingswinford (glass)
   Barnett Lane, Kingswinford, West Midlands DY6 9QA
Cannon Hall Museum, Barnsley (glass)
   Cawthorne, Barnsley, South Yorkshire S75 4AT
Design Museum, London (product design, furniture, textiles)
   Butlers Wharf, Shad Thames, London SE1 2YD
Manchester City Art Galleries, Manchester (ceramics, glass, furniture)
   Mosley Street, Manchester M2 3JL
Royal Museum of Scotland, Edinburgh (ceramics, glass)
   Chambers Street, Edinburgh E1 1UF
Science Museum, London (textiles, wallpapers, glass)
   Exhibition Road, South Kensington, London SW7 2DD
Silver Studio Archive, London (wallpapers)
   University of Middlesex, Bounds Green Road, London N11 2NQ
Stoke-on-Trent City Museum and Art Gallery, Hanley (ceramics)
   Bethesda Street, Hanley, Stoke-on-Trent, Staffordshire ST1 3DW
Turner Museum of Glass, Sheffield (glass)
   Sir Robert Hadfield Building, Mapin Court, Sheffield, S1 4DU
Victoria and Albert Museum, London (general decorative arts)
   Exhibition Road, South Kensington, London SW7 2RL
Warner Archive, Milton Keynes (textiles)
   Bradbourne Drive, Tillbrook, Milton Keynes MK7 8BE
Whitworth Art Gallery, Manchester (textiles, wallpapers)
   University of Manchester, Oxford Road, Manchester M15 6EF
Worshipful Company of Goldsmiths, London (silver)
   Goldsmiths Hall, Foster Lane, London EC2V 6BN

Another useful contact in the UK is the Twentieth Century Society, 70 Cowcross Street, London EC1M 6BP. This society is concerned with the preservation of and research into modern buildings, including those dating from the post-war period.

USA
Brooklyn Museum, New York (general decorative arts)
   200 Eastern Parkway, Brooklyn, New York NY 11238
Cooper Hewitt Museum, New York (general decorative arts)
   2 East Street, New York NY 10128
The Corning Museum of Glass, New York (glass),
   Museum Way, Corning NY 14830-2253
Metropolitan Museum of Art, New York (general decorative arts)
   5th Avenue at 82nd Street, New York NY 10028
Museum of Modern Art, New York (general decorative arts)
   11 West 53rd Street, New York NY 10019
Philadelphia Museum of Art, Philadelphia (general decorative arts)
   Benjamin Franklin Parkway, Box 7646, Philadelphia PA 19101

Due to the fact that most houses built during the 1950s are still privately owned, public access to the properties mentioned in this book is not usually possible except by prior arrangement with the owners. The public and commercial buildings listed below can, in most cases, be viewed from the exterior, access to view the interiors of private buildings being by prior arrangement with the owners. However, it is important to bear in mind that both the interiors and exteriors of many 1950s buildings have been significantly altered since they were originally designed.

Brazil
Brasilia
    (Lucio Costa and Oscar Niemeyer, 1956 onwards)

Denmark
Munkegård School
    Vangedevej, Gentofte, Copenhagen
    (Arne Jacobsen, 1952–6)
Søholm Terraced Houses
    Strandvejen, Klampenborg
    (Arne Jacobsen, 1949)

Finland
Chapel of the Technical University Otaniemi
    (Kaija and Heikki Siren, 1957)
House of Culture Sturenkatu
    Helsinki
    (Alvar Aalto, 1958)
Jyväskylä University and Teachers' College
    Seminaarinkatu, Jyväskylä
    (Alvar Aalto, 1957)
Knitted Goods Factory
    Hanko, Hopearanta
    (Viljo Revell, 1956)
Säynätsalo Town Hall
    Säynätsalo
    (Alvar Aalto, 1950–52)
Tapiola Garden City
    Tapiola
    (Aarne Ervi, 1956–62)

France
Cité de l'Abreuvoir
    Avenue Édouard Vaillant , Paris-Bobigny
    (Émile Aillaud, 1959)
Cité des Courtilières
    near Fort d'Aubervilliers, Paris-Pantin
    (Émile Aillaud, 1959)
Le Couvent Sainte Marie de la Tourette
    Éveux-sur-l'Arbresle
    (Le Corbusier, 1960)
Notre-Dame du Haut
    Ronchamp, Vosges
    (Le Corbusier, 1955)
Royan Covered Market
    Boulevard A Briand, Royan
    (Simon and Morisseau, c 1956)

Unesco Building
    Place de Fontenoy, Paris
    (Marcel Breuer, Bernard Zehrfuss and Pier Luigi Nervi, 1958)
Unité d'Habitation
    Boulevard Michelet, Marseilles
    (Le Corbusier, 1946–52)

Germany
Holy Cross Church
    Scharnhölzstrasse, Bottrop
    (Rudolf Schwarz, 1957)
Münster City Theatre
    Neubrückenstrasse, Münster
    (Harald Deilmann, Max von Hausen, Ortwin Rave and Werner Ruhnau, 1956)
St Albert
    Jägersfreuderstrasse, Saarbrücken
    (Gottfried Böhm, 1957)
St Anna, Annaplatz
    Düren
    (Rudolf Schwarz, 1956)
St Maria Königin
    Goethestrasse, Cologne-Marienburg
    (Dominikus Böhm, 1954)
St Maria Königin
    Kohlweg, Saarbrücken
    (Rudolph Schwarz, 1959)
St Michael
    Rotlinstrasse, Frankfurt
    (Rudolf Schwarz, 1954)

Ireland
Bus Terminal
    Beresford Place, Dublin
    (Michael Scott, 1953)

Italy
Olivetti Workers Dining and Recreation Hall
    Via Jervis, Ivrea
    (Ignazio Gardella, 1959)
Olivetti Workers Housing
    Canton Vesco, Ivrea
    (Nizzoli and Fiocchi, 1952)
Palazzo delle Esposizioni
    Corso Massimo d'Azeglio, Turin
    (Pier Luigi Nervi, 1948–50)
Palazzetto dello Sport
    Viale Tiziano, Rome
    (Pier Luigi Nervi, 1952)
Palazzo dello Sport
    Via Cristoforo, Colombo, Rome
    (Pier Luigi Nervi, 1960)
Pescia Covered Market
    Piazza del Mercato, Pescia
    (Brizzi, Gori, Gori, Ricci and Savioli, 1951)
Pirelli Building
    Piazza Duca d'Aosta, Milan
    (Gio Ponti and Pier Luigi Nervi, 1958–61)

Termini Station
Piazza dei Cinquecento, Rome
(Montuori and Calini, 1950)
Torre Velasca
Via Velasca, Milan
(BBPR, 1958)

Japan
Kurashiki City Hall
Okayama Prefecture
(Kenzo Tange, 1958–60)

Norway
United States Embassy
Drammensveien, Oslo
(Eero Saarinen, 1959)

Spain
Iglesia de la Coronación
Calle de Eulogio Serdan, Vitoria
(Miguel Fisac, 1960)
Instituto Técnico de la Construcción y del Cemento
Costillares, Madrid
(Eduardo Torroja, 1951)

Sweden
Baronbäckarna Housing
Hedgatan, Örebro
(Ekholm and White, 1957)
Cardboard Factory
Fors
(Ralph Erskine, 1953)
Fröslunda Centre
Skogstorpsvägen, Eskilstuna
(Jan Höjer and Sture Ljungqvist, 1957)
Nya Läroverk High School
Norra Esplanaden 2, Växjö
(Åke E Lindqvist, 1958)
Gröndal Apartments
Gröndalsvägen, Stockholm
(Backström and Reinius, 1947)
Orrefors Exhibition Hall and Museum
Orrefors Glassworks, Orrefors
(Bengt Gate, 1957)
Vällingby
Bergslagsvägen, Stockholm
(Sven Markelius and Stockholm Town Planning Office, 1953–9)

Switzerland
Apartments
Flamatt
(Atelier 5, 1957)
Bruder Klaus Church
Hardstrasse, Birsfelden, Basel
(Hermann Baur, 1958)

Electric Power Station
River Rhine, Birsfelden, Basel
(Hans Hofmann, 1956)
Freudenberg High School
Bederstrasse, Zurich
(Jacques Schader, 1960)
Geigy Paint Warehouse
Sandgrubenstrasse, Basel
(Burckhardt Office, 1959)
Siedlung Halen
Halenbrücke, Länggasse, Bern
(Atelier 5, 1961)

UK
Aboyne Lodge Infants School
St Albans, Hertfordshire
(Hertfordshire County Council Architects Department, 1949–50)
Boat House for Corpus Christi and Sidney Colleges
Victoria Avenue, Cambridge
(David Roberts, 1959)
Brasenose College (staircases L16–17)
Oxford
(Powell and Moya, 1961)
Churchill Gardens Housing Estate
Grosvenor Road, Pimlico, London SW1
(Powell and Moya, 1946–62)
Gatwick Airport
near Crawley, Surrey
(Yorke, Rosenberg and Mardall, 1958)
Golden Lane Housing
near Barbican, London EC1
(Chamberlin, Powell and Bon, 1961)
Harlow New Town, Harlow, Essex
(Frederick Gibberd, 1957 onwards)
Harvey Court Residential Building
Gonville and Caius College, West Road, Cambridge
(Sir Leslie Martin and Colin St John Wilson, 1961)
Hollings Faculty
University of Manchester, Wilmslow Road, Manchester
(Manchester City Council Architects Department, 1960)
Hurst Gunson Cooper Taber Seed Warehouse
Station Road, Witham, Essex
(Chamberlin, Powell and Bon, 1956)
Oxford Road Station
Oxford Road, Manchester
(Max Clendinning, 1960)
Park Hill Housing Estate,
Duke Street/South Street, Sheffield
(Sheffield Corporation Architects Department, 1960)
Plymouth Town Centre
(various architects, 1945 onwards)
Roehampton Housing Estate
Portsmouth Road, London SW15
(London County Council Architects Department, 1952–9)
Royal College of Physicians
St Andrew's Place, London NW1
(Denys Lasdun and Partners, 1960)

Royal Festival Hall
   South Bank, London SE1
   (London County Council Architects Department, 1951)
Rubber Factory,
   Waen Pond, Brynmawr, Brecknockshire, Wales
   (Architects' Co-Partnership and Ove Arup, 1951)
Secondary School
   Kings Lynn Road, Hunstanton, Norfolk
   (Peter and Alison Smithson, 1954)
St Catherine's College
   Oxford
   (Arne Jacobsen, 1964)
St Michael's Cathedral
   Cathedral Square, Coventry
   (Sir Basil Spence and Partners, 1962)
Summerswood Junior School
   Boreham Wood, Hertfordshire
   (Hertfordshire County Council Architects Department, 1951–2)
TUC Building
   Great Russell Street, London WC1
   (David Du R Aberdeen, 1957)
United States Embassy
   Grosvenor Square, London W1
   (Eero Saarinen, 1960)

USA
Apartment Houses
   860–880 Lake Shore Drive, Chicago, Illinois
   (Ludwig Mies van der Rohe, 1951)
Baker House
   Massachusetts Institute of Technology, Cambridge, Massachusetts
   (Alvar Aalto, 1948)
Christ Church Lutheran
   3244 34th Avenue South, Minneapolis, Minnesota
   (Eliel and Eero Saarinen, 1949)
Connecticut General Life Assurance Company Headquarters
   Hartford, Connecticut
   (Skidmore, Owings and Merrill, 1954–6)
Dulles International Airport
   Chantilly, Virginia
   (Eero Saarinen, 1961–2)
Equitable Savings and Loan Building (now Far West Federal Bank)
   421 SW Sixth Avenue, Portland, Oregon
   (Pietro Belluschi, 1948)
Fontainbleau Hotel
   4441 Collins Avenue, Miami Beach, Florida
   (Morris Lapidus, 1954)
General Motors Technical Centre
   6250 Chicago Road, Warren, Michigan
   (Eero Saarinen, 1951–7)
Inland Steel Building
   30 West Monroe Street, Chicago, Illinois
   (Skidmore, Owings and Merrill, 1956–8)
Jewish Community Centre Bath House (now Trenton Bath House)
   999 Lower Ferry Road, Ewing, New Jersey
   (Louis Kahn, 1955)

Kresge Auditorium and Church
   Massachusetts Institute of Technology, Cambridge, Massachusetts
   (Eero Saarinen, 1955)
Lever House
   390 Park Avenue, New York
   (Skidmore, Owings and Merrill, 1951–2)
Manufacturers Hanover Trust Company Bank (now Chemical Bank)
   Fifth Avenue, New York
   (Skidmore, Owings and Merrill, 1954)
Pepsi Cola World Headquarters (now Walt Disney Corporation)
   500 Park Avenue, New York
   (Skidmore, Owings and Merrill, 1959)
Seagram Building
   375 Park Avenue, New York
   (Ludwig Mies van der Rohe and Philip Johnson, 1958)
Solomon R Guggenheim Museum
   1071 Fifth Avenue, New York
   (Frank Lloyd Wright, 1959)
Space Needle
   219 Fourth Avenue North, Seattle, Washington
   (John Graham Associates, 1962)
S R Crown Hall
   Illinois Institute of Technology, State Street, Chicago, Illinois
   (Ludwig Mies van der Rohe, 1956)
TWA Terminal
   John F Kennedy International Airport New York
   (Eero Saarinen, 1962)
Union Tank Car Dome
   Brooklawn Road, Baton Rouge, Louisiana
   (R Buckminster Fuller, 1958)
United Nations Secretariat
   First Avenue, New York
   (Wallace K Harrison, Le Corbusier, Oscar Niemeyer and Sven Markelius, 1950)
United States Air Force Academy Chapel
   Colorado Springs, Colorado
   (Skidmore, Owings and Merrill, 1962)
Yale University Art Gallery Extension
   Yale University, Chapel Street, New Haven, Connecticut
   (Louis Kahn, 1953)

selected bibliography

1950s Architecture

Aloi, Roberto, *Nuove Architetture a Milano* (Hoepli, Milan, 1959)

Arkitektens Forlag, *Contemporary Danish Architecture* (Arkitektens Forlag, Copenhagen, 1958)

Banham, Reyner, *Theory and Design in the First Machine Age* (The Architectural Press, London, 1960)

Banham, Reyner, *Guide to Modern Architecture* (The Architectural Press, London, 1962)

Banham, Reyner, *Los Angeles: The Architecture of Four Ecologies* (Harper and Row, New York, 1971)

Becker and Schlote, *Contemporary Finnish Houses* (Kramer Verlag, Stuttgart, 1958)

Blake, Peter, *Master Builders* (Gollancz, London, 1960)

Blake, Peter, *Frank Lloyd Wright – Architecture and Space* (Penguin, Harmondsworth, 1960)

Blake, Peter, *Mies van der Rohe* (Penguin, Harmondsworth, 1963)

Boyd, Robin, *Kenzo Tange* (George Braziller, New York, 1962)

Cantacuzino, Sherban, *Modern Houses of the World* (Studio Vista, London, 1964)

Cantacuzino, Sherban, *Great Modern Architecture* (Studio Vista, London, 1966)

Carrington, Noel, *Design and Decoration in the Home* (Batsford, London, 1952)

Carrington, Noel, *Colour and Pattern in the Home* (Batsford, London, 1954)

Choay, Françoise, *Le Corbusier* (George Braziller, New York, 1960)

Clark, Robert Judson, ed, *Design in America – The Cranbrook Vision 1925–1950* (Harry N Abrams, New York, 1983)

Crosby, Theo, and Pidgeon, Monica, *An Anthology of Houses* (Batsford, London, 1960)

Dannatt, Trevor, *Modern Architecture in Britain* (Batsford, London, 1959)

Drexler, Arthur, *Ludwig Mies van der Rohe* (George Braziller, New York, 1960)

Drexler, Arthur, and Hine, Thomas, *The Architecture of Richard Neutra: From International Style to California Modern* (The Metropolitan Museum of Art, New York, 1982)

Von Eckardt, Wolf, ed, *Mid-Century Architecture in America* (The John Hopkins Press, Baltimore, 1961)

Faber, T, *Arne Jacobsen* (Gerd Hatje, Stuttgart, 1964)

Fitch, J M, *Walter Gropius* (George Braziller, New York, 1960)

Gable, Emerson, ed, *A Treasury of Contemporary Houses* (F W Dodge Corporation, New York, 1954)

Gardiner, Stephen, *Le Corbusier* (Fontana/Collins, London, 1974)

Gibberd, Frederick, *Town Design* (The Architectural Press, London, 1953)

Giedion, Sigfried, *Walter Gropius* (The Architectural Press, London, 1954)

Giedion, Sigfried, *Space, Time and Architecture* (Harvard University Press, Cambridge, MA, 1963 [4th edition])

Gilchrist Wilson, J, *Exposed Concrete Finishes* (C R Books, London, 1964, 2 vols)

Goldstein, Barbara, and McCoy, Esther, *Guide to US Architecture 1940–1980* (Arts and Architecture Press, Santa Monica, 1982)

Gropius, Walter, *The New Architecture and the Bauhaus* (Faber and Faber, London, 1935)

Gutheim, Frederick, *Alvar Aalto* (George Braziller, New York, 1960)

Hammond, Peter, *Liturgy and Architecture* (Barrie and Rockcliff, London, 1960)

Hammond, Peter, ed, *Towards a Church Architecture* (The Architectural Press, London, 1962)

Harling, Robert, *The House and Garden Book of Small Houses* (Condé Nast, London, 1961)

Hatje, Hoffmann and Kasper, *New German Architecture* (The Architectural Press, London, 1956)

Hine, Thomas, *Richard Neutra and the Search for Modern Architecture* (Oxford University Press, New York, 1982)

Hitchcock, Henry Russell, *Architecture: Nineteenth and Twentieth Centuries* (Penguin, Harmondsworth, 1958)

Hitchcock, Henry Russell, and Johnson, Philip C, *The International Style* (The Museum of Modern Art, New York, 1932)

Huxtable, Ada Louise, *Pier Luigi Nervi* (Mayflower, London, 1960)

Joedicke, Jurgen, *A History of Modern Architecture* (translated by James C Palmer) (The Architectural Press, London, 1959)

Joedicke, Jurgen, *Architecture Since 1945 – Sources and Directions* (Pall Mall Press, London, 1969)

Johnson, Philip C, *Mies van der Rohe* (The Museum of Modern Art, New York, 1947)

Jones, Cranston, *Architecture Today and Tomorrow* (McGraw-Hill, New York, 1961)

Kaplan, Sam Hall, *LA Lost and Found: An Architectural History of Los Angeles* (Crown Publishers, New York, 1987)

Kidder Smith, G E, *Switzerland Builds* (The Architectural Press, London, 1950)

Kidder Smith, G E, *Italy Builds* (The Architectural Press, London, 1954)

Kidder Smith, G E, *Sweden Builds* (The Architectural Press, London, 1957 [2nd edition])

Kidder Smith, G E, *The New Architecture of Europe* (Prentice-Hall, London, 1962)

Landau, Royston, *New Directions in British Architecture* (Studio Vista, London, 1968)

Le Corbusier, *Oeuvres Completes 1910–1957* (Girsberger, Zurich, 1953)

Lerner, Mel, Rolfes, Herbert, and Zim, Larry, *The World of Tomorrow – The 1939 New York World's Fair* (Harper and Row, New York, 1988)

McCallum, Ian, *Architecture USA* (The Architectural Press, London, 1959)

McCoy, Esther, *Craig Ellwood* (Walker and Co, New York, 1968)

McCoy, Esther, *Case Study Houses 1945–1962* (Hennessey and Ingalls, Los Angeles, 1977 (2nd edition))

McCoy, Esther, *The Second Generation* (Gibbs M Smith, Salt Lake City, 1984)

Maguire, Robert, and Murray, Keith, *Modern Churches of the World* (Studio Vista, London, 1965)

Mills, Edward D, *The Modern Church* (The Architectural Press, London, 1956)

Mock, Elizabeth B, *If You Want To Build A House* (Museum of Modern Art, New York, 1946)

Murray, Peter, and Trombley, Stephen, *Modern British Architecture Since 1945* (RIBA, London, 1984)

Nairn, Ian, *Outrage* (The Architectural Press, London, 1955)

Nairn, Ian, ed, *Counter Attack Against Subtopia* (The Architectural Press, London, 1956)

Nelson, George, and Wright, Henry, *Tomorrow's House – A Complete Guide for the Homebuilder* (Simon and Schuster, New York, 1945)

Nervi, Pier Luigi, *Structures* (F W Dodge Corporation, New York, 1956)

Neutra, Richard, *Survival Through Design* (Oxford University Press, New York, 1954)

O'Callaghan, Judith, ed, *The Australian Dream – Design of the Fifties* (Powerhouse Museum, Sydney, 1993)

Pagani, C, *Italy's Architecture Today* (Hoepli, Milan, 1955)

Pederson, Johan, *Arne Jacobsen* (Arkitektens Forlag, Copenhagen, 1954)

Penn, Colin, *Houses of To-day – A Practical Guide* (Batsford, London, 1954)

Peter, John, *Masters of Modern Architecture* (Batsford, London, 1959)

Pevsner, Nikolaus, *Pioneers of Modern Design* (Penguin, Harmondsworth, 1960)

Ponti, L L, *Gio Ponti* (Thames and Hudson, London, 1990)

Pulos, A J, *The American Design Adventure* (MIT, Cambridge, MA, 1988)

Richards, J M, *An Introduction to Modern Architecture* (Penguin, Harmondsworth, 1959)

Rogers, Ernesto N, *The Works of Pier Nervi* (The Architectural Press, London, 1958)

Saarinen, Eero, *Eero Saarinen on his Work* (Yale University Press, New Haven, 1962)

Scully, Vincent, *Frank Lloyd Wright* (George Braziller, New York, 1960)

Schwarz, Rudolf, *The Church Incarnate: The Sacred Nature of Christian Architecture*, (translated by Cynthia Harris) (Henry Regnery Co, Chicago, 1958)

Smith, Elizabeth A T, ed, *Blueprints for Modern Living – History and Legacy of the Case Study Houses* (MIT Press, Cambridge, MA, 1989)

Smith, Trevor, *The Daily Mail Book of House Plans* (Associated Newspapers, London, 1956)

Skidmore, Owings and Merrill, *Architecture of Skidmore, Owings and Merrill, 1950–62* (The Architectural Press, London, 1963)

Spade, Rupert, *Oscar Niemeyer* (Thames and Hudson, London, 1971)

Spade, Rupert, *Eero Saarinen* (Thames and Hudson, London, 1971)

Tempel, Egon, *New Finnish Architecture* (The Architectural Press, London, 1968)

Temko, Allan, *Eero Saarinen* (George Braziller, New York, 1962)

Torroja, Eduardo, *The Structures of Eduardo Torroja* (F W Dodge Corporation, New York, 1958)

Werner, Bruno E, *Modern Architecture in Germany* (Bruckmann, Munich, 1956)

Yorke, F R S, *The Modern House* (The Architectural Press, London, 1948 [6th edition, revised])

Yorke, F R S, *Modern Flats* (The Architectural Press, London, 1958)

1950s Design

Adlerova, A, *Masters of Czech Glass 1945–1965* (Dan Klein, London, 1983)

Aloi, Roberto, *Esempi di Arredamento Moderno di Tutto il Mondo*, 6 vols (Hoepli, Milan, 1950–53)

Aloi, Roberto, *Esempi di Decorazione Moderna di Tutto il Mondo: Gioelli, Sbalzi, Argenti* (Hoepli, Milan, 1954)

Aloi, Roberto, *Esempi di Arredamento Moderno di Tutto il Mondo: Tavoli, Tavolini, Carelli* (Hoepli, Milan, 1955)

Aloi, Roberto, *Esempi di Decorazione Moderna di Tutto il Mondo: Vetri d'Oggi* (Hoepli, Milan, 1955)

Aloi, Roberto, *Mobili Tipo*, 6 vols (Hoepli, Milan, 1956)

Aloi, Roberto, *Esempi di Arredamento Moderno di Tutto il Mondo: Sedie, Poltrone, Divani* (Hoepli, Milan, 1957)

Arceneaux, M, *Atomic Age: Art and Design of the Fifties* (Troubadour, San Francisco, 1975)

Arnošt, F, Drahotova, O, and Langhamer, A, *Bohemian Glass* (Crystalex, Nový Bor, 1985)

Aveline, M, ed, *La Verrerie Européenne des Années 50* (Musées de Marseilles, Marseilles, 1988)

Bangert, A, *Der Stil der 50er Jahre* (Band 2, Design und Kunsthandverk, Heyne Buch, Munich, 1983)

Bangert, A, *Die 50er Jahre – Mobel und Ambiente, Design und Kunsthandwerk* (Munich, 1990)

Banham, Mary, and Hillier, Bevis, *Festival of Britain – A Tonic to the Nation* (Thames and Hudson, London, 1976)

Baroni, D, *Arflex '51 '81* (Arflex, Milan, 1981)

Baroni, D, *L'Oggetto Lampada – Forma e Funzione* (Electa, Milan, 1981)

Beard, Geoffrey, *Modern Glass* (Studio Vista, London, 1968)

Besetti, C, *Forme Nuove in Italia* (Rome, 1957)

Bill, Max, *Die Gute Form* (Zurich, 1949)

Bill, Max, *Form*, (Werner, Basel, 1952)

Von Bock, G Reineking, *Keramik des 20 Jahrhunderts in Deutschland* (Munich, 1979)

Bodelsen, M, *Dansk Keramik* (Glyndendal, Copenhagen, 1960)

Boj, A, *Glas Av Monica Bratt* (Bellmansmiljo, 1981)

Borngräber, Christian, *Stilnovo: Design in den 50er Jahre* (Fricke, Frankfurt, 1979)

Burns, M, and Di Bonis, L, *50's Homestyle* (Thames and Hudson, London, 1988)

Caplan, R, *The Design of Herman Miller* (Whitney Library of Design, New York, 1976)

Castelli, V, ed, *Il Design Italiano Degli Anni '50* (IGIS, Milan, 1981)

Centre Georges Pompidou, *Les Années Cinquantes* (Centre Georges Pompidou, Paris, 1988)

Centre Georges Pompidou, *Mollino –L'Étrange Univers de l'Architecte Carlo Mollino* (Centre Georges Pompidou, Paris, 1989)

Christopher, J and R, *Design for Modern Marriage* (Hurst and Blackett, London, 1958)

Clarke, G, and Hughto, M, *A Century of Ceramics in the United States 1878–1978* (E P Dutton, New York, 1979)

Compagnia Nazionale Artigiana, *Italian Contemporary Design* (Italian Institute, London, 1955)

Compagnia Nazionale Artigiana, *Modern Italian Design* (Manchester City Art Galleries, Manchester, 1956)

Conway, Hazel, *Ernest Race* (Design Council, London, 1982)

Cooke, F, *Glass – Twentieth Century Design* (Bell and Hyman, London, 1986)

Corning Museum of Glass, *Glass 1959* (Corning Museum, New York, 1959)

Council of Industrial Design, *Design in the Festival* (HMSO, London, 1951)

Dal Fabbro, Mario, *Furniture for Modern Interiors* (Reinhold, New York, 1954)

Deboni, F, *Venini Glass* (Basel, 1990)

Detroit Institute of Arts, *Design in America: The Cranbrook Vision* (Harry Abrams, New York, 1983)

Ditzel, Nanna and Jorgen, eds, *Danish Chairs* (Høst, Copenhagen, 1954)

Domus, *Quaderni di Domus: Libri Nella Casa – Camini – Illuminazione – Tavoli – Letti* (Domus, Milan, 1945–51)

Domus, *Vetri alla 9a Triennale* (Domus, Milan, 1952)

Dorigato, A, *Ercole Barovier 1889–1974* (Venice, 1989)

Drexler, A, and Daniel, G, *Introduction to Twentieth Century Design from the Collection of the Museum of Modern Art* (Museum of Modern Art, New York, 1959)

Drexler, A, *Charles Eames Furniture from the Design Collection* (Museum of Modern Art, New York, 1973)

Eatwell, Ann, *Susie Cooper Productions* (Victoria and Albert Museum, London, 1987)

Eidelberg, Martin, *Eva Zeisel: Designer for Industry* (Le Château Dufresne, Montreal, 1984)

Eidelberg, Martin, ed, *Design 1935–1965: What Modern Was* (Le Château Dufresne, Montreal, 1991)

Eilmann, H, and Votteler, A, *Wege Zum Modernen Möbel – 100 Jahre Designgeschichte* (Stuttgart, 1989)

Eilmann, H, Fandrey, C, Marquard, C, Reiser, R, and Votteler, A, *Möbeldesign – Made in Germany* (Stuttgart, 1985)

Ericsson, A M, *Arthur Percy – Konstnar Och Formgivare* (Nordiska Museum, Stockholm, 1980)

Erlhoff, M, *Designed in Germany since 1949* (Rat für Formgebung, Munich, 1990)

Farr, Michael, *Design in British Industry: A Mid-Century Survey* (Cambridge University Press, Cambridge, 1955)

Fehrman, C and K, *Postwar Interior Design 1945–1960* (Van Nostrand Reinhold, New York, 1987)

Fischer, W, and Sembach, K-J, *Seit Langem Bewährt – Klassische Produkte Moderner Formgebung* (Munich, 1968)

Frey, G, *Schweizer Möbeldesign 1927–1984* (Benteli, Lausanne, 1986)

Funkat, W, *Kunsthandwerk in der Deutschen Demokratischen Republik*, (Berlin, 1970)

Gandy, C D, and Zimmermann-Stidham, S, *Contemporary Classics: Furniture of the Masters* (McGraw-Hill, New York, 1981)

Garner, Philippe *Contemporary Decorative Arts: 1940 to the Present Day* (Quarto, London, 1980)

selected bibliography

Garner, Philippe, *Twentieth Century Furniture* (Van Nostrand Reinhold, New York, 1980)

Gasparetto, A, *Il Vetro di Murano* (Venice, 1958)

Gerber, D, *Wohnen in unserer Zeit – Wohnungsgestaltung der Interbau* (Darmstadt, 1957)

Germanisches Nationalmuseum, *Cuno Fischer* (Germanisches Nationalmuseum, Nuremberg, 1984)

Goodden, S, *A History of Heal's* (Heal and Son, London, 1984)

Gorlich, G G, *So Wohnt Man Heute – Form und Farbe in der Modernen Wohnungsgestaltung* (Ravensburg, 1962)

Gramigna, G, *1950–1980 Repertory: Pictures and Ideas Regarding the History of Italian Furniture* (Arnoldo Mondadori, Milan, 1985)

Grandison, William, and Kenna, Richard, *Somethin' Else: 50s Life and Style* (Richard Drew, Glasgow, 1989)

Grassi, A, and Pansera, A, *Atlante del Design Italiano, 1940–1980* (Milan, 1980)

Gregotti, V, *Il Designo del Prodotto Industriale Italiano, Italia 1860-1980* (Electa, Milan, 1982)

Greenberg, Carla, *Mid-Century Modern* (Thames and Hudson, London, 1984)

Gronert V, and Ricke, H, *Glass in Schweden 1915–1960* (Prestel-Verlag, Munich, 1986)

Hald, A, and Skawonius, S E, *Contemporary Swedish Design* (Nordisk-Rotogravyr, Stockholm, 1957)

Hamilton, J, and Oman, C, *Wallpaper – A History and Illustrated Catalogue of the Collection in the Victoria and Albert Museum* (Sotheby's, London, 1982)

Hannah, Frances, *Ceramics – Twentieth Century Design* (Bell and Hyman, London, 1986)

Harris, Jennifer, *Lucienne Day – A Career in Design* (Whitworth Art Gallery, Manchester, 1993)

Hatje, Gerd, ed, *New Furniture* (Niggli, Teufen, 1952–9)

Hatje, Gerd, *So Wohnen* (Band 6, Mobel, Stuttgart, 1962)

Hawkins, Jennifer, *The Poole Potteries* (Barrie and Jenkins, London, 1980)

Haycraft, J, *Finnish Jewellery and Silverware* (Helsinki, 1960)

Heiremans, M, *Murano Glas 1945–1970* (M Heiremans, Antwerp, 1989)

Hennessey, W J, *Russel Wright, American Designer* (Massachusetts Institute of Technology, Cambridge, MA, 1983)

Herlitz-Gezelius, A M, *Orrefors – A Swedish Glassplant* (Atlantis, Stockholm, 1986)

Hiesinger, K B, and Marcus, G H, *Design Since 1945* (Philadelphia Museum of Art, Philadelphia, 1984)

Hillier, Bevis, *Austerity/Binge* (Studio Vista, London, 1975)

Hinchcliffe, Frances, *Fifties Furnishing Fabrics* (Victoria and Albert Museum, London, 1989)

Hine, Thomas, *Populuxe* (Alfred Knopf, New York, 1986)

Hiort, Esben, *Modern Danish Silver* (Zwemmer, London, 1954)

Hiort, Esben, *Modern Dansk Keramik* (Jul Gjellerups, Copenhagen, 1955)

Hiort, Esben, *Modern Dänische Möbelkunst* (Stuttgart, 1956)

Hirzel, S, *Kunsthandwerk und Manufaktur in Deutschland seit 1945* (Berlin, 1953)

Hokkaido Museum of Art, *Lyricism of Modern Design: Swedish Glass 1900–1970* (Hokkaido Museum of Art, Sapporo, 1992)

Hölmer, Gunnel, *Från Boda Till New York – Konstnaren Erik Höglund* (Carlsson, Stockholm, 1986)

Hölmer, Gunnel, *Paul Kedelv – Från Trä Till Glas* (Smålands Museum, Växjö, 1990)

Horn, Richard, *Fifties Style: Then and Now* (Columbus, London, 1975)

Hoskins, Lesley, Pinney, Mark, and Turner, Mark, *A Popular Art – British Wallpapers 1930–1960* (Silver Studio Archive, Middlesex, 1989)

Huldt, A H, and Stavenow, A, *Design in Sweden* (Gothia, Stockholm, 1961)

Huldt, A H, *Nils Landberg* (Kalmar Konstmuseum, Kalmar, 1986)

Hughes, Graham, *Modern Silver throughout the World 1880–1967* (Studio Vista, London, 1967)

Iittala Glass Museum, *Iittala in the Triennales* (Iittala Glass Museum, Iittala, 1987)

Jackson, Lesley, *The New Look – Design in the Fifties* (Thames and Hudson, London, 1991)

Jalk, Grete, *The Copenhagen Cabinetmakers' Guild Exhibitions*, vols 3–4, 1947–66 (Technologisk Instituts Forlag, Copenhagen, 1987)

Karlsen, A, Silicath, B, and Utzon-Frank, M, *Contemporary Danish Design* (Danish Society of Arts and Crafts and Industrial Design, Copenhagen, 1960)

Karlsen, A, *Mobler Tegnet af Borge Mogensen* (Arkitektens Forlag, Copenhagen, 1982)

Katzenbach, L and W, *The Practical Book of American Wallpapers* (J B Lippincott Co, Philadelphia, 1951)

Kaufmann, Edgar, *Prize Designs for Modern Furniture from the International Competition for Low-Cost Furniture Design* (Museum of Modern Art, New York, 1950)

Kestner Museum, *Venini Murano – Orrefors Schweden – Glas* (Kestner Museum, Hannover, 1957)

Kestner Museum, *Rosenthal – Hundert Jahre Porzellan* (Kestner Museum, Hannover, 1982)

Klatt, J, and Staeffler, G, *Braun und Design Collection – Braun Produkte von 1955 bis Heute* (Hamburg, 1990)

Koch, A, *Dekorationsstoffe Tappen/Teppiche* (Koch, Stuttgart, 1953)

Koivisto, Kaisa, and Niemisto, K, *The Modern Spirit – Glass from Finland* (Finnish Glass Museum, Riihimäki, 1985)

Koivisto, Kaisa and Matiskainen, Heikki, eds, *Gunnel Nyman – Glass Research IV* (Finnish Glass Museum, Riihimäki, 1987)

Koivisto, Kaisa, *Fran Modern till Nutid – Glas Fran Finland 1920–1990* (Finnish Glass Museum, Riihimäki, 1992)

Kulturzentrum, Ludwigsburg, *Fifty Fifty: Formen und Farben der 50er Jahre* (Kultnrzentrum, Ludwigsburg, 1987)

Kumela, M, Paatero, K, and Rissanen, K, *Arabia* (Oy Wartsila AB, Helsinki, 1987)

Kunstgewerbemuseum, Zurich, *Finnisches Kunstgewerbe* (Kunstgewerbemuseum, Zurich, 1951)

Kunstgewerbemuseum, Zurich, *Angewandte, Kunst aus Danemark* (Kunstgewerbemuseum, Zurich, 1954)

Kunstgewerbemuseum, Zurich, *Industrieware von Wilhelm Wagenfeld* (Kunstgewerbemuseum, Zurich, 1960)

Larrabee, E, and Vignelli, M, *Knoll Design* (Harry N Abrams, New York, 1981)

Larsen, Jack Lenor, *Jack Lenor Larsen: 30 Years of Creative Textiles* (Jack Lenor Larsen, New York, 1981)

Larson, L, *Lighting and its Design* (Whitney Library of Design, New York, 1964)

Lassen, E, and Schluter, Mogens, *Dansk Glas 1926-1985* (Arnold Busck, Copenhagen, 1987)

Laszlo, A, *Svenskt Konstglas* (Sellin and Blomqvist, Stockholm, 1989)

Lindinger, H, *Hochschule für Gestaltung Ulm – Die Moral der Gegenstände* (Ernst & Sohn, Berlin, 1987)

Lindinger, H, *Ulm Design – The Morality of Objects – Hochschule fur Gestaltung Ulm 1953–1958* (MIT Press, Cambridge, MA, 1991)

Loffelhardt, H, *Gedanken und Bilder sur Austellung 'Wie Wohnen'* (Stuttgart and Karlsruhe, 1949–50)

Lyall, S, *Hille: 75 Years of British Furniture* (Victoria and Albert Museum, London, 1984)

Lutteman, Helena Dahlbäck, *Stig Lindberg – Formgivare* (Nationalmuseum, Stockholm, 1982)

selected bibliography

Lutteman, Helena Dahlbäck, *The Lunning Prize* (Nationalmuseum, Stockholm, 1986)

MacDonald, Sally, and Porter, Julia, *Putting on the Style: Setting Up Home in the 1950s* (Geffrye Museum, London, 1990)

MacFadden, David Revere, ed, *Scandinavian Modern Design* (Cooper Hewitt Museum, New York, 1982)

Maenz, P, *Die 50er Jahre: Formen Eines Jahrzehnts* (Gerd Hatje, Stuttgart, 1978)

Mäki, O, *Finnish Design Today* (Söderström, Helsinki, 1954)

Malmö Museum, *Gunnar Nylund* (Malmö Museum, Malmö, 1973)

Mang, K, *History of Modern Furniture* (Harry Abrams, New York, 1978)

Manske, B, and Scholz, G, *Täglich in der Hand – Industrieform von Wilhelm Wagenfeld aus Sechs Jahrzehnten* (Bremen, 1987)

Marelli, E, *Lino Sabattini: Intimations and Craftsmanship* (Mariano Commense, 1979)

Mariacher, G, *Vetri di Murano* (Bestetti, Milan, 1967)

Martin, E, and Sydhoff, B, *Swedish Textile Art* (Liberforlag, Stockholm, 1980)

Miestamo, R, *The Form and Substance of Finnish Furniture* (Asko, Lahti, 1980)

Miller, R Craig, *Modern Design in the Metropolitan Museum of Art* (Metropolitan Museum of Art, New York, 1990)

Møller, H S, *Danish Design* (Rhodos, Copenhagen, 1975)

Møller, V S, *Henning Koppel* (Carlsberg Foundation, Copenhagen, 1965)

Mundt, Barbara, *Produkt-Design 1900–1990 – Eine Auswahl* (Kunstgewerbemuseum, Berlin, 1991)

Mundt, Barbara, *Interieur und Design in Deutschland 1945–1960* (Kunstgewerbemuseum, Berlin, 1993)

Musée Curtius, *Aspects de la Verrerie Contemporaine* (Musée Curtius, Liège, 1958)

Musée des Arts Décoratifs, Bordeaux, *Jean Prouvé – Meubles* (Musée des Arts Décoratifs, Bordeaux, 1989)

Museum of Applied Arts, Helsinki, *Timo Sarpaneva: Sculpture in Vetro* (Museum of Applied Arts, Helsinki, 1987)

Museum of Decorative Arts, Copenhagen, *Hans J Wegner en Stolemager* (Museum of Decorative Arts, Copenhagen, 1989)

Museum of Modern Art, New York, *Textiles USA* (Museum of Modern Art, New York, 1956)

Museum of Modern Art, New York, *Alvar Aalto: Furniture and Glass* (Museum of Modern Art, New York, 1984)

Museum Villa Stuck, *Die Funfziger: Stilkonturen Eines Jahrzehnts* (Museum Villa Stuck, Munich, 1984)

Nationalmuseum, Stockholm, *Gustavsberg 150ar* (Nationalmuseum, Stockholm, 1975)

Nationalmuseum, Stockholm, *Dansk 50 Tal* (Nationalmuseum, Stockholm, 1981)

Nationalmuseum, Stockholm, *Astrid Sampe – Swedish Industrial Textiles* (Nationalmuseum, Stockholm, 1984)

Niblett, Kathy, *Dynamic Design – The British Pottery Industry 1940–1980* (Stoke-on-Trent City Museum and Art Gallery, Stoke-on-Trent, 1990)

Nelson, George, *Chairs* (Whitney Publications, New York, 1953)

Nelson, George, *Storage* (Whitney Publications, New York, 1954)

Nelson, George, *Living Spaces* (Whitney Publications, New York, 1952)

Neuhart, J and M, and Eames, Ray, *Eames Design* (Thames and Hudson, London, 1989)

Neuwith, Waltraud, *Italian Glass 1950–1960* (Waltraud Neuwith, Vienna, 1987)

Niilonen, K, *Finnish Glass* (Kustannusonakeyhtio Tanmi, Helsinki, 1967)

Noyes, Eliot, *Organic Design in Home Furnishings* (Museum of Modern Art, New York, 1941)

Opie, Jennifer, *Scandinavia – Ceramics and Glass in the Twentieth Century* (Victoria and Albert Museum, London, 1989)

Ornamo, *Suomen Taideteollissutta* (Ornamo, Helsingfors, 1955)

Ornamo, *The Ornamo Book of Finnish Design* (Ornamo, Helsinki, 1962)

Pansera, Anty, *Design e Design* (Compasso d'Oro) (Milan, 1979)

Pearce, Christopher, *Fifties Sourcebook* (Quarto, London, 1990)

Peat, Alan, *Midwinter – A Collector's Guide* (Cameron Books, Moffat, 1992)

Peat, Alan, *David Whitehead Fabrics* (Oldham Art Gallery, Oldham, 1993)

Peel, L, and Powell, P, *50's and 60's Style* (Apple Press, London, 1988)

Peltonen, J, *Ilmari Tapiovaara* (Museum of Applied Arts, Helsinki, 1984)

Persson, Sigurd, *Modern Swedish Silver* (Lindqvists, Stockholm, 1951)

Persson, Sigurd, *Sigurd Persson Silver* (Arne Tryckare, Stockholm, 1979)

Pica, A, *Storia della Triennale di Milano 1918–1957* (Il Milione, Milan, 1957)

Piranova, C, *Compasso d'Oro 1954–1984* (Cracow, 1985)

Potente, J, *Design der 50er Jahre* (Cologne, 1989)

Pulos, A J, *The American Design Adventure* (Massachusetts Institute of Technology, Cambridge, MA, 1988)

Raban, J, ed, *Modern Bohemian Glass* (Artia, Prague, 1963)

Reihnér, Anders, *Edvin Öhrström* (Orrefors Glasbruk, Orrefors, 1987)

Reihnér, Anders, *Ingeborg Lundin* (Orrefors Glasbruk, Orrefors, 1989)

Remlow, A, *Design in Scandinavia* (Oslo, 1954)

Ricke, H, and Thor, Lar, *Swedish Glass Factories: Production Catalogues 1915–60* (Prestel-Verlag, Munich, 1987)

Rogers, M R, *Italy at Work* (Compagnia Nazionale Artigiana, Rome, 1950)

Santini, P C, *The Years of Italian Design – A Portrait of Cesare Cassina* (Electa, Milan, 1981)

Sarpaneva, Timo, *Lasiaika – Glaszeit* (Cramers Kunstanstalt, Dortmund, 1985)

Schoeser, Mary, *Marianne Straub* (Design Council, London, 1984)

Schoeser, Mary, *Fifties Furnishing Textiles* (Warner and Sons, London, 1984)

Schoeser, Mary, *Fabrics and Wallpapers – Twentieth Century Design* (Bell and Hyman, London, 1986)

Schulz, B, *Grauzonen, Farbwelten – Kunst und Zeitbilder 1945–1955* (NGBK/Medusa, Berlin, 1983)

Schumann, C W, *Wilhelm Wagenfeld – 50 Jahre Mitarbeit in Fabriken* (Cologne, 1973)

Schwarz, W, *Georg Jensen* (Jensen and Wendel, Copenhagen, 1958)

Segerstad, U H A, *Skandinävische Gebrauchkunst* (Frankfurt, 1961)

Segerstad, U H A, *Modern Scandinavian Furniture* (Nordisk Rotogravyr, Stockholm, 1963)

Segerstad, U H A, *Modern Finnish Design* (Weidenfield and Nicholson, London, 1969)

Sembach, K-J, *Contemporary Furniture – An International Review of Modern Furniture, 1950 to the Present Day* (Design Council, London, 1982)

Service Culturel CGER, *Les Fifties en Belgique* (Service Culturel CGER, Brussels, 1988)

Siemen, W, *100 Jahre Porzellanfabrik Arzberg, 1887–1987* (Museum der Deutschen Porzellanindustrie, Hohenberg, 1987)

Siemen, W, *So Fing Es An, So Ging Es Weiter – Deutsches Porzellan und Deutsche Porzellanfabriken 1945–1960* (Museum der Deutschen Porzellanindustrie, Hohenberg, 1988)

Smålands Museum, *Erik Höglund – 30ar Med Glas Och Brons* (Smålands Museum, Växjö, 1990)

Smithsonian Institute, *Georg Jensen Silversmithy: 77 Artists, 77 Years* (Washington, DC, 1980)

Society of Industrial Artists, Designers in Britain, vols 1–5 (Wingate, London, 1947–57)

Society of Industrial Designers, *Industrial Design in America* (Farrer, Straus & Young Inc, New York, 1954)

Sparke, Penny, *Furniture – Twentieth Century Design* (Bell and Hyman, London, 1986)

Sparke, Penny, *Italian Design* (Thames and Hudson, London, 1989)

Staal G, and Walters, H, eds, *Holland in Vorm: Dutch Design 1945–1987* (Stichting Holland in Vorm, The Hague, 1987)

Stadt Museum, Offenbach, *Fünfziger Jahre* (Stadt Museum, Offenbach, 1984)

Stennett-Willson, Ronald, *The Beauty of Modern Glass* (Studio Publications, London, 1958)

Suhonen, P, *Tapio Wirkkala* (Finnish Society of Crafts and Design, Helsinki, 1985)

Teague, Walter Dorwin, *US Industrial Design* (New York, 1951)

Thiry, M, *De l'Art Deco aux Années 50: Le Verre et le Crystal Belges dans le Monde* (Charleroi, 1987)

Thor, Lars, *Legend I Glas – En Bok Om Vicke Lindstrand* (Liberforlag, Stockholm, 1982)

Tucci, G Duplani, *Venini* (Milan, 1989)

Untrach, O, *Saara Hopea* (WSOY, Porvoo, 1988)

Victoria and Albert Musem, *Finlandia: Modern Finnish Design* (Victoria and Albert Museum, London, 1961)

Warnecke, A, *Kultur in Glas und Porzellan 1925–1965* (Hamburg, 1965)

Welch, Robert, *Hand and Machine* (Robert Welch, Chipping Campden, 1986)

Wichmnann, H, *Italien Design 1945 Bis Heute* (Neues Sammlung, Munich, 1988)

Widman, D, *Sven Palmqvist 1906–1984* (Kalmar Konstmuseum, Kalmar, 1984)

Whitechapel Art Gallery, *Modern Chairs: 1918–1970* (Whitechapel Art Gallery, London, 1970)

Woods, Christine, *Sanderson 1860–1985* (Sanderson, London, 1985)

Worshipful Company of Goldsmiths, *Modern British Silver* (WCG, London, 1963)

Worshipful Company of Goldsmiths, *The Goldsmith Today* (WCG, London, 1967)

Worshipful Company of Goldsmiths, *Stuart Devlin in London* (WCG, London, 1983)

Zahle, E, ed, *Scandinavian Domestic Design* (Methuen, London, 1963)

index

index

acknowledgements

In order to convey the mood of the post-war period accurately and explain the thinking behind the architectural expression of the time, this book draws extensively on quotations from contemporary sources. I am indebted to the authors of these commentaries and to the publishers of their books for allowing these quotations to be reproduced in the present work, details of which are given below. The use of first-hand accounts was felt to be of vital importance in conjuring up a reliable picture of the buildings and interiors created during the 1950s, many of which have now been significantly modified. Hence also the reliance on period photographs to show domestic interiors as they were then, rather than as they are now. In this context, special mention must be made of the work of Julius Shulman, the Los Angeles-based photographer who made such a significant and creative contribution to the recording of 'Contemporary' architecture in the USA. I am extremely grateful to Mr Shulman for his assistance in the selection of the images for this book, and for allowing his work to be reproduced so extensively. I am also indebted to Elizabeth Smith at the Museum of Contemporary Art in Los Angeles and the late Esther McCoy for their invaluable work on the Case Study Houses. I would particularly like to thank my picture researcher, Juliet Brightmore, for her hard work in tracking down the images for this book. Her enthusiasm and dedication are much appreciated. Finally, I would like to thank my partner, Ian Fishwick, for his support during the preparation of this work, and for his help in locating obscure books and printing out my manuscript.

Sources for Quotations

Architectural Forum (93, September 1950), p 97

Architectural Review (February 1945), p 41, and (May 1950), p 325

Arts and Architecture (December 1949), p 29 and (February 1959), p 19

Cantacuzino, Sherban, *Modern Houses of the World* (Studio Vista, London, 1964), pp 15, 77

Cantacuzino, Sherban, *Great Modern Architecture* (Studio Vista, London, 1966), pp 63, 64

Crosby, Theo, and Pidgeon, Monica, eds, *An Anthology of Houses* (Batsford, London, 1960), pp 105, 107

Gable, Emerson, *A Treasury of Contemporary Houses* (F W Dodge Corporation, New York, 1954), pp v, 20, 26, 59, 81

Giedion, Sigfried, *Space, Time and Architecture* (Harvard University Press, Cambridge, MA, 4th edition, 1963), pp xxvi, xxvii, xxxi, xlii, 605, 606, 607

Harling, Robert, ed, *The House and Garden Book of Small Houses* (Condé Nast, London, 1961), pp 11, 50, 52, 161, 162, 182, 183, 184

Hatje, Gerd, ed, *New Furniture* (Niggli and Verkauf, Vienna, 1952), pp vi, vii

Huxtable, Ada Louise, *Pier Luigi Nervi* (The Mayflower Publishing Company, London, 1965), p 30

Ideal Home Yearbook (1957), pp 6, 9

Jones, Cranston, *Architecture Today and Tomorrow* (McGraw-Hill, New York, 1961), pp 1, 85, 90, 96, 223, 227, 228

Kidder Smith, G E, *The New Architecture of Europe* (Prentice-Hall, London, 1962), pp 35, 37, 39, 205

Maguire, Robert and Murray, Keith, *Modern Churches of the World* (Studio Vista, London, 1965), p 14

Nelson, George, and Wright, Henry, *Tomorrow's House – A Complete Guide for the Home Builder* (Simon and Schuster, New York, 1945), Foreword and pp 1, 2, 4, 5, 6, 7, 9, 15, 22, 54, 69, 74, 75, 78, 180 Copyright © 1945 by G Nelson and H Wright. Reprinted by permission of Simon and Schuster, Inc.

Penn, Colin, *Houses of Today* (Batsford, London, 1954), p 117, 118

Progressive Architecture (40, March 1959, no 3), pp 10–15

Saarinen, Eero, *Eero Saarinen on his Work* (Yale Univeristy Press, New Haven, 1962)

Smith, Elizabeth, ed, *Blueprints for Modern Living – History and Legacy of the Case Study Houses* (MIT Press, Cambridge, MA, 1989), pp 16, 27, 33, 37, 72

The Decorative Art Studio Yearbook (1951–2), pp 5, 8

Von Eckhardt, Wolf, ed, *Mid-Century Architecture in America* (The John Hopkins Press, Baltimore, 1961), pp 6, 12, 18, 21, 22, 23, 24, 25, 26

Yorke, F R S, *The Modern House* (The Architectural Press, London, 6th edition, 1948), pp 1, 8, 10, 14, 16, 32, 34, 36, 44, 56, 60

Picture Acknowledgements

a: above, b: bottom, l: left, r: right, c: centre

© Wayne Andrews/ESTO: 194 (ar and b); Peter Aprahamian: 62, 78, 86, 87; Archipress Paris: 186, Luc Boegly 197 (b), F Bouchart 206 (b), S Couturier 10, 13 (bl), 206 (a); Architectural Press: 12, 23, 32 (a), 33, 146, 178 (a and br), 179, 191 (b), 202 (a), 205 (a), Kenneth Brown 181 (b), de Burgh Galway 88 (b), 91, 108, 180 (b), 188 (a), 191 (a), 202 (bl), G Gherardi-A Fiorelli 216 (br), Riccardo Moncalvo 216 (a), John R Pantlin 161 (a), 174, 189, 203, Peter Pitt 187 (b), Oscar Savio 204 (b), 216 (bl), W J Toomey 187 (a), 193, Wainwright 180 (a); *Architectural Press/Architectural Review*, with acknowledgement to: Adamsez Ltd 134 (b), Bakelite Ltd 132 (bl), British Reinforced Concrete Engineering Company Ltd 205 (b), Copperad Ltd 137 (a), Falk, Stadelmann and Company Ltd 148 (bl), Formica Ltd 132 (br), Henry Hope and Sons Ltd 188 (b), Intertol Company Ltd 178 (bl), International Paints Ltd 117 (b), John Line and Sons Ltd 114 (a), Marley Tile Company Ltd 117 (a), 120 (b), Pilkington Brothers Ltd 92, 133, 134 (a), Pilkington's Tiles Ltd 114 (b), Ernest Race Ltd 160 (b), Radiation Ltd 137 (b), Rotaflex (Great Britain) Ltd 148 (bc), R S Stevens Ltd/S J Stockwell and Company/Tibor Ltd 168 (a), David Whitehead Fabrics 168 (b); Arflex spa, Limbiate-Milan/Giancarlo De Carlo: 151 (r); Bethlehem Steel: 74 (b); Cassina spa, Milan: 144 (b); Martin Charles: 13 (a and br), 20 (bl and r), 22, 24–25; Peter Cook: 31, 184; William Curtis: 185; Editoriale DOMUS SpA: 150; Fallingwater/Robert P Ruschak, courtesy The Western Pennsylvania Conservancy: 30; courtesy The Ginnel Gallery, Manchester: 120 (b), 123 (a); Fondation Le Corbusier, Paris/© SPADEM: 20 (al); General Electric: 42 (r); Soloman R Guggenheim Museum/Robert E Mates: 202 (br); Hackman Designor Oy Ab, Iittala Finland: 173 (a); Fritz Hansen A/S Denmark/Strüwing: 154–155; Hedrich-Blessing Photograph courtesy Chicago Historical Society: 76 (a); Collection Thomas Hine, Philadelphia: 42 (r); Angelo Hornak: 214–215; Kalmar Konstmuseum, Sweden: 163 (r), 170 (br); Knoll International: 152, 201 (b); Jack Lenor Larsen, New York/David Arky: 169 (bc and br); Le Klint A/S Denmark: 149 (br); *Los Angeles Examiner/Pictorial Living*, April 19, 1959: 66; © Manchester City Art Galleries: 160 (a), 161 (br), Burgess and Leigh Ltd 171 (ar), Terence Conran/Waterford Wedgwood 171 (br), Andrew Cox 81, 138 (a), Paul Kedelv/Flygsfors 173 (bl), Sven Palmquist/Orrefors 173 (br), Jessie Tait/Midwinter 170 (a and bl), THELMA 120 (a); © Bill Maris/ESTO: 27, 28–29; Herman Miller, Zeeland, Michigan: 147 (a), 148 (al), 151 (a and bl) 156 (bl), 157; Jon Miller © Hedrich-Blessing: 60–61; Museum of Applied Arts, Helsinki (Taideteollisuusmuseo): 148 (ar), 156 (br); by courtesy The Museum Of Contemporary Art (MOCA), Los Angeles: 42 (l), 46, 47 (a), 74 (b), 128 (a), 176 (a); Museum of Finnish Architecture, Helsinki: 183 (l and ar), © P Ingervo 111 (b), 207, 208 (b), © Pietinen 182, 208 (a); National Magazine Company Ltd/*House Beautiful:* Jan–Feb 1960 131 (l), Feb 1958 144 (a); National Trade Press Ltd/*Furnishing:* Sept 1957 123 (a); Orrefors Sweden: 172 (l and ar); Frank den Oudsten, Amsterdam: 14, 15; Louis Poulsen and Company A/S, Copenhagen: 149 (al, ar and bl); Radiation Ltd: 128 (b); © 1949 RKO Radio Pictures Inc Ren 1975, RKO General Inc: 42 (al); Marvin Rand: 63; Range/Bettmann/UPI: 45 (a and r); Harry Seidler and

Associates, NSW Australia: 5, 112 (b); Julius Shulman: 2, 6, 8, 17, 34–35, 37, 38, 40, 41, 48, 49, 50–51, 54 (a), 55, 56, 57, 58, 59, 64, 65, 66, 67, 68–69, 70, 71, 72, 74 (a), 75, 80, 82, 83, 84, 85, 89, 90, 94, 95, 96-97, 98, 99, 100, 101, 102–103, 105, 106, 109, 110, 111 (a), 112 (a), 118–119, 124, 125 (a), 126–127, 129, 130, 131 (r), 135, 136 (a), 139, 140, 141, 142, 148 (br), 153, 158, 159, 177, 196, 210 (a), 222, 223; Staatliche Muzeen zu Berlin-Preussischer Kulturbesitz Kunstgewerbemuseum: Saturia Linke 172 (bc and br), Helge Mundt 145, 171 (l); Stapleton Collection: 115 (cl), 169 (l); Esra Stoller © ESTO: 18, 24 (a), 26, 76 (b), 88 (a), 192, 194 (l), 195, 197 (a), 198, 199, 200, 201 (a), 209, 210 (b), 211, 212, 213; Tim Street-Porter: 16, 52, 53, 54 (b); Strüwing Foto Aps, Denmark: 93, 104, 183 (br), 190, 204 (a); Swedish Museum of Architecture, Stockholm: 181 (a); Tempo Carpet Trades Ltd: 122; Topham Picture Point: 218; by courtesy of the Board of Trustees of the Victoria and Albert Museum, London: 115 (ar), 123 (b), 162, 163 (bl), 164, 165, 166–167; © 1949 Warner Bros Inc Ren 1976, United Artists Television, courtesy Turner Entertainment; 45 (l); Warner Fabrics plc: 169 (ar); The Whitworth Art Gallery, University of Manchester: Endpapers © Lucienne Day, 115 (al, cr, bl and br), 116, 163 (al); F Wrighton and Sons Ltd: 132 (a).

Every reasonable effort has been made to acknowledge the ownership of copyright photographs included in this volume. Any errors that may have occurred are inadvertent, and will be corrected in subsequent editions provided notification is sent to the publisher.